GLENCOE LANGUAGE ARTS

Grammar

AND

Composition

Handbook

GRADE 8

Glencoe
McGraw-Hill

New York, New York
Columbus, Ohio
Woodland Hills, California
Peoria, Illinois

Photo Credits
Cover Index Stock; **all other photos** Amanita Pictures.

Glencoe/McGraw-Hill

*A Division of The **McGraw·Hill** Companies*

Printed in the United States of America.

Send all inquiries to:
Glencoe/McGraw-Hill
8787 Orion Place
Columbus, OH 43240–4027

ISBN 0-07-825115-X

2 3 4 5 6 7 8 9 10 042 06 05 04 03 02 01

Table of Contents at a Glance

Table of Contents

Part One

● ● ● ● ● ● ● ● ● ● ● ● ● ● ●

Ready Reference

The **Ready Reference** consists of three parts.
The **Glossary of Terms** is a list of language arts
terms with definitions and examples. Page
references show you where to find more
information about the terms elsewhere
in the book. The **Usage Glossary**
lists words that are easily
confused or often used
incorrectly and explains how
to use the words correctly.
The third part is **Abbreviations**,
which consists of lists of many
commonly used abbreviations.

20,000 +
WORDS
SPELLED AND DIVIDED
FOR QUICK REFERENCE
NINTH
EDITION

20,000 + WORDS

NEW FEATURES OF 20,000 + WORDS, 9/E

IMPROVED FEATURES OF 20,000 + WORDS, 9/E

GLENCOE

ISBN 0-09-840050-0

ZOUBEK · HOSLER

A DICTIONARY
OF SYNONYMS
AND ANTONYMS

by Joseph Devlin

REFERENCE · WARNER BOOKS

A DICTIONARY O
SYNONYMS AND ANTO

Merriam-Webster

webster · 0-877/9-911-3 · USA $5.99 · (CAN)

Merriam-Webster

Dictionary

Merriam-Webster
Webster

Merria

Thesau

SIGNET
REFERENCE
AE
6554
SLANG AND EUPHEMISM RICHARD A. SPEARS
U.S.

Merriam-
Webster

Merria

Vocabulary

GLOSSARY OF TERMS

abbreviation An abbreviation is a shortened form of a word or phrase. Many abbreviations are followed by periods (pages 276–278).

EXAMPLES Mrs., Tues., Dec., Mont., NBA, ft., St., RI

abstract noun An abstract noun names an idea, a quality, or a feeling that can't be seen or touched (page 82).

EXAMPLE Her **bravery** and **courage** filled us with **admiration.**

action verb An action verb is a verb that expresses action. An action verb may consist of more than one word (pages 97–98).

EXAMPLES The director **shouts** at the members of the cast.

The lights **are flashing** above the stage.

The play **has begun.**

active voice A verb is in the active voice when the subject performs the action of the verb (pages 111–112).

EXAMPLE Thornton Wilder **composed** that play.

adjective An adjective is a word that describes, or modifies, a noun or a pronoun (pages 144–152, 164–165).

HOW ADJECTIVES MODIFY NOUNS

WHAT KIND?   We studied **ancient** history.

HOW MANY?   I read **four** chapters.

WHICH ONE?   **That** invention changed history.

adjective clause An adjective clause is a subordinate clause that modifies, or describes, a noun or a pronoun in the main clause of a complex sentence (pages 195, 197).

EXAMPLE The Aqua-Lung, **which divers strap on,** holds oxygen.

adjective phrase An adjective phrase is a prepositional phrase or a participial phrase that modifies, or describes, a noun or a pronoun (pages 178, 206–207).

EXAMPLES The servers **at the new restaurant** are courteous.
[prepositional phrase modifying *servers*]

The musician **seated at the piano** is Erik. **[participial phrase modifying *musician*]**

adverb An adverb is a word that modifies a verb, an adjective, or another adverb (pages 158–167, 179–180).

WHAT ADVERBS MODIFY

VERBS	People *handle* old violins **carefully.**
ADJECTIVES	**Very** *old* violins are valuable.
ADVERBS	Orchestras **almost** *always* include violins.

WAYS ADVERBS MODIFY VERBS

ADVERBS TELL	EXAMPLES
HOW	grandly, easily, completely, neatly, gratefully, sadly
WHEN	soon, now, immediately, often, never, usually, early
WHERE	here, there, everywhere, inside, downstairs, above

adverb clause An adverb clause is a subordinate clause that often modifies the verb in the main clause of a complex sentence. It tells *how, when, where, why,* or *under what conditions* the action occurs (pages 198–199).

EXAMPLE **After we won the meet,** we shook hands with our opponents.

An adverb clause can also modify an adjective or an adverb.

EXAMPLES Carson is younger **than I am. [The adverb clause *than I am* modifies the adjective *younger*.]**

Sherry walks faster **than her brother runs. [The adverb clause *than her brother runs* modifies the adverb *faster*.]**

adverb phrase An adverb phrase is a prepositional phrase that modifies a verb, an adjective, or another adverb (page 178).

ADVERB PHRASES

MODIFIES A VERB	The servers *dress* **like movie characters.**
MODIFIES AN ADJECTIVE	The restaurant is *popular* **with young people.**
MODIFIES AN ADVERB	The restaurant opens *early* **in the morning.**

agreement Agreement is the match between grammatical forms. A verb must agree with its subject. A pronoun must agree with its antecedent (pages 73, 132–133, 181, 216–224).

EXAMPLES Both **ducks** and **swans swim** in this lake. **[subject-verb agreement]**

Jerry and his **brother** visited **their** grandparents. **[pronoun-antecedent agreement]**

antecedent An antecedent is the word a pronoun refers to. The word *antecedent* means "going before" (pages 128–130).

EXAMPLE **Max** likes to read books. **He** particularly likes novels. **[*He* refers to *Max*. *Max* is the antecedent of *He*.]**

apostrophe An apostrophe (') is a punctuation mark used in possessive nouns, possessive indefinite pronouns, and contractions. In contractions an apostrophe shows that one or more letters have been left out (pages 273–274).

EXAMPLES Shefali's friends don't always understand her.

Cameron's asking for everyone's help.

appositive An appositive is a noun that is placed next to another noun to identify it or add information about it (pages 89–90).

EXAMPLE James Madison's wife, **Dolley,** was a famous first lady.

appositive phrase An appositive phrase is a group of words that includes an appositive and other words that modify the appositive (pages 89–90).

EXAMPLE Madison, **our fourth president,** held many other offices.

article The words *a, an,* and *the* make up a special group of adjectives called articles. *A* and *an* are called **indefinite articles** because they refer to one of a general group of people, places, things, or ideas. *A* is used before words beginning with a consonant sound. *An* is used before words beginning with a vowel sound (page 147).

EXAMPLES **a** union   **a** picture   **an** hour   **an** easel

    The is called the **definite article** because it identifies specific people, places, things, or ideas (page 147).

auxiliary verb *See helping verb.*

base form A base form is the simplest form of a word. *Small* is a base form; other forms of *small* are *smaller* and *smallest. Be* is a base form; other forms of *be* are *am, is, are, was, were, being,* and *been* (pages 104, 113–116, 149–150, 163).

clause A clause is a group of words that has a subject and a verb (pages 192–201). *See also adjective clause, adverb clause, main clause, noun clause, and subordinate clause.*

closing A closing is a way to end a letter. It begins with a capital letter and is followed by a comma (page 249).

EXAMPLES

Yours truly,   Sincerely,   With love,   Your friend,

collective noun A collective noun names a group of people, animals, or things. It may be singular or plural, depending on the meaning of the sentence (pages 85, 220–221).

EXAMPLES The **team** shares the field with its opponent.

The **team** share their jokes with one another.

colon A colon (:) is a punctuation mark. It's used to introduce a list and to separate the hour and the minutes when you write the time of day. It's also used after the salutation of a business letter (page 269).

EXAMPLES Please buy these fruits: apples, bananas, grapes, peaches.

It's now exactly 2:43 P.M.

Dear Editor:

comma A comma (,) is a punctuation mark that's used to separate items or to set them off from the rest of a sentence (pages 262–267).

EXAMPLES Shoes, socks, hats, and gloves lay in the bottom of the closet.

Tessa's great-grandmother, who is ninety, loves to travel.

common noun A common noun names any person, place, thing, or idea. Common nouns can be either concrete or abstract (pages 81–82).

EXAMPLE **Children** learn **handwriting** in school.

comparative form The comparative form of an adjective compares one person or thing with another. The comparative form of an adverb compares one action with another (pages 149–152, 162–163).

EXAMPLES Is Venezuela **larger** than Peru? [adjective]

The pianist arrived **earlier** than the violinist. [adverb]

complete predicate *See predicate.*

complete subject *See subject.*

complex sentence A complex sentence has one main clause and one or more subordinate clauses (pages 193–194).

EXAMPLE Since Mariah moved to Springfield, she has made many new friends. [**She has made many new friends** is a main clause. **Since Mariah moved to Springfield** is a subordinate clause.]

compound-complex sentence A compound-complex sentence has two or more main clauses and one or more subordinate clauses (page 194).

EXAMPLE Ahmal has never scored a goal, but he plays soccer because he loves the game. [**The two main clauses are Ahmal has never scored a goal** and **he plays soccer. Because he loves the game** is a subordinate clause.]

compound noun A compound noun is a noun made of two or more words (pages 82, 85).

EXAMPLES storybook, showcase, bookmark

ice cream, dining room, high school

sister-in-law, seventh-grader, push-ups

compound predicate A compound predicate consists of two or more simple predicates, or verbs, that have the same subject. The verbs may be connected by *and, or, but, both . . . and, either . . . or,* or *neither . . . nor* (page 73).

EXAMPLE Many students **read** the novel *Jane Eyre* and **enjoy** it.

compound sentence A compound sentence is a sentence that contains two or more main clauses joined by a comma and a coordinating conjunction or by a semicolon (pages 75, 181, 183–184, 192).

EXAMPLES **Eudora Welty is a novelist,** but **she also writes essays.**
[A comma and the coordinating conjunction *but* join the two main clauses, *Eudora Welty is a novelist* and *she also writes essays.*]

Eudora Welty is a novelist; she also writes essays.

compound subject A compound subject consists of two or more simple subjects that have the same predicate. The subjects may be joined by *and, or, both . . . and, either . . . or,* or *neither . . . nor* (pages 73, 181, 223–224).

EXAMPLE **Charlotte Brontë** and **Emily Brontë** were sisters.

compound verb *See compound predicate.*

concrete noun A concrete noun names something you can see or touch (page 82).

EXAMPLE **Julio** wore a **cap** on his **head** and a **scarf** around his **neck.**

conjunction A conjunction is a connecting word. *See coordinating conjunction, correlative conjunction, and subordinating conjunction.*

conjunctive adverb A conjunctive adverb may be used to join the simple sentences in a compound sentence (pages 183–184).

EXAMPLE The school cafeteria sometimes serves Chinese food; **however,** these meals are not very tasty.

contraction A contraction is a word formed from one or more words by omitting one or more letters and substituting an apostrophe (pages 87–88, 166, 274).

EXAMPLES We **can't** find the map. [*Can't* is a contraction of *cannot.*]

Carmella's visited every state. [*Carmella's* is a contraction of *Carmella has.*]

coordinating conjunction A coordinating conjunction is a word used to connect compound parts of a sentence. *And, but, or, nor,* and *for* are coordinating conjunctions. *So* and *yet* are also sometimes used as coordinating conjunctions (pages 181, 223–224).

EXAMPLE   Juan **or** Lisa collects the money **and** distributes the tickets.

correlative conjunction Correlative conjunctions are pairs of words used to connect compound parts of a sentence. Correlative conjunctions include *both . . . and, either . . . or, neither . . . nor,* and *not only . . . but also* (pages 181, 223–224).

EXAMPLE   Examples of great architecture exist in **both** New York **and** Paris.

dash A dash (—) is a punctuation mark. It's usually used in pairs to set off a sudden break or change in thought or speech (page 275).

EXAMPLE   Billy Adams—he lives next door—is our team manager.

declarative sentence A declarative sentence makes a statement. It ends with a period (pages 66, 261).

EXAMPLE   Edgar Allan Poe wrote suspenseful short stories.

demonstrative adjective A demonstrative adjective points out something and modifies a noun by answering the question *which one?* or *which ones? This, that, these,* and *those* are demonstrative adjectives when they modify nouns (page 147).

EXAMPLES   Take **this** umbrella with you.   **That** answer is wrong.

Take **these** boots too.   **Those** clouds are lovely.

demonstrative pronoun A demonstrative pronoun is a pronoun that points out something. *This, that, these,* and *those* are demonstrative pronouns when they take the place of nouns (pages 136, 148).

EXAMPLES Take **this** with you.　　**That** is the wrong answer.

Take **these** too.　　**Those** are lovely clouds.

dependent clause *See subordinate clause.*

direct address Direct address is a name used in speaking directly to a person. Direct address may also be a word or a phrase used in place of a name. Words used in direct address are set off by commas (page 263).

EXAMPLES **Suzy,** please hand me a dish towel.

Here, **my dear mother,** is your birthday present.

Don't do that again, **Samson.**

direct object A direct object receives the action of a verb. It answers the question *whom?* or *what?* after an action verb (pages 98–100).

EXAMPLE The actor rehearsed his **lines** from the play.

direct quotation A direct quotation gives a speaker's exact words (pages 248, 270).

EXAMPLE **"Spiders,"** explained Raul, **"have eight legs."**

double negative A double negative is the use of two negative words to express the same idea. Only one negative word is necessary (pages 166–167).

EXAMPLES

INCORRECT I **don't** have **no** homework.

CORRECT I **don't** have **any** homework.

CORRECT I have **no** homework.

end mark An end mark is a punctuation mark used at the end of a sentence. Periods, question marks, and exclamation points are end marks (pages 66–67, 261).

EXAMPLES Tell me a story**.**

Where have you been**?**

What a hot day this has been**!**

essential clause An essential clause is a clause that is necessary to make the meaning of a sentence clear. Don't use commas to set off essential clauses (page 197).

EXAMPLE The girl **who is standing beside the coach** is our best swimmer.

essential phrase An essential phrase is a phrase that is necessary to make the meaning of a sentence clear. Don't use commas to set off essential phrases (page 207).

EXAMPLE The boy **seated at the piano** is Erik.

exclamation point An exclamation point (!) is a punctuation mark used to end a sentence that shows strong feeling (exclamatory). It's also used after strong interjections (pages 67, 261).

EXAMPLES My**!** What a hot day it is**!**

exclamatory sentence An exclamatory sentence expresses strong feeling. It ends with an exclamation point (pages 67, 261).

EXAMPLES What a great writer Poe was!

How I enjoy his stories!

future perfect tense The future perfect tense of a verb expresses action that will be completed before another future event begins (page 110).

EXAMPLE   The production **will have closed** by next week.

future tense The future tense of a verb expresses action that will take place in the future (page 110).

EXAMPLE   Mr. and Mrs. Pao **will attend** the performance.

gender The gender of a noun may be masculine (male), feminine (female), or neuter (referring to things) (page 130).

EXAMPLES   boy (male), woman (female), desk (neuter)

gerund A gerund is a verb form that ends in -*ing* and is used as a noun (pages 208–209).

EXAMPLE   **Exercising** builds strength, endurance, and flexibility.

gerund phrase A gerund phrase is a group of words that includes a gerund and other words that complete its meaning (pages 208–209).

EXAMPLE   **Exercising on a bike** is fun for all ages.

helping verb A helping verb is a verb that helps the main verb express action or make a statement (pages 104–106, 217).

EXAMPLES   Telma **is acting** in another play today. [*Is* **is the helping verb;** *acting* **is the main verb.**]

Emilio **has written** a story. [*Has* **is the helping verb;** *written* **is the main verb.**]

hyphen A hyphen (-) is a punctuation mark that's used in some compound words (page 275).

EXAMPLE Mrs. Gilmore's **mother-in-law** is **sixty-two** years old.

imperative sentence An imperative sentence gives a command or makes a request. It ends with a period (pages 66, 72, 261).

EXAMPLE Read "The Pit and the Pendulum."

indefinite pronoun An indefinite pronoun is a pronoun that does not refer to a particular person, place, or thing (pages 132–133, 222, 274).

SOME INDEFINITE PRONOUNS

SINGULAR			PLURAL
another	everybody	no one	both
anybody	everyone	nothing	few
anyone	everything	one	many
anything	much	somebody	others
each	neither	someone	several
either	nobody	something	

SINGULAR OR PLURAL all, any, most, none, some

indirect object An indirect object answers the question *to whom?* or *for whom?* or *to what?* or *for what?* an action is done (page 100).

EXAMPLE Friends sent the **actors** flowers.

indirect quotation An indirect quotation does not give a speaker's exact words (page 248).

EXAMPLE Raul said **that spiders have eight legs.**

infinitive An infinitive is formed with the word *to* and the base form of a verb. Infinitives are often used as nouns in sentences (pages 210–211).

EXAMPLE **To write** is Alice's ambition.

infinitive phrase An infinitive phrase is a group of words that includes an infinitive and other words that complete its meaning (pages 210–211).

EXAMPLE **To write a great novel** was Alice's ambition.

intensive pronoun An intensive pronoun ends with *-self* or *-selves* and is used to draw special attention to a noun or a pronoun already named (page 134).

EXAMPLE Yolanda **herself** repaired the engine.

interjection An interjection is a word or group of words that expresses emotion. It has no grammatical connection to other words in a sentence (pages 185–186, 261).

EXAMPLE **Good grief!** My favorite restaurant has closed.

interrogative pronoun An interrogative pronoun is a pronoun used to introduce an interrogative sentence. *Who, whom, which, what,* and *whose* are interrogative pronouns (pages 135–136).

EXAMPLE **Who** borrowed the book?

interrogative sentence An interrogative sentence asks a question. It ends with a question mark (pages 66, 71–72, 219, 261).

EXAMPLE Did Poe also write poetry?

intransitive verb An intransitive verb is a verb that does not have a direct object (pages 98–99).

EXAMPLE The audience **applauds** loudly.

inverted sentence An inverted sentence is a sentence in which the subject follows the verb (pages 72, 218–219).

EXAMPLES There **are** many **immigrants** among my ancestors.

Across the ocean **sailed** the three **ships.**

irregular verb An irregular verb is a verb whose past and past participle are formed in a way other than by adding *-d* or *-ed* to the base form (pages 113–116).

SOME IRREGULAR VERBS

BASE	PAST	PAST PARTICIPLE
go	went	gone
write	wrote	written
begin	began	begun

italics Italics are printed letters that slant to the right. *This sentence is printed in italic type.* Italics are used for the titles of certain kinds of published works and works of art. In handwriting, underlining is a substitute for italics (page 272).

EXAMPLE On the desk were a copy of *Robinson Crusoe* and several issues of *Time* magazine.

linking verb A linking verb connects the subject of a sentence with a noun or an adjective in the predicate (pages 101–102).

EXAMPLE Juana Ortiz **was** the director.

main clause A main clause has a subject and a predicate and can stand alone as a sentence (pages 192–194).

EXAMPLE After the storm passed, **the governor surveyed the damage.**

main verb A main verb is the last word in a verb phrase. If a verb stands alone, it's a main verb (pages 104–106, 217).

EXAMPLES The professor is **studying** ancient history.

The professor **studies** ancient history.

negative word A negative word expresses the idea of "no" or "not" (pages 166–167).

SOME COMMON NEGATIVE WORDS			
barely	no	no one	nowhere
hardly	nobody	not	scarcely
never	none	nothing	

nonessential clause A nonessential clause is a clause that is not necessary to make the meaning of a sentence clear. Use commas to set off nonessential clauses (pages 197, 265).

EXAMPLE Janice, **who is standing beside the coach,** is our best swimmer.

nonessential phrase A nonessential phrase is a phrase that is not necessary to make the meaning of a sentence clear. Use commas to set off nonessential phrases (pages 207, 263, 264).

EXAMPLE Erik, **dreaming of fame,** sits at the piano.

nonrestrictive clause *See nonessential clause.*

nonrestrictive phrase *See nonessential phrase.*

noun A noun is a word that names a person, a place, a thing, or an idea (pages 81–90).

NOUNS	
PERSONS	sister, mayor, player, coach, pianist, children
PLACES	park, zoo, lake, school, playground, desert, city
THINGS	magazine, boots, rose, pencil, peach, baseball, car
IDEAS	honesty, truth, democracy, pride, maturity, progress

noun clause A noun clause is a subordinate clause used as a noun (pages 200–201).

EXAMPLE **Whoever plays hockey** wears protective equipment.

number Number is the form of a word that shows whether it's singular or plural (page 130).

EXAMPLES **This book is a mystery. [singular words]**

These books are mysteries. [plural words]

object An object is a noun or a pronoun that follows a verb or a preposition. *See direct object, indirect object, and object of a preposition.*

EXAMPLE Mario gave the **horse** a **carrot** for a **treat.** [*Horse* **is an indirect object;** *carrot* **is a direct object;** *treat* **is the object of a preposition.]**

object of a preposition The object of a preposition is the noun or pronoun that ends a prepositional phrase (pages 175, 176–177).

EXAMPLE Hang the painting outside the **auditorium.**

object pronoun *Me, us, you, him, her, it, them,* and *whom* are object pronouns. Object pronouns are used as direct objects, indirect objects, and objects of prepositions (pages 125–127, 176–177).

EXAMPLE Sally gave **her** and **me** a picture of **them.**

parentheses Parentheses ( ) are punctuation marks used to set off words that define or explain another word (page 276).

EXAMPLE This container holds one gallon **(**3.785 liters**).**

participial phrase A participial phrase is a group of words that includes a participle and other words that complete its meaning (pages 206–207, 263).

EXAMPLE **Sitting at the piano,** Erik loses himself in the music.

participle A participle is a verb form that can act as the main verb in a verb phrase or as an adjective to modify a noun or a pronoun (pages 206–207, 263). *See also past participle and present participle.*

EXAMPLES Erik has **played** several pieces on the piano. **[main verb]**

His **playing** skill improves daily. **[adjective]**

passive voice A verb is in the passive voice when the subject receives the action of the verb (pages 111–112).

EXAMPLE That play **was composed** by Thornton Wilder.

past participle A past participle is usually formed by adding -*d* or -*ed* to the base form of a verb. Some past participles are formed irregularly. When the past participle acts as a verb, one or more helping verbs are always used before the past participle. A past participle may also be used as an adjective (pages 104–105, 113–116, 145, 206–207).

EXAMPLES Kimi has **baked** cookies for us. **[*Baked* is the past participle of *bake*.]**

Mrs. Gonzales had **planted** tomatoes in the spring. **[*Planted* is the past participle of *plant*.]**

Two students have **written** a play. **[*Written* is the past participle of *write*.]**

Erik practices on a **rented** piano. **[*Rented* is an adjective modifying *piano*.]**

past perfect tense The past perfect tense of a verb expresses action that happened before another action or event in the past (page 109).

EXAMPLES The actors **had rehearsed** for many weeks.

We **had** just **arrived** when the play started.

past progressive The past progressive form of a verb expresses action or a condition that was continuing at some time in the past (page 107).

EXAMPLE We **were watching** a scary show.

past tense The past tense of a verb expresses action that already happened (pages 103, 113–116).

EXAMPLE The actors **rehearsed.**

perfect tenses The perfect tenses are the present perfect tense, the past perfect tense, and the future perfect tense. The perfect tenses consist of a form of the verb *have* and a past participle (pages 108–110).

EXAMPLES Lynn **has played** the trumpet for three years. **[present perfect]**

His father **had played** the trumpet as a boy. **[past perfect]**

By the end of high school, Lynn **will have played** the trumpet for seven years. **[future perfect]**

period A period (.) is a punctuation mark used to end a sentence that makes a statement (declarative) or gives a command (imperative). It's also used at the end of many abbreviations (pages 66, 261, 276–278).

EXAMPLES The day was hot and humid. **[declarative]**

Bring me some lemonade. **[imperative]**

personal pronoun A personal pronoun is a pronoun that refers to people or things. *I, me, you, he, she, him, her, it, we, us, they,* and *them* are personal pronouns (pages 125–126).

EXAMPLE **I** saw **you** with **her** and **him.**

phrase A phrase is a group of words that is used as a single part of speech and does not contain a verb and its subject. *See adjective phrase, adverb phrase, appositive phrase, gerund phrase, infinitive phrase, participial phrase, prepositional phrase, and verb phrase.*

EXAMPLE Three students **wearing backpacks were hiking through the woods.** [*Wearing backpacks* is a participial phrase acting as an adjective to modify the noun *students*. *Were hiking* is a verb phrase. *Through the woods* is a prepositional phrase acting as an adverb to modify the verb *were hiking*.]

plural noun A plural noun is a noun that means more than one of something (pages 83–88).

EXAMPLE The **students** and their **parents** heard the **candidates** give their **speeches.**

possessive noun A possessive noun is a noun that shows ownership (pages 86–88, 273).

EXAMPLE **Tiffany's** friend distributed the **children's** toys.

possessive pronoun A possessive pronoun is a pronoun that shows ownership. *My, mine, our, ours, your, yours, his, her, hers, its, their, theirs,* and *whose* are possessive pronouns (pages 131, 274).

predicate The predicate part of a sentence tells what the subject does or has. It can also tell what the subject is or is like. The **complete predicate** includes all the words in the predicate of a sentence. The **simple predicate** is the main word or word group in the complete predicate. The simple predicate is always a verb (pages 68–73).

EXAMPLE Emily Dickinson **wrote hundreds of poems.** [The complete predicate is *wrote hundreds of poems*. The simple predicate is *wrote*.]

predicate adjective A predicate adjective is an adjective that follows a linking verb and modifies the subject of the sentence (pages 101–102, 145).

EXAMPLE   Ms. Ortiz is **stern** but **fair.**

predicate noun A predicate noun is a noun that follows a linking verb and renames or identifies the subject of the sentence (pages 101–102).

EXAMPLE   Ms. Ortiz is the **director.**

preposition A preposition is a word that relates a noun or a pronoun to another word in a sentence (pages 174–180).

EXAMPLE   A boy **with** red hair stood **near** the window.

prepositional phrase A prepositional phrase is a group of words that begins with a preposition and ends with a noun or a pronoun, which is called the **object of the preposition** (pages 174–180, 218–219, 263).

EXAMPLE   Hang the painting **outside the new auditorium.**

present participle A present participle is formed by adding -*ing* to the base form of a verb. A helping verb is always used with the present participle when it acts as a verb. A present participle may also be used as an adjective (pages 104–105, 145, 206–207).

EXAMPLES   Mr. Omara is **teaching** algebra this year. [*Teaching* **is the present participle of** *teach*.]

The students were **making** decorations. [*Making* **is the present participle of** *make*.]

Erik's **playing** skill improves daily. [*Playing* **is an adjective modifying** *skill*.]

present perfect tense The present perfect tense of a verb expresses action that happened at an indefinite time in the past (page 108).

EXAMPLE   The actors **have rehearsed** for many hours.

present progressive The present progressive form of a verb expresses action or a condition that is continuing in the present (pages 106–107, 110).

EXAMPLE   Althea **is finishing** her song.

present tense The present tense of a verb expresses action that happens regularly. It can also express a general truth (pages 103, 110).

EXAMPLE   A great actor **wins** awards.

principal parts of a verb The principal parts of a verb are the base form, the present participle, the past, and the past participle. The principal parts are used to form verb tenses (pages 104, 113–116).

BASE	PRESENT PARTICIPLE	PAST	PAST PARTICIPLE
play	playing	played	played
go	going	went	gone

progressive forms Progressive forms of verbs express continuing action. They consist of a form of the verb *be* and a present participle (pages 106–107). *See also past progressive and present progressive.*

EXAMPLES   Carla **is leaving,** but Mr. and Mrs. Tsai **are staying.**

Ahmed **was studying,** but his brothers **were playing** basketball.

pronoun A pronoun is a word that takes the place of one or more nouns (pages 125–136).

EXAMPLE   Max likes books. **He** particularly enjoys novels. **[The pronoun *He* takes the place of the noun *Max*.]**

proper adjective A proper adjective is an adjective formed from a proper noun. It begins with a capital letter (pages 145–146, 254).

EXAMPLE   The **Florida** sun beat down on the **Japanese** tourists.

proper noun A proper noun names a particular person, place, thing, or idea. The first word and all other important words in a proper noun are capitalized (pages 81–82, 250–254).

EXAMPLE Did **Edgar Allan Poe** ever see the **Statue of Liberty**?

question mark A question mark (?) is a punctuation mark used to end a sentence that asks a question (interrogative) (pages 66, 261).

EXAMPLE Do you like green eggs and ham**?**

quotation marks Quotation marks (" ") are punctuation marks used to enclose the exact words of a speaker. They're also used for certain titles (pages 270–271).

EXAMPLES "A spider," said Sean, "has eight legs."
Have you read the story "To Build a Fire"?

reflexive pronoun A reflexive pronoun ends with *-self* or *-selves* and refers to the subject of a sentence. In a sentence with a reflexive pronoun, the action of the verb returns to the subject (page 134).

EXAMPLE Yolanda bought **herself** a book on engine repair.

regular verb A regular verb is a verb whose past and past participle are formed by adding *-d* or *-ed* (page 103).

EXAMPLES I **believed** her.
The twins **have learned** a lesson.

relative pronoun A relative pronoun is a pronoun that may be used to introduce an adjective clause (page 195).

EXAMPLE Divers prefer equipment **that** is lightweight.

restrictive clause *See essential clause.*

restrictive phrase *See essential phrase.*

run-on sentence A run-on sentence is two or more sentences incorrectly written as one sentence (page 75).

EXAMPLES Welty wrote novels, she wrote essays. **[run-on]**

Welty wrote novels she wrote essays. **[run-on]**

Welty wrote novels. She wrote essays. **[correct]**

Welty wrote novels, and she wrote essays. **[correct]**

Welty wrote novels; she wrote essays. **[correct]**

salutation A salutation is the greeting in a letter. The first word and any proper nouns in a salutation should be capitalized (pages 249, 267).

EXAMPLES My dear aunt Julia,   Dear Professor Higgins:

semicolon A semicolon (;) is a punctuation mark used to join the main clauses of a compound sentence (pages 268–269).

EXAMPLE Kendra weeded the garden; Geronimo mowed the lawn.

sentence A sentence is a group of words that expresses a complete thought (pages 66–68).

EXAMPLE Edgar Allan Poe wrote many short stories.

sentence fragment A sentence fragment does not express a complete thought. It may also be missing a subject, a predicate, or both (page 68).

EXAMPLES The poems. **[fragment]**

Lay in Dickinson's bureau for years. **[fragment]**

The poems lay in Dickinson's bureau for years. **[sentence]**

simple predicate *See predicate.*

simple sentence A simple sentence has one subject and one predicate (pages 74, 192).

EXAMPLE Eudora Welty lived in Jackson, Mississippi.

simple subject *See subject.*

singular noun A singular noun is a noun that means only one of something (pages 83–86).

EXAMPLE The **child** and his **father** saw a **rabbit** in the **garden.**

subject The subject part of a sentence names whom or what the sentence is about. The **complete subject** includes all the words in the subject of a sentence. The **simple subject** is the main word or word group in the complete subject (pages 68–73, 216–224).

EXAMPLE **A large ship with many sails** appeared on the horizon. [The complete subject is *A large ship with many sails.* The simple subject is *ship.*]

subject pronoun *I, we, you, he, she, it, they,* and *who* are subject pronouns. Subject pronouns are used as subjects and predicate pronouns (pages 125–127).

EXAMPLE **He** and **I** know **who you** are.

subordinate clause A subordinate clause is a group of words that has a subject and a predicate but does not express a complete thought and cannot stand alone as a sentence. A subordinate clause is always combined with a main clause in a sentence (pages 193–201).

EXAMPLE Mariah, **who moved here from Montana,** is very popular.

subordinating conjunction A subordinating conjunction is a word that is used to introduce a subordinate clause (page 199).

SUBORDINATING CONJUNCTIONS

after	because	though	whenever
although	before	till	where
as	if	unless	whereas
as if	since	until	wherever
as though	than	when	while

superlative form The superlative form of an adjective compares one person or thing with several others. The superlative form of an adverb compares one action with several others (pages 149–152, 162–163).

EXAMPLES Is Brazil the **richest** country in South America? **[adjective]**

The drummer arrived **earliest** of all the players. **[adverb]**

tense Tense shows the time of the action of a verb (pages 103–110).

EXAMPLES The team often **wins** games. **[present tense]**

The team **won** the game. **[past tense]**

The team **will win** this game. **[future tense]**

transitive verb A transitive verb is an action verb that transfers action to a direct object (pages 98–99).

EXAMPLE The audience **applauds** the actors.

verb A verb is a word that expresses action or a state of being (pages 97–116, 216–224).

EXAMPLES Juanita **plays** soccer.

Kwami **is** a good student.

verbal A verbal is a verb form used as a noun, an adjective, or an adverb. Participles, gerunds, and infinitives are verbals (pages 206–211).

EXAMPLES The **swimming** instructor showed us **diving** techniques. **[participles used as adjectives]**

Mr. McCoy teaches **swimming** and **diving**. **[gerunds used as nouns]**

Mr. McCoy taught us **to swim** and **to dive**. **[infinitives used as nouns]**

verb phrase A verb phrase consists of one or more helping verbs followed by a main verb (page 105).

EXAMPLE Telma **is acting** in another play today. **[*Is* is the helping verb; *acting* is the main verb.]**

voice *See active voice and passive voice.*

USAGE GLOSSARY

This glossary will guide you in choosing between words that are often confused. It will also tell you about certain words and expressions you should avoid when you speak or write for school or business.

a, an Use *a* before words that begin with a consonant sound. Use *an* before words that begin with a vowel sound.

EXAMPLES **a** poem, **a** house, **a** yacht, **a** union, **a** one-track mind

an apple, **an** icicle, **an** honor, **an** umbrella, **an** only child

accept, except *Accept* is a verb that means "to receive" or "to agree to." *Except* is a preposition that means "but." *Except* may also be a verb that means "to leave out or exclude."

EXAMPLES Please **accept** this gift.

Will you **accept** our decision?

Everyone will be there **except** you. **[preposition]**

Some students may be **excepted** from taking physical education. **[verb]**

advice, advise *Advice*, a noun, means "an opinion offered as a guide." *Advise*, a verb, means "to give advice."

EXAMPLE Why should I **advise** you when you never accept my **advice**?

affect, effect *Affect* is a verb that means "to cause a change in" or "to influence the emotions of." *Effect* may be a noun or a verb. As a noun, it means "result." As a verb, it means "to bring about or accomplish."

EXAMPLES The mayor's policies have **affected** every city agency.

The mayor's policies have had a positive **effect** on every city agency. **[noun]**

The mayor has **effected** positive changes in every city agency. **[verb]**

ain't *Ain't* is unacceptable in speaking and writing unless you're quoting someone's exact words or writing dialogue. Use *I'm not; you, we,* or *they aren't; he, she,* or *it isn't.*

all ready, already *All ready* means "completely ready." *Already* means "before" or "by this time."

EXAMPLE The band was **all ready** to play its last number, but the fans were **already** leaving the stadium.

all right, alright The spelling *alright* is not acceptable in formal writing. Use *all right.*

EXAMPLE Don't worry; everything will be **all right.**

all together, altogether Use *all together* to mean "in a group." Use *altogether* to mean "completely" or "in all."

EXAMPLES Let's cheer **all together.**

You are being **altogether** silly.

I have three dollars in quarters and two dollars in dimes; that's five dollars **altogether.**

almost, most Don't use *most* in place of *almost.*

EXAMPLE Marty **almost [*not* most]** always makes the honor roll.

a lot, alot *A lot* should always be written as two words. It means "a large number or amount." Avoid using *a lot* in formal writing; be specific.

EXAMPLES **A lot** of snow fell last night.

Ten inches of snow fell last night.

altar, alter An *altar* is a raised structure at which religious ceremonies are performed. *Alter* means "to change."

EXAMPLES The bride and groom approached the **altar.**

Mom **altered** my old coat to fit my little sister.

among, between Use *among* to show a relationship in which more than two persons or things are considered as a group.

EXAMPLES The committee will distribute the used clothing **among** the poor families in the community.

There was confusion **among** the players on the field.

In general, use *between* to show a relationship involving two persons or things, to compare one person or thing with an entire group, or to compare more than two items within a single group.

EXAMPLES Mr. and Mrs. Ohara live halfway **between** Seattle and Portland. **[relationship involving two places]**

What was the difference **between** Elvis Presley and other singers of the twentieth century? **[one person compared with a group]**

Emilio could not decide **between** the collie, the cocker spaniel, and the beagle. **[items within a group]**

anxious, eager *Anxious* means "fearful." It is not a synonym for *eager,* which means "filled with enthusiasm."

EXAMPLES Jean was **anxious** about her test results.

Kirk was **eager** [*not* **anxious**] to visit his cousin.

anyways, anywheres, everywheres, nowheres, somewheres
Write these words without the final *s: anyway, anywhere, everywhere, nowhere, somewhere.*

a while, awhile Use *a while* after a preposition. Use *awhile* as an adverb.

EXAMPLES She read for **a while.**

She read **awhile.**

bad, badly *Bad* is an adjective; use it before nouns and after linking verbs to modify the subject. *Badly* is an adverb; use it to modify action verbs.

EXAMPLES Clara felt **bad** about the broken vase.

The team performed **badly** in the first half.

bare, bear *Bare* means "naked." A *bear* is an animal.

EXAMPLES Don't expose your **bare** skin to the sun.

There are many **bears** in Yellowstone National Park.

base, bass One meaning of *base* is "a part on which something rests or stands." *Bass* pronounced to rhyme with *face* is a type of voice. When *bass* is pronounced to rhyme with *glass*, it's a kind of fish.

EXAMPLES Who is playing first **base**?

We need a **bass** singer for the part.

We caught several **bass** on our fishing trip.

beside, besides *Beside* means "at the side of" or "next to." *Besides* means "in addition to."

EXAMPLES Katrina sat **beside** her brother at the table.

Besides apples and bananas, the lunchroom serves dry cereal and doughnuts.

blew, blue *Blue* is the color of a clear sky. *Blew* is the past tense of *blow*.

EXAMPLES She wore a **blue** shirt.

The dead leaves **blew** along the driveway.

boar, bore A *boar* is a male pig. *Bore* means "to tire out with dullness"; it can also mean "a dull person."

EXAMPLES Wild **boars** are common in parts of Africa.

Please don't **bore** me with your silly jokes.

bow When *bow* is pronounced to rhyme with *low*, it means "a knot with two loops" or "an instrument for shooting arrows." When *bow* rhymes with *how*, it means "to bend at the waist."

EXAMPLES Can you tie a good **bow**?

Have you ever shot an arrow with a **bow**?

Actors **bow** at the end of a play.

brake, break As a noun, a *brake* is a device for stopping something or slowing it down. As a verb, *brake* means "to stop or slow down"; its principal parts are *brake, braking, braked,* and *braked.* The noun *break* has several meanings: "the result of breaking," "a fortunate chance," "a short rest." The verb *break* also has many meanings. A few are "to smash or shatter," "to destroy or disrupt," "to force a way through or into," "to surpass or excel." Its principal parts are *break, breaking, broke,* and *broken.*

EXAMPLES Rachel, please put a **brake** on your enthusiasm. **[noun]**

He couldn't **brake** the car in time to avoid the accident. **[verb]**

To fix the **break** in the drainpipe will cost a great deal of money. **[noun]**

Don't **break** my concentration while I'm studying. **[verb]**

bring, take *Bring* means "to carry from a distant place to a closer one." *Take* means "to carry from a nearby place to a more distant one."

EXAMPLES Will you **bring** me some perfume when you return from Paris?

Remember to **take** your passport when you go to Europe.

bust, busted Don't use these words in place of *break, broke, broken,* or *burst.*

EXAMPLES Don't **break** [*not* **bust**] that vase!

Who **broke** [*not* **busted**] this vase?

Someone has **broken** [*not* **busted**] this vase.

The balloon **burst** [*not* **busted**] with a loud pop.

The child **burst** [*not* **busted**] into tears.

buy, by *Buy* is a verb. *By* is a preposition.

EXAMPLES I'll **buy** the gift tomorrow.

Stand **by** me.

can, may *Can* indicates ability. *May* expresses permission or possibility.

EXAMPLES I **can** tie six kinds of knots.

"You **may** be excused," said Dad. [**permission**]

Luanna **may** play in the band next year. [**possibility**]

"We don't say 'CAN I,' Jeffy.
It's 'MAY I' 'cause this
is May."

capital, capitol A *capital* is a city that is the seat of a government. *Capitol,* on the other hand, refers only to a building in which a legislature meets.

EXAMPLES What is the **capital** of Vermont?

The **capitol** has a gold dome.

cent, scent, sent A *cent* is a penny. A *scent* is an odor. *Sent* is the past and past participle of *send*.

EXAMPLES I haven't got one **cent** in my pocket.

The **scent** of a skunk is unpleasant.

I **sent** my grandma a birthday card.

choose, chose *Choose* is the base form; *chose* is the past tense. The principal parts are *choose, choosing, chose,* and *chosen*.

EXAMPLES Please **choose** a poem to recite in class.

Brian **chose** to recite a poem by Emily Dickinson.

cite, sight, site *Cite* means "to quote an authority." *Sight* is the act of seeing or the ability to see; it can also mean "to see" and "something seen." A *site* is a location; it also means "to place or locate."

EXAMPLES Consuela **cited** three sources of information in her report.

My **sight** is perfect.

The board of education has chosen a **site** for the new high school.

clothes, cloths *Clothes* are what you wear. *Cloths* are pieces of fabric.

EXAMPLES Please hang all your **clothes** in your closet.

Use these **cloths** to wash the car.

coarse, course *Coarse* means "rough." *Course* can mean "a school subject," "a path or way," "order or development," or "part of a meal." *Course* is also used in the phrase *of course.*

EXAMPLES To begin, I'll need some **coarse** sandpaper.

I'd like to take a photography **course.**

The hikers chose a difficult **course** through the mountains.

complement, complementary; compliment, complimentary As a noun, *complement* means "something that completes"; as a verb, it means "to complete." As a noun, *compliment* means "a flattering remark"; as a verb, it means "to praise." *Complementary* and *complimentary* are the adjective forms of the words.

EXAMPLES This flowered scarf will be the perfect **complement** for your outfit. **[noun]**

This flowered scarf **complements** your outfit perfectly. **[verb]**

Phyllis received many **compliments** on her speech. **[noun]**

Many people **complimented** Phyllis on her speech. **[verb]**

consul; council, councilor; counsel, counselor A *consul* is a government official living in a foreign city to protect his or her country's interests and citizens. A *council* is a group of people gathered for the purpose of giving advice. A *councilor* is one who serves on a council. As a noun, *counsel* means "advice." As a verb, *counsel* means "to give advice." A *counselor* is one who gives counsel.

EXAMPLES The **consul** protested to the foreign government about the treatment of her fellow citizens.

The city **council** met to discuss the lack of parking facilities at the sports field.

The defendant received **counsel** from his attorney. **[noun]**

The attorney **counseled** his client to plead innocent. **[verb]**

could of, might of, must of, should of, would of After the words *could*, *might*, *must*, *should*, and *would*, use the helping verb *have* or its contraction, *'ve*, not the word *of*.

EXAMPLES **Could** you **have** prevented the accident?

You **might have** swerved to avoid the other car.

You **must have** seen it coming.

I **should've** warned you.

dear, deer *Dear* is a word of affection and is used to begin a letter. It can also mean "expensive." A *deer* is an animal.

EXAMPLES Talia is my **dear** friend.

We saw a **deer** at the edge of the woods.

desert, dessert *Desert* has two meanings. As a noun, it means "dry, arid land" and is stressed on the first syllable. As a verb, it means "to leave" or "to abandon" and is stressed on the second syllable. A *dessert* is something sweet eaten after a meal.

EXAMPLES This photograph shows a sandstorm in the **desert.**
[noun]

I won't **desert** you in your time of need. **[verb]**

Strawberry shortcake was served for **dessert.**

diner, dinner A *diner* is someone who dines or a place to eat. A *dinner* is a meal.

EXAMPLES The **diners** at the corner **diner** enjoy the friendly atmosphere.

Dinner will be served at eight.

doe, dough A *doe* is a female deer. *Dough* is a mixture of flour and a liquid.

EXAMPLES A **doe** and a stag were visible among the trees.

Knead the **dough** for three minutes.

doesn't, don't *Doesn't* is a contraction of *does not.* It is used with *he, she, it,* and all singular nouns. *Don't* is a contraction of *do not.* It is used with *I, you, we, they,* and all plural nouns.

EXAMPLES She **doesn't** know the answer to your question.

The twins **don't** like broccoli.

eye, I An *eye* is what you see with; it's also a small opening in a needle. *I* is a personal pronoun.

EXAMPLE **I** have something in my **eye.**

fewer, less Use *fewer* with nouns that can be counted. Use *less* with nouns that can't be counted.

EXAMPLES There are **fewer** students in my English class than in my math class.

I used **less** sugar than the recipe recommended.

flour, flower *Flour* is used to bake bread. A *flower* grows in a garden.

EXAMPLES Sift two cups of **flour** into a bowl.

A daisy is a **flower.**

for, four *For* is a preposition. *Four* is a number.

EXAMPLES Wait **for** me.

I have **four** grandparents.

formally, formerly *Formally* is the adverb form of *formal,* which has several meanings: "according to custom, rule, or etiquette," "requiring special ceremony or fancy clothing," "official." *Formerly* means "previously."

EXAMPLES The class officers will be **formally** installed on Thursday.

Mrs. Johnson was **formerly** Miss Malone.

go, say Don't use forms of *go* in place of forms of *say*.

EXAMPLES I tell her the answer, and she **says** [*not* goes], "I don't believe you."

I told her the news, and she **said** [*not* went], "Are you serious?"

good, well *Good* is an adjective; use it before nouns and after linking verbs to modify the subject. *Well* is an adverb; use it to modify action verbs. *Well* may also be an adjective meaning "in good health."

EXAMPLES You look **good** in that costume.

Joby plays the piano **well.**

You're looking **well** in spite of your cold.

grate, great A *grate* is a framework of bars set over an opening. *Grate* also means "to shred by rubbing against a rough surface." *Great* means "wonderful" or "large."

EXAMPLES The little girl dropped her lollipop through the **grate.**

Will you **grate** this cheese for me?

You did a **great** job!

had of Don't use *of* between *had* and a past participle.

EXAMPLE I wish I **had known** [*not* had of known] about this sooner.

had ought, hadn't ought, shouldn't ought *Ought* never needs a helping verb. Use *ought* by itself.

EXAMPLES You **ought** to win the match easily.

You **ought** not to blame yourself. *or* You **shouldn't** blame yourself.

hardly, scarcely *Hardly* and *scarcely* have negative meanings. They shouldn't be used with other negative words, like *not* or the contraction *n't,* to express the same idea.

EXAMPLES I **can** [*not* **can't**] **hardly** lift this box.

The driver **could** [*not* **couldn't**] **scarcely** see through the thick fog.

he, she, it, they Don't use a pronoun subject immediately after a noun subject, as in *The **girls they** baked the cookies.* Omit the unnecessary pronoun: *The **girls** baked the cookies.*

hear, here *Hear* is a verb meaning "to be aware of sound by means of the ear." *Here* is an adverb meaning "in or at this place."

EXAMPLES I can **hear** you perfectly well.

Please put your books **here.**

how come In formal speech and writing, use *why* instead of *how come.*

EXAMPLE **Why** weren't you at the meeting? [*not* **How come you weren't at the meeting?**]

in, into, in to Use *in* to mean "inside" or "within." Use *into* to show movement from the outside to a point within. Don't write *into* when you mean *in to.*

EXAMPLES Jeanine was sitting outdoors **in** a lawn chair.

When it got too hot, she went **into** the house.

She went **in to** get out of the heat.

its, it's *Its* is the possessive form of *it. It's* is a contraction of *it is* or *it has.*

EXAMPLES The dishwasher has finished **its** cycle.

It's **[It is]** raining again.

It's **[It has]** been a pleasure to meet you, Ms. Donatello.

kind of, sort of Don't use these expressions as adverbs. Use *somewhat* or *rather* instead.

EXAMPLE We were **rather** sorry to see him go. [*not* **We were kind of sorry to see him go.**]

knead, need *Knead* means "to mix or work into a uniform mass." As a noun, a *need* is a requirement. As a verb, *need* means "to require."

EXAMPLES **Knead** the clay to make it soft.

I **need** a new jacket.

knew, new *Knew* is the past tense of *know. New* means "unused" or "unfamiliar."

EXAMPLES I **knew** the answer.

I need a **new** pencil.

There's a **new** student in our class.

knight, night A *knight* was a warrior of the Middle Ages. *Night* is the time of day during which it is dark.

EXAMPLES A handsome **knight** rescued the fair maiden.

Night fell, and the moon rose.

lay, lie *Lay* means "to put" or "to place." Its principal parts are *lay, laying, laid,* and *laid.* Forms of *lay* are usually followed by a direct object. *Lie* means "to recline" or "to be positioned." Its principal parts are *lie, lying, lay,* and *lain.* Forms of *lie* are never followed by a direct object.

EXAMPLES **Lay** your coat on the bed.

The children are **laying** their beach towels in the sun to dry.

Dad **laid** the baby in her crib.

Myrna had **laid** the book beside her purse.

Lie down for a few minutes.

The lake **lies** to the north.

The dog is **lying** on the back porch.

This morning I **lay** in bed listening to the birds.

You have **lain** on the couch for an hour.

lead, led As a noun, *lead* has two pronunciations and several meanings. When it's pronounced to rhyme with *head,* it means "a metallic element." When it's pronounced to rhyme with *bead,* it can mean "position of being in first place in a race or contest," "example," "clue," "leash," or "the main role in a play."

EXAMPLES **Lead** is no longer allowed as an ingredient in paint.

Jason took the **lead** as the runners entered the stadium.

Follow my **lead.**

The detective had no **leads** in the case.

Only dogs on **leads** are permitted in the park.

Who will win the **lead** in the play?

As a verb, *lead* means "to show the way," "to guide or conduct," "to be first." Its principal parts are *lead, leading, led,* and *led.*

EXAMPLES Ms. Bachman **leads** the orchestra.

The trainer was **leading** the horse around the track.

An usher **led** us to our seats.

Gray has **led** the league in hitting for two years.

learn, teach *Learn* means "to receive knowledge." *Teach* means "to give knowledge."

EXAMPLES   Manny **learned** to play the piano at the age of six.

Ms. Guerrero **teaches** American history.

leave, let *Leave* means "to go away." *Let* means "to allow to."

EXAMPLES   I'll miss you when you **leave.**

Let me help you with those heavy bags.

like, as, as if, as though *Like* can be a verb or a preposition. It should not be used as a subordinating conjunction. Use *as, as if,* or *as though* to introduce a subordinate clause.

EXAMPLES   I **like** piano music. **[verb]**

Teresa plays the piano **like** a professional. **[preposition]**

Moira plays **as [*not* like]** her teacher taught her to play.

He looked at me **as if [*not* like]** he'd never seen me before.

loose, lose The adjective *loose* means "free," "not firmly attached," or "not fitting tightly." The verb *lose* means "to misplace" or "to fail to win."

EXAMPLES   Don't **lose** that **loose** button on your shirt.

If we **lose** this game, we'll be out of the tournament.

mail, male *Mail* is what turns up in your mailbox. *Mail* also means "send." A *male* is a boy or a man.

EXAMPLES   We received four pieces of **mail** today.

Sunny **mailed** a gift to her aunt Netta.

The **males** in the chorus wore red ties.

main, mane *Main* means "most important." A *mane* is the long hair on the neck of certain animals.

EXAMPLES What is your **main** job around the house?

The horse's **mane** was braided with colorful ribbons.

many, much Use *many* with nouns that can be counted. Use *much* with nouns that can't be counted.

EXAMPLES **Many** of the events are entertaining.

Much of the money goes to charity.

meat, meet *Meat* is food from an animal. Some meanings of *meet* are "to come face to face with," "to make the acquaintance of," and "to keep an appointment."

EXAMPLES Some people don't eat **meat.**

Meet me at the library at three o'clock.

minute The word *minute* (min´it) means "sixty seconds" or "a short period of time." The word *minute* (mī no͞ot´) means "very small."

EXAMPLES I'll be with you in a **minute.**

Don't bother me with **minute** details.

object *Object* is stressed on the first syllable when it means "a thing." *Object* is stressed on the second syllable when it means "oppose."

EXAMPLES Have you ever seen an unidentified flying **object**?

Mom **objected** to the proposal.

of Don't use *of* after the prepositions *off, inside,* and *outside.*

EXAMPLES He jumped **off** [*not* off of] the diving board.

The cat found a mouse **inside** [*not* inside of] the garage.

Outside [*not* outside of] the school, there is an old-fashioned drinking fountain.

off Don't use *off* in place of *from.*

EXAMPLE I'll borrow some money **from** [*not* **off**] my brother.

ought to of Don't use *of* in place of *have* after *ought to.*

EXAMPLE You **ought to have** [*not* **ought to of**] known better.

pair, pare, pear A *pair* is two. *Pare* means "to peel." A *pear* is a fruit.

EXAMPLES I bought a new **pair** of socks.

Pare the potatoes and cut them in quarters.

Would you like a **pear** or a banana?

passed, past *Passed* is the past tense and the past participle of the verb *pass. Past* can be an adjective, a preposition, an adverb, or a noun.

EXAMPLES We **passed** your house on the way to school. **[verb]**

The **past** week has been a busy one for me. **[adjective]**

We drove **past** your house. **[preposition]**

At what time did you drive **past**? **[adverb]**

I love Great-grandma's stories about the **past. [noun]**

pause, paws A *pause* is a short space of time. *Pause* also means "to wait for a short time." *Paws* are animal feet.

EXAMPLES We **pause** now for station identification.

I wiped the dog's muddy **paws.**

peace, piece *Peace* means "calmness" or "the absence of conflict." A *piece* is a part of something.

EXAMPLES We enjoy the **peace** of the countryside.

The two nations have finally made **peace.**

May I have another **piece** of pie?

plain, plane *Plain* means "not fancy," "clear," or "a large area of flat land." A *plane* is an airplane or a device for smoothing wood; it can also mean "a two-dimensional figure."

EXAMPLES He wore a **plain** blue tie.

The solution is perfectly **plain** to me.

Buffalo once roamed the **plains.**

We took a **plane** to Chicago.

Jeff used a **plane** to smooth the rough wood.

How do you find the area of a **plane** with four equal sides?

precede, proceed *Precede* means "to go before" or "to come before." *Proceed* means "to continue" or "to move along."

EXAMPLE Our band **preceded** the decorated floats as the parade **proceeded** through town.

principal, principle As a noun, *principal* means "head of a school." As an adjective, *principal* means "main" or "chief." *Principle* is a noun meaning "basic truth or belief" or "rule of conduct."

EXAMPLES Mr. Washington, our **principal,** will speak at the morning assembly. **[noun]**

What was your **principal** reason for joining the club? **[adjective]**

The **principle** of fair play is important in sports.

quiet, quit, quite The adjective *quiet* means "silent" or "motionless." The verb *quit* means "to stop" or "to give up or resign." The adverb *quite* means "very" or "completely."

EXAMPLES Please be **quiet** so I can think.

Shirelle has **quit** the swim team.

We were **quite** sorry to lose her.

raise, rise *Raise* means "to cause to move upward." It can also mean "to breed or grow" and "to bring up or rear." Its principal parts are *raise, raising, raised,* and *raised.* Forms of *raise* are usually followed by a direct object. *Rise* means "to move upward." Its principal parts are *rise, rising, rose,* and *risen.* Forms of *rise* are never followed by a direct object.

EXAMPLES **Raise** your hand if you know the answer.

My uncle is **raising** chickens.

Grandma and Grandpa Schwartz **raised** nine children.

Steam **rises** from boiling water.

The sun is **rising.**

The children **rose** from their seats when the principal entered the room.

In a short time, Loretta had **risen** to the rank of captain.

rap, wrap *Rap* means "to knock." *Wrap* means "to cover."

EXAMPLES **Rap** on the door.

Wrap the presents.

read, reed *Read* means "to understand the meaning of something written" or "to speak aloud something that is written or printed." A *reed* is a stalk of tall grass.

EXAMPLES Will you **read** Jimmy a story?

We found a frog in the **reeds** beside the lake.

real, really *Real* is an adjective; use it before nouns and after linking verbs to modify the subject. *Really* is an adverb; use it to modify action verbs, adjectives, and other adverbs.

EXAMPLES Winona has **real** musical talent.

She is **really** talented.

real, reel *Real* means "actual." A *reel* is a spool to wind something on, such as a fishing line.

EXAMPLES I have a **real** four-leaf clover.

My dad bought me a new fishing **reel.**

reason is because Don't use *because* after *reason is.* Use *that* after *reason is,* or use *because* alone.

EXAMPLES The **reason** I'm tired is **that** I didn't sleep well last night.

I'm tired **because** I didn't sleep well last night.

row When *row* is pronounced to rhyme with *low,* it means "a series of things arranged in a line" or "to move a boat by using oars." When *row* is pronounced to rhyme with *how,* it means "a noisy quarrel."

EXAMPLES We sat in the last **row** of the theater.

Let's **row** across the lake.

My sister and I had a serious **row** yesterday, but today we've forgotten about it.

S

sail, sale A *sail* is part of a boat. It also means "to travel in a boat." A *sale* is a transfer of ownership in exchange for money.

EXAMPLES As the boat **sails** away, the crew raise the **sails.**

The **sale** of the house was completed on Friday.

sea, see A *sea* is a body of water. *See* means "to be aware of with the eyes."

EXAMPLES The **sea** is rough today.

I can **see** you.

set, sit *Set* means "to place" or "to put." Its principal parts are *set, setting, set,* and *set.* Forms of *set* are usually followed by a direct object. *Sit* means "to place oneself in a seated position." Its principal parts are *sit, sitting, sat,* and *sat.* Forms of *sit* are not followed by a direct object.

EXAMPLES Lani **set** the pots on the stove.

The children **sit** quietly at the table.

sew, sow *Sew* means "to work with needle and thread." When *sow* is pronounced to rhyme with *how,* it means "a female pig." When *sow* is pronounced to rhyme with *low,* it means "to plant."

EXAMPLES Can you **sew** a button on a shirt?

The **sow** has five piglets.

Some farmers **sow** corn in their fields.

shined, shone, shown Both *shined* and *shone* are past tense forms and past participles of *shine.* Use *shined* when you mean "polished"; use *shone* in all other instances.

EXAMPLES Clete **shined** his shoes.

The sun **shone** brightly.

Her face **shone** with happiness.

Shown is the past participle of *show;* its principal parts are *show, showing, showed,* and *shown.*

EXAMPLES You **showed** me these photographs yesterday.

You have **shown** me these photographs before.

some, somewhat Don't use *some* as an adverb in place of *somewhat.*

EXAMPLE The team has improved **somewhat** [*not* some] since last season.

son, sun A *son* is a male child. A *sun* is a star.

EXAMPLES Kino is Mr. and Mrs. Akawa's **son.**

Our **sun** is 93 million miles away.

stationary, stationery *Stationary* means "fixed" or "unmoving." *Stationery* is writing paper.

EXAMPLES This classroom has **stationary** desks.

Rhonda likes to write letters on pretty **stationery.**

sure, surely *Sure* is an adjective; use it before nouns and after linking verbs to modify the subject. *Surely* is an adverb; use it to modify action verbs, adjectives, and other adverbs.

EXAMPLES Are you **sure** about that answer?

You are **surely** smart.

tail, tale A *tail* is what a dog wags. A *tale* is a story.

EXAMPLES The dog's **tail** curled over its back.

Everyone knows the **tale** of Goldilocks and the three bears.

tear When *tear* is pronounced to rhyme with *ear,* it's a drop of fluid from the eye. When *tear* is pronounced to rhyme with *bear,* it means "a rip" or "to rip."

EXAMPLES A **tear** fell from the child's eye.

Tear this rag in half.

than, then *Than* is a conjunction used to introduce the second part of a comparison. *Then* is an adverb meaning "at that time."

EXAMPLES LaTrisha is taller **than** LaToya.

My grandmother was a young girl **then.**

that, which, who *That* may refer to people or things. *Which* refers only to things. *Who* refers only to people.

EXAMPLES The poet **that** wrote *Leaves of Grass* is Walt Whitman.

I have already seen the movie **that** is playing at the Palace.

The new play, **which** closed after a week, received poor reviews.

Students **who** do well on the test will receive scholarships.

that there, this here Don't use *there* or *here* after *that, this, those,* or *these.*

EXAMPLES I can't decide whether to read **this** [*not* **this here**] magazine or **that** [*not* **that there**] book.

Fold **these** [*not* **these here**] towels and hang **those** [*not* **those there**] shirts in the closet.

their, there, they're *Their* is a possessive form of *they;* it's used to modify nouns. *There* means "in or at that place." *They're* is a contraction of *they are.*

EXAMPLES A hurricane damaged **their** house.

Put your books **there.**

They're our next-door neighbors.

theirs, there's *Theirs* is a possessive form of *they* used as a pronoun. *There's* is a contraction of *there is* or *there has.*

EXAMPLES **Theirs** is the white house with the green shutters.

There's [There is] your friend Chad.

There's [There has] been an accident.

them Don't use *them* as an adjective in place of *those.*

EXAMPLE I'll take one of **those** [*not* **them**] hamburgers.

this kind, these kinds Use the singular forms *this* and *that* with the singular nouns *kind, sort,* and *type.* Use the plural forms *these* and *those* with the plural nouns *kinds, sorts,* and *types.*

EXAMPLES Use **this kind** of lightbulb in your lamp.

Do you like **these kinds** of lamps?

Many Pakistani restaurants serve **that sort** of food.

Those sorts of foods are nutritious.

This type of dog makes a good pet.

These types of dogs are good with children.

thorough, through *Thorough* means "complete." *Through* is a preposition meaning "into at one side and out at another."

EXAMPLES We gave the bedrooms a **thorough** cleaning.

A breeze blew **through** the house.

threw, through *Threw* is the past tense of *throw*. *Through* is a preposition meaning "into at one side and out at another." *Through* can also mean "finished."

EXAMPLES Lacey **threw** the ball.

Ira walked **through** the room.

At last I'm **through** with my homework.

to, too, two *To* means "in the direction of"; it is also part of the infinitive form of a verb. *Too* means "very" or "also." *Two* is the number after *one*.

EXAMPLES Jaleela walks **to** school.

She likes **to** study.

The soup is **too** salty.

May I go **too**?

We have **two** kittens.

try and Use *try to.*

EXAMPLE Please **try to** [*not* try and] be on time.

unless, without Don't use *without* in place of *unless.*

EXAMPLE **Unless** [*not* Without] I clean my room, I can't go to the mall.

used to, use to The correct form is *used to.*

EXAMPLE   We **used to** [*not* **use to**] live in Cleveland, Ohio.

waist, waste Your *waist* is where you wear your belt. As a noun, *waste* means "careless or unnecessary spending" or "trash." As a verb, it means "to spend or use carelessly or unnecessarily."

EXAMPLES   She tied a colorful scarf around her **waist.**

Buying that computer game was a **waste** of money.

Put your **waste** in the dumpster.

Don't **waste** time worrying.

wait, weight *Wait* means "to stay or remain." *Weight* is a measurement.

EXAMPLES   **Wait** right here.

Her **weight** is 110 pounds.

wait for, wait on *Wait for* means "to remain in a place looking forward to something expected." *Wait on* means "to act as a server."

EXAMPLES   **Wait for** me at the bus stop.

Nat and Tammy **wait on** diners at The Golden Griddle.

way, ways Use *way,* not *ways,* in referring to distance.

EXAMPLE   It's a long **way** [*not* **ways**] to Tipperary.

weak, week *Weak* means "feeble" or "not strong." A *week* is seven days.

EXAMPLE   She felt **weak** for a **week** after the operation.

weather, whether *Weather* is the condition of the atmosphere. *Whether* means "if"; it is also used to introduce the first of two choices.

EXAMPLES The **weather** in Portland is mild and rainy.

Tell me **whether** you can go.

I can't decide **whether** to go or stay.

when, where Don't use *when* or *where* incorrectly in writing a definition.

EXAMPLES A compliment is a flattering remark. [*not* A compliment is when you make a flattering remark.]

Spelunking is the hobby of exploring caves. [*not* Spelunking is where you explore caves.]

where Don't use *where* in place of *that*.

EXAMPLE I see **that** [*not* where] the Yankees are in first place in their division.

where . . . at Don't use *at* after *where*.

EXAMPLE **Where** is your mother? [*not* Where is your mother at?]

who's, whose *Who's* is a contraction of *who is* or *who has*. *Whose* is the possessive form of *who*.

EXAMPLES **Who's [Who is]** conducting the orchestra?

Who's [Who has] read this book?

Whose umbrella is this?

wind When *wind* has a short-*i* sound, it means "moving air." When *wind* has a long-*i* sound, it means "to wrap around."

EXAMPLES The **wind** is strong today.

Wind the bandage around your ankle.

wood, would *Wood* comes from trees. *Would* is a helping verb.

EXAMPLE **Would** you prefer a **wood** bookcase or a metal one?

wound When *wound* is pronounced to rhyme with *sound*, it is the past tense of *wind*. The word *wound* (wo͞ond) means "an injury in which the skin is broken."

EXAMPLE I **wound** the bandage around my ankle to cover the **wound.**

your, you're *Your* is a possessive form of *you*. *You're* is a contraction of *you are*.

EXAMPLES **Your** arguments are convincing.

You're doing a fine job.

ABBREVIATIONS

An abbreviation is a short way to write a word or a group of words. Abbreviations should be used sparingly in formal writing except for a few that are actually more appropriate than their longer forms. These are *Mr., Mrs.,* and *Dr. (doctor)* before names, *A.M.* and *P.M.,* and *B.C.* and *A.D.*

Some abbreviations are written with capital letters and periods, and some with capital letters and no periods; some are written with lowercase letters and periods, and some with lowercase letters and no periods. A few may be written in any one of these four ways and still be acceptable. For example, to abbreviate *miles per hour,* you may write *MPH, M.P.H., mph,* or *m.p.h.*

Some abbreviations may be spelled in more than one way. For example, *Tuesday* may be abbreviated *Tues.* or *Tue. Thursday* may be written *Thurs.* or *Thu.* In the following lists, only the most common way of writing each abbreviation is given.

When you need information about an abbreviation, consult a dictionary. Some dictionaries list abbreviations in a special section in the back. Others list them in the main part of the book.

MONTHS

Jan.	January	none	July
Feb.	February	Aug.	August
Mar.	March	Sept.	September
Apr.	April	Oct.	October
none	May	Nov.	November
none	June	Dec.	December

DAYS

Sun.	Sunday	Thurs.	Thursday
Mon.	Monday	Fri.	Friday
Tues.	Tuesday	Sat.	Saturday
Wed.	Wednesday		

TIME AND DIRECTION

CDT	central daylight time
CST	central standard time
DST	daylight saving time
EDT	eastern daylight time
EST	eastern standard time
MDT	mountain daylight time
MST	mountain standard time
PDT	Pacific daylight time
PST	Pacific standard time
ST	standard time
NE	northeast
NW	northwest
SE	southeast
SW	southwest
A.D.	in the year of the Lord (Latin *anno Domini*)
B.C.	before Christ
B.C.E.	before the common era
C.E.	common era
A.M.	before noon (Latin *ante meridiem*)
P.M.	after noon (Latin *post meridiem*)

MEASUREMENT

The same abbreviation is used for both the singular and the plural meaning of measurements. Therefore, *ft.* stands for both *foot* and *feet,* and *in.* stands for both *inch* and *inches.* Note that abbreviations of metric measurements are commonly written without periods. U.S. measurements, on the other hand, are usually written with periods.

Metric System

Mass and Weight

t	metric ton
kg	kilogram
g	gram
cg	centigram
mg	milligram

Capacity

kl	kiloliter
l	liter
cl	centiliter
ml	milliliter

Length

km	kilometer
m	meter
cm	centimeter
mm	millimeter

U.S. Weights and Measures

Weight

wt.	weight
lb.	pound
oz.	ounce

Capacity

gal.	gallon
qt.	quart
pt.	pint
c.	cup
tbsp.	tablespoon
tsp.	teaspoon
fl. oz.	fluid ounce

Length

mi.	mile
rd.	rod
yd.	yard
ft.	foot
in.	inch

MISCELLANEOUS MEASUREMENTS

p.s.i.	pounds per square inch
MPH	miles per hour
MPG	miles per gallon
rpm	revolutions per minute
C	Celsius, centigrade
F	Fahrenheit
K	Kelvin
kn	knot

COMPUTER AND INTERNET

CPU	central processing unit
CRT	cathode ray tube
DOS	disk operating system
e-mail	electronic mail
K	kilobyte
URL	uniform resource locator
DVD	digital video disc
d.p.i	dots per inch
WWW	World Wide Web
ISP	internet service provider
DNS	domain name system

ADDITIONAL ABBREVIATIONS

ac	alternating current
dc	direct current
AM	amplitude modulation
FM	frequency modulation
ASAP	as soon as possible
e.g.	for example (Latin *exempli gratia*)
etc.	and others, and so forth (Latin *et cetera*)
i.e.	that is (Latin *id est*)
Inc.	incorporated
ISBN	International Standard Book Number

lc	lowercase
misc.	miscellaneous
p.	page
pp.	pages
R.S.V.P.	please reply (French *répondez s'il vous plaît*)
SOS	international distress signal
TM	trademark
uc	uppercase
vs.	versus
w/o	without

UNITED STATES (U.S.)

In most cases, state names and street addresses should be spelled out. The postal abbreviations in the following list should be used with ZIP codes in addressing envelopes. They may also be used with ZIP codes for return addresses and inside addresses in business letters. The traditional state abbreviations are seldom used nowadays, but occasionally it's helpful to know them.

State	Traditional	Postal
Alabama	Ala.	AL
Alaska	none	AK
Arizona	Ariz.	AZ
Arkansas	Ark.	AR
California	Calif.	CA
Colorado	Colo.	CO
Connecticut	Conn.	CT
Delaware	Del.	DE
District of Columbia	D.C.	DC
Florida	Fla.	FL
Georgia	Ga.	GA
Hawaii	none	HI
Idaho	none	ID
Illinois	Ill.	IL
Indiana	Ind.	IN

Iowa	none	IA
Kansas	Kans.	KS
Kentucky	Ky.	KY
Louisiana	La.	LA
Maine	none	ME
Maryland	Md.	MD
Massachusetts	Mass.	MA
Michigan	Mich.	MI
Minnesota	Minn.	MN
Mississippi	Miss.	MS
Missouri	Mo.	MO
Montana	Mont.	MT
Nebraska	Nebr.	NE
Nevada	Nev.	NV
New Hampshire	N.H.	NH
New Jersey	N.J.	NJ
New Mexico	N. Mex.	NM
New York	N.Y.	NY
North Carolina	N.C.	NC
North Dakota	N. Dak.	ND
Ohio	none	OH
Oklahoma	Okla.	OK
Oregon	Oreg.	OR
Pennsylvania	Pa.	PA
Rhode Island	R.I.	RI
South Carolina	S.C.	SC
South Dakota	S. Dak.	SD
Tennessee	Tenn.	TN
Texas	Tex.	TX
Utah	none	UT
Vermont	Vt.	VT
Virginia	Va.	VA
Washington	Wash.	WA
West Virginia	W. Va.	WV
Wisconsin	Wis.	WI
Wyoming	Wyo.	WY

Part Two

• • • • • • • • • • • • •

Grammar, Usage, and Mechanics

Subjects, Predicates, and Sentences

• • • • • • • • • • • • • • •

PRETEST **Kinds of Sentences**

Write declarative, interrogative, imperative, *or* exclamatory *to identify each sentence.*

1. Have you ever heard about the horse Clever Hans?
2. Could it really count and read?
3. Its owner gave signals to the horse.
4. What a good trick it was!
5. Read an article about the horse.

PRETEST **Sentences and Sentence Fragments**

Write sentence *or* fragment *for each item. Rewrite each fragment to make it a sentence.*

6. A new hobby.
7. George learned how to cut glass.

8. He will also drill holes and sand the glass.
   9. To have special equipment.
  10. He made sun catchers for windows.
  11. Presents for friends.
  12. My sister likes to knit.
  13. Her friend taught knitting classes last year.
  14. Sweaters and scarves in many colors.
  15. She uses many colors of yarn.

PRETEST Subjects and Predicates

Write each sentence. Underline the simple subjects once and the simple predicates twice.

  16. A musical is a play set to music.
  17. We saw a musical last week.
  18. The singers gave a great performance.
  19. Buy a ticket for the next show.
  20. What do you like best—opera, rhythm and blues, rock 'n' roll, or country music?
  21. Rodgers and Hammerstein wrote the musicals *Oklahoma* and *South Pacific*.
  22. The set turned on a hidden platform.
  23. Sit next to me in the theater.
  24. Laura enjoyed the performance of *Cats*.
  25. Here are our seats.

PRETEST Simple, Compound, and Run-on Sentences

Write simple, compound, *or* run-on *to identify each numbered item. If an item is a run-on, rewrite it correctly.*

  26. The science class studies astronomy in September.
  27. The students study maps of the skies they also review charts of the northern constellations.
  28. Everyone was familiar with the Big Dipper, but many students did not know about other star formations.

29. Lynn and I decided to learn myths and stories about stars.
30. I read about Orion, Lynn read about Scorpion.
31. We prepared a report and a talk.
32. Lynn found more information on the Internet, and she shared it with me.
33. We also learned about Greek astronomers.
34. The class enjoyed our report, but they wanted more information about certain constellations.
35. They should read articles and watch special reports about astronomy.

1.1 KINDS OF SENTENCES

A **sentence** is a group of words that expresses a complete thought.

Different kinds of sentences have different purposes. A sentence can make a statement, ask a question, or give a command. A sentence can also express strong feeling. All sentences begin with a capital letter and end with a punctuation mark. The punctuation mark depends on the purpose of the sentence.

A **declarative sentence** makes a statement. It ends with a period.

EXAMPLE   Edgar Allan Poe wrote suspenseful short stories.

An **interrogative sentence** asks a question. It ends with a question mark.

EXAMPLE   Did Poe also write poetry?

An **imperative sentence** gives a command or makes a request. It ends with a period.

EXAMPLE   Read "The Pit and the Pendulum."

An **exclamatory sentence** expresses strong feeling. It ends with an exclamation point.

EXAMPLE   What a great writer Poe was!

EXAMPLE   How I enjoy his stories!

"Now that we've been introduced, Mr. Kelvey, I'd like to bring an old friend of mine—the interrogative sentence—into our conversation."

PRACTICE Identifying Kinds of Sentences

Write declarative, interrogative, imperative, *or* exclamatory *to identify each sentence.*

1. Have you seen Venus Williams on the tennis court?
2. She won a Grand Slam tennis title in 2000.
3. What a fabulous player she is!
4. She can hit a serve of 121 miles per hour.
5. How exciting it is to watch her play!

6. Her sister Serena won the U.S. Open in 1999.
7. Sign up for tennis lessons this summer.
8. The game takes skill and concentration.
9. Plan to practice as often as possible.
10. Will I see you on the courts?

1.2 SENTENCES AND SENTENCE FRAGMENTS

Every sentence has two parts: a subject and a predicate.

EXAMPLE

Sentence

Emily Dickinson wrote poetry.

Subject ‖ Predicate

The **subject part** of a sentence names whom or what the sentence is about.

The **predicate part** of a sentence tells what the subject does or has. It can also tell what the subject is or is like.

A **sentence fragment** does not express a complete thought. It may also be missing a subject, a predicate, or both.

CORRECTING SENTENCE FRAGMENTS

FRAGMENT	PROBLEM	SENTENCE
The poems.	The fragment lacks a predicate. *What did the poems do?*	The poems lay in Dickinson's bureau for years.
Wrote about her emotions.	The fragment lacks a subject. *Who wrote about her emotions?*	This famous poet wrote about her emotions.
Of meaning.	The fragment lacks a subject and a predicate.	Her poems contain many layers of meaning.

Identifying Sentences and Fragments

Write sentence *or* fragment *for each item. Write each sentence and underline the subject part once and the predicate part twice. For each fragment, add a subject or a predicate or both to make it a sentence.*

1. The word *dinosaur* means "terrible lizard."
2. Weighed thousands of pounds.
3. Some dinosaurs were twenty feet tall.
4. Many dinosaurs ate plants.
5. Huge jaws and sharp teeth.
6. Dinosaurs may have been cold-blooded creatures.
7. Dinosaurs disappeared a long time ago.
8. Were good fighters.
9. Many ideas and theories about dinosaurs.
10. The dinosaurs may have starved to death.

1.3 SUBJECTS AND PREDICATES

A sentence consists of a subject and a predicate that together express a complete thought. Both a subject and a predicate may consist of more than one word.

	┌──── Complete Subject ────┐	┌──── Complete Predicate ────┐
EXAMPLE	Charles Dickens's **novels**	**are** still popular today.
EXAMPLE	My English **teacher**	**wrote** an article about Dickens.

The **complete subject** includes all the words in the subject of a sentence.

The **complete predicate** includes all the words in the predicate of a sentence.

Not all words in the subject or the predicate are equally important.

GRAMMAR/USAGE/MECHANICS

Complete
Subject

Complete
Predicate

EXAMPLE   The young **Charles Dickens**   **wrote** many articles.

Simple Subject   Simple Predicate

The **simple subject** is the main word or word group in the complete subject.

The simple subject is usually a noun or a pronoun. A **noun** is a word that names a person, a place, a thing, or an idea. A **pronoun** is a word that takes the place of one or more nouns.

The **simple predicate** is the main word or word group in the complete predicate.

The simple predicate is always a verb. A **verb** is a word that expresses action or a state of being.

Sometimes the simple subject is the same as the complete subject. Sometimes the simple predicate is the same as the complete predicate.

PRACTICE **Identifying Complete Subjects and Complete Predicates**

Write each sentence. Underline the complete subject once and the complete predicate twice.

1. Some teachers do not assign homework.
2. Others give students hours of homework.
3. Family time is important to many parents.
4. Many students spend over two hours a night on homework.
5. One grade school in California has a different program.
6. Students attend school 220 days a year.

GRAMMAR/USAGE/MECHANICS

7. Families take vacations at any time.

8. Homework is not given in any class.

9. Summer vacation lasts one week.

10. The school has a long waiting list.

PRACTICE **Identifying Simple Subjects and Simple Predicates**

Write each sentence. Underline the simple subject once and the simple predicate twice.

1. Everyone brought a notebook to the lecture.

2. The presentation lasted an hour.

3. Many people send cards or gifts on Valentine's Day.

4. We learned about customs in various countries.

5. The bald eagle is the national emblem of the United States.

6. The long wanderings of Odysseus lasted ten years.

7. Many Japanese women still wear traditional kimonos on special occasions.

8. The family's pictures were stored inside an old suitcase.

9. I also bought several souvenirs.

10. That silver ring should fit me perfectly.

1.4 IDENTIFYING THE SUBJECT

In most sentences, the subject comes before the predicate.

```
            ┌──── Subject ────┐   ┌────────── Predicate ──────────┐
EXAMPLE   Washington Irving     described New York in his stories.
```

Other kinds of sentences, such as questions, begin with part or all of the predicate. The subject comes next, followed by the rest of the predicate.

```
          Predicate  Subject   ┌──────Predicate──────┐
EXAMPLE   Are        people    still reading his stories?
```

Chapter 1 Subjects, Predicates, and Sentences **71**

To locate the subject of a question, rearrange the words to form a statement.

PREDICATE	SUBJECT	PREDICATE
Did	Irving	write many funny stories?
	Irving	did write many funny stories.

The predicate also comes before the subject in sentences with inverted word order and in declarative sentences that begin with *Here is, Here are, There is,* and *There are.*

EXAMPLE   Over the paper raced   Irving's pen.

― Predicate ―   ― Subject ―

EXAMPLE   There is   Irving's original manuscript.

― Predicate ―   ― Subject ―

In imperative sentences (requests and commands), the subject is usually not stated. The predicate is the entire sentence. The word *you* is understood to be the subject.

Understood Subject   ― Predicate ―

EXAMPLE   (You)   Look for the author's name on the cover.

PRACTICE   Identifying the Subject

Write each sentence. Underline the complete subject. Write (You) *before any sentence with an understood subject.*

1. Some animals hardly ever see the daylight.
2. They live in nests in underground tunnels.
3. There is the small mole, for example.
4. Into a tunnel scampers the hard-working mole.
5. Do insects really make up part of the mole's diet?
6. How energetic the mole is!
7. Find more information about moles in the library.
8. Their eyes are extremely tiny.
9. They can only distinguish light from dark.
10. Has anyone seen a nature video about moles?

1.5 COMPOUND SUBJECTS AND COMPOUND PREDICATES

A sentence may have more than one simple subject or simple predicate.

A **compound subject** consists of two or more simple subjects that have the same predicate. The subjects may be joined by *and, or, both . . . and, either . . . or,* or *neither . . . nor.*

Compound Subject

EXAMPLE **Charlotte Brontë** and **Emily Brontë** were sisters.

When the two simple subjects are joined by *and* or by *both . . . and,* the compound subject is plural. Use the plural form of the verb to agree with the plural compound subject.

When simple subjects are joined by *or, either . . . or,* or *neither . . . nor,* the verb must agree with the nearer simple subject.

EXAMPLE Neither **Charlotte** nor **Emily is** my favorite author.

EXAMPLE Neither her **sisters** nor **Charlotte was** outgoing.

EXAMPLE Neither **Charlotte** nor her **sisters were** outgoing.

In the first sentence, *Emily* is the nearer subject, so the singular form of the verb is used. In the second sentence, *Charlotte* is the nearer subject, so the singular form of the verb is used here too. In the third sentence, *sisters* is the nearer subject, so the plural form of the verb is used.

A **compound predicate** consists of two or more simple predicates, or verbs, that have the same subject. The verbs may be connected by *and, or, but, both . . . and, either . . . or,* or *neither . . . nor.*

Compound Predicate

EXAMPLE Many students **read** and **enjoy** novels.

The compound predicate in this sentence consists of *read* and *enjoy.* Both verbs agree with the plural subject, *students.*

Chapter 1 Subjects, Predicates, and Sentences **73**

Write each sentence, using the correct form of the verb in parentheses. Then underline the compound subjects once and the compound predicates twice.

1. Andrea and Josh (is, are) good friends.
2. Job applicants either (applies, apply) in person or (sends, send) résumés by mail.
3. Both Mrs. Chan and Mr. Edgar (studies, study) and (teaches, teach) history.
4. A teacher or a parent (directs, direct) the junior-high play and (prepares, prepare) the program.
5. Tessa (likes, like) the new school but (misses, miss) her old friends.
6. Neither his friends nor Abdul (walks, walk) or (rides, ride) a bike to school.
7. Abdul and his friends (takes, take) the bus or (gets, get) rides from their parents.
8. The students and families both (speaks, speak) and (reads, read) French.
9. Neither Alexia nor Raul (was, were) joining the team.
10. Aaron both (writes, write) and (performs, perform) in plays.

1.6 SIMPLE, COMPOUND, AND RUN-ON SENTENCES

A **simple sentence** has one subject and one predicate.

——————— Simple Sentence ———————
EXAMPLE Eudora Welty   lived in Jackson, Mississippi.

A simple sentence may have a compound subject, a compound predicate, or both, as in the following example.

——————— Simple Sentence ———————
EXAMPLE **Jeff** and **I**   **read** and **enjoy** Welty's stories.
         Compound Subject   Compound Predicate

A **compound sentence** is a sentence that contains two or more simple sentences joined by a comma and a coordinating conjunction (*and, but, or*) or by a semicolon.

┌─────────── Compound Sentence ───────────┐

EXAMPLE Welty is a novelist, but she also writes essays.

EXAMPLE Welty is a novelist; she also writes essays.

└── Simple Sentence ──┘ └── Simple Sentence ──┘

A run-on sentence is two or more sentences incorrectly written as one sentence. To correct a run-on, write separate sentences or combine the sentences.

CORRECTING RUN-ON SENTENCES

RUN-ON	CORRECT
Welty wrote novels she wrote essays. Welty wrote novels, she wrote essays.	Welty wrote novels. She wrote essays. Welty wrote novels, **and** she wrote essays. Welty wrote novels; she wrote essays.

PRACTICE Identifying Simple, Compound, and Run-on Sentences

Write simple, compound, *or* run-on *to identify each numbered item. If an item is a run-on, rewrite it correctly.*

1. Many male baseball players were in the armed services during World War II.
2. During that time, the All-American Girls Professional Baseball League was created and helped keep professional baseball alive.
3. The Racine Belles and the Rockford Peaches were two of the teams.
4. The women played in baseball stadiums in the Midwest they earned from $55 to $125 per week.

5. The women played hard, but they had to wear feminine attire.
6. The "Darlings of the Diamonds" wore short skirts as part of their uniforms.
7. Do you play in an organized baseball league, or do you prefer informal games?
8. Every day after school, I practice my pitching and batting.
9. Our team won the playoffs, and we hung our winning banner at school.
10. Did you watch the game, or did you read the story about it in the newspaper?

PRACTICE Proofreading

Rewrite the following passage, correcting errors in spelling, capitalization, grammar, and usage. Add any missing punctuation. Write legibly to be sure one letter is not mistaken for another. There are ten mistakes.

Jane Addams

[1]Many men and women has made a difference in the lives of others. [2]Jane Addams is an example of one such woman. [3]her work changed people's lives.

[4]Her degree from the Rockford Female Seminary in Illinois in 1882. [5]Addams visited Europe, she was affected by the poverty there. [6]A trip to a settlement house in London changed her life and the lives of others?

[7]Settlement houses were needed to help workers who moved to the cities. [8]Addams reterned to Chicago. [9]She opened a settlement in Hull House, she moved into the mansion and used her own money and the contributions from others to keep it running. [10]Addams even became a garbage inspector and helped to clean up the filthy streets?

[11]Hull House continued to grow and eventually included thirteen buildings. [12]Addams continued to work for change. [13]She spoke about the rights of workers and children she also helped to create the first juvenile court. [14]In 1931, she were awarded the Nobel Peace Prize.

Write declarative, interrogative, imperative, *or* exclamatory *to identify each sentence.*

1. I bought a new radio for use during emergencies.
2. What a wonderful idea!
3. Turn on the radio and listen to this program.
4. Does the radio work without electricity?
5. The radio operates by solar power.

POSTTEST Sentences and Sentence Fragments

Write sentence *or* fragment *for each item. Rewrite each fragment to make it a sentence.*

6. Near the lake not far from the shore.
7. Use the kayak or the canoe.
8. Kayaks sit deep in the water.
9. The new paddle for the kayak.
10. The camping gear fits in the canoe.
11. The new tent takes up very little space.
12. Folds into a small rectangle.
13. Put the lantern under the seat.
14. The campsite is available for three nights.
15. Wood and kindling for the campfire.

POSTTEST Subjects and Predicates

Write each sentence. Underline the simple subjects once and the simple predicates twice.

16. Have you visited the seashore along the Atlantic or Pacific Oceans in recent years?
17. Crabs often live in rock pools along the shore.
18. Does calcium carbonate make the shells of crabs and lobsters hard and stony?
19. There are the muddy shores of some tropical seacoasts.

GRAMMAR/USAGE/MECHANICS

20. The shallow waters of tropical coasts may be covered with mangrove plants.
21. Roots hold the mangroves in the mud.
22. Through the mangrove swamps swim alligators.
23. Look for other unusual animals.
24. Oil spills from tankers can damage the seashore and its life forms.
25. The oil poisons birds and seals.

POSTTEST Simple, Compound, and Run-on Sentences

Write simple, compound, *or run-on to identify each numbered item. If an item is a run-on, rewrite it correctly.*

26. Nineteen students are appearing in this year's class play.
27. Paul is working on lights, and Emma is helping with the sets and props.
28. I tried out for the play I got a small part as the daughter of one of the main characters.
29. My family and some of my friends will attend both performances of the play.
30. Ken and Maureen made the posters and hung them around the school.
31. Janine sold tickets Alec put an ad in the school paper.
32. We will perform on Friday night and Saturday afternoon.
33. Did Kim make her own costume, or did her mother and aunt make it for her?
34. Jessie bought a ticket for Friday, but she came on Saturday instead.
35. Ms. Hanson directed the play, and Mr. Akeem and Mr. Williams directed the music.

Chapter 2

Nouns

• • • • • • • • • • • • • • • •

PRETEST **Kinds of Nouns**

Write each noun. Label the common nouns C *and the proper nouns* P.

1. Paul discovered the next morning that five sheep had escaped.
2. The family is going to travel around the United States and Mexico in a mobile home.
3. Is the ozone layer over the Arctic thinning as much as the layer over the Antarctic?
4. Sunspot Airlines offers more room throughout the cabins of their airplanes than any other airline.
5. The Alcyon Theater has a first-come, first-serve policy for seating people.

PRETEST **Possessive Nouns**

Write the possessive form of the noun in parentheses.

6. The (boy) favorite cousin went away to college.
7. (Wes) sister is the president of the firm.

8. The (car) interior is gray and black.
9. A raccoon ate (Riley) food.
10. The new intern had trouble finding the (doctors) lounge.
11. The (Woods) cabin is on the north shore of the lake.
12. The judge did not allow the (companies) financial records to be used as evidence.
13. Her (boss) house is the stone mansion at the end of the road.
14. The (girls) dance performance won awards for creativity and originality.
15. The police officer listened to the (women) stories.

PRETEST Recognizing Plurals, Possessives, and Contractions

Identify the italicized word in each sentence by writing plural noun, singular possessive noun, plural possessive noun, *or* contraction.

16. I saw my *sister's* friend at the rodeo.
17. Has anyone seen *Petra's* hairbrush?
18. *Today's* the last day to sign up for summer school.
19. *Beekeepers* wear special suits to protect their bodies.
20. The *children's* story time was interrupted by the fire alarm.
21. I presented my paper at the *writers'* conference.
22. Molten rock bubbles out of cracks in *Earth's* crust.
23. The *farmers'* market is closed on Monday.
24. The *dogs* chased the fox through the woods.
25. *Maria's* leaving on the ten o'clock train.

PRETEST Appositives

Write the appositive or appositive phrase in each sentence.

26. The Renaissance, a renewed interest in learning, began in Italy and spread across Europe.
27. Mira's favorite dinosaur, *Tyrannosaurus rex,* had razor-sharp teeth and powerful claws.

28. Her brother James is a legal secretary.

29. After Justine finished writing her latest book, a twelve-hundred-page novel, she took some time off.

30. Have you read A. A. Milne's book *Winnie-the-Pooh*?

31. Jules Verne, a French author, wrote over sixty-five books inspired by technological progress.

32. Last year, the year of the big hurricane, was the year I entered high school.

33. The early works of the Dutch painter Vincent van Gogh were influenced by Impressionism.

34. A star on both stage and screen, Angela Lansbury works hard to keep in touch with her fans.

35. Abraham Lincoln, the sixteenth president of the United States, laid the foundation for a free, modern nation.

2.1 KINDS OF NOUNS

A **noun** is a word that names a person, a place, a thing, or an idea.

NOUNS	
PERSONS	sister, mayor, player, coach, pianist, children
PLACES	park, zoo, lake, school, playground, desert, city
THINGS	magazine, boots, rose, pencil, peach, baseball, car
IDEAS	honesty, truth, democracy, pride, maturity, progress

A **common noun** names *any* person, place, thing, or idea.
A **proper noun** names a *particular* person, place, thing, or idea.

The first word and all other important words in a proper noun are capitalized: *Edgar Allan Poe, Statue of Liberty.*

Common nouns can be either concrete or abstract.

Concrete nouns name things you can see or touch.
Abstract nouns name ideas, qualities, and feelings that can't be seen or touched.

KINDS OF NOUNS		
COMMON NOUNS		**PROPER NOUNS**
Abstract	**Concrete**	
truth	document	Supreme Court
courage	crown	Queen Elizabeth I
time	snow	December
history	museum	Museum of Modern Art
entertainment	actor	Meryl Streep
education	school	Howard University
comedy	comedian	Jerry Seinfeld
friendship	friend	Jessica
tragedy	ship	*Titanic*

Compound nouns are nouns made of two or more words.

A compound noun can be one word, like *storybook*, or more than one word, like *ice cream*. A compound noun can also be joined by one or more hyphens, like *runner-up*.

COMPOUND NOUNS	
ONE WORD	housekeeper, showcase, bookmark, outdoors, teammate
MORE THAN ONE WORD	post office, dining room, maid of honor, high school
HYPHENATED	sister-in-law, great-aunt, kilowatt-hour, walkie-talkie

Write each noun. Label the common nouns C *and the proper nouns* P.

1. Both lions and house cats are members of the scientific family Felidae.
2. The Superdome in New Orleans is the largest indoor arena.
3. All the students want to help out at the local fund-raising event.
4. Bill has been saving his money because he wants to buy a new guitar.
5. Egypt is home to some of the most beautiful structures in the world.
6. Crispus Attucks was an American protester killed in the Boston Massacre.
7. The first time we went to Arizona, the temperature was in the hundreds on most days.
8. Lise and Hillary went as a hedgehog and a raccoon for Halloween.
9. Aunt Mary made soup with the vegetables she bought at the vegetable stand in Matoon.
10. The beaches in Hawaii are great places to swim, snorkel, and surf.

2.2 SINGULAR AND PLURAL NOUNS

A **singular noun** names one person, place, thing, or idea. A **plural noun** names more than one.

To form the plural of most nouns, you simply add -*s*. Other plural nouns are formed in different ways.

FORMING PLURAL NOUNS

NOUNS ENDING WITH	TO FORM PLURAL	EXAMPLES		
s, z, ch, sh, x	Add *-es.*	bus bus**es**	buzz buzz**es**	box box**es**
o preceded by a vowel	Add *-s.*	rodeo rodeo**s**	studio studio**s**	radio radio**s**
o preceded by a consonant	Usually add *-es.*	hero hero**es**	potato potato**es**	echo echo**es**
	Sometimes add *-s.*	zero zero**s**	photo photo**s**	piano piano**s**
y preceded by a vowel	Add *-s.*	day day**s**	turkey turkey**s**	toy toy**s**
y preceded by a consonant	Usually change *y* to *i* and add *-es.*	city cit**ies**	diary diar**ies**	penny penn**ies**
f or *fe*	Usually change *f* to *v* and add *-s* or *-es.*	wife wi**ves**	leaf lea**ves**	half hal**ves**
	Sometimes add *-s.*	roof roof**s**	chief chief**s**	belief belief**s**

FoxTrot

by Bill Amend

Foxtrot © 1998 & 1993 Bill Amend. Reprinted with permission of Universal Press Syndicate. All rights reserved.

To form the plural of compound nouns written as one word, usually add -*s* or -*es*. To form the plural of compound nouns that are written as more than one word or are hyphenated, make the main noun in the compound word plural, or check a dictionary.

COMPOUND NOUNS	
ONE WORD	doorbell**s**, necklace**s**, rosebush**es**; *Exception:* passer**s**by
MORE THAN ONE WORD	post office**s**, dining room**s**, maid**s** of honor, high school**s**
HYPHENATED	brother**s**-in-law, great-aunt**s**, eighth-grader**s**, push-up**s**

Words such as *family* and *team* are called collective nouns.

A **collective noun** names a group of people, animals, or things.

A collective noun subject may be followed by a singular verb or a plural verb, depending on the meaning. The subject is singular when the members of the group act as a single unit. The subject is plural when each member of the group acts separately. Other words in a sentence can sometimes help you decide whether a collective noun is singular or plural.

EXAMPLE   The **team shares** the field with **its** opponent.
[shares, its, singular]

EXAMPLE   The **team share their** jokes with one another.
[share, their, plural]

PRACTICE Forming Plural Nouns

Write the plural form of each noun.

1. insect
2. ego
3. toothbrush
4. shelf
5. tornado

6. strategy
7. chef
8. knife
9. highway
10. attorney-at-law

Write each collective noun. Label it S *if it's singular and* P *if it's plural.*

1. The swim team travels to Plano once a month.
2. The marching band buy their own instruments.
3. The ant colony stores food for the long winter.
4. The class present their speeches.
5. The crowd wants to hear another song.
6. The art committee vote for their favorite painting.
7. The crew works seven days a week.
8. The group drive separately to the performance.
9. The congregation holds a garage sale for charity.
10. The Ramirez family wants to move to Alaska.

2.3 POSSESSIVE NOUNS

A noun can show ownership or possession of things or qualities. This kind of noun is called a possessive noun.

A **possessive noun** tells who or what owns or has something.

Possessive nouns may be common nouns or proper nouns. They may also be singular or plural. Notice the possessive nouns in the following sentences:

SINGULAR NOUN	**Rita** has a book about baseball.
SINGULAR POSSESSIVE NOUN	**Rita's** book is about baseball.
PLURAL NOUN	Several **cities** have baseball teams.
PLURAL POSSESSIVE NOUN	These **cities'** teams attract fans.

Possessive nouns are formed in one of two ways. To form the possessive of singular nouns and plural nouns not ending in *s*, add an apostrophe and *s* (*'s*). To form the possessive of plural nouns ending in *s*, add just an apostrophe at the end of the word.

FORMING POSSESSIVE NOUNS

NOUNS	TO FORM POSSESSIVE	EXAMPLES
All singular nouns; plural nouns not ending in **s**	Add an apostrophe and **s** (**'s**).	a girl–a girl**'s** name Germany–Germany**'s** exports the bus–the bus**'s** capacity Ms. Ames–Ms. Ames**'s** class children–children**'s** toys women–women**'s** coats
Plural nouns ending in **s**	Add just an apostrophe (') at the end of the plural noun.	babies–babies**'** birth weight the Joneses–the Joneses**'** car

---

PRACTICE **Writing Possessive Nouns**

Write the possessive form of the noun in parentheses.

1. The hawk stole the eggs from that (bird) nest.
2. (Dennis) entry in the soapbox derby won first place.
3. The rose (bush) thorns were very sharp.
4. The (lawyers) meeting was cancelled because of schedule conflicts.
5. (France) largest and most celebrated city is Paris.
6. The (states) position on the matter is clear.
7. The (Jacobs) home was not damaged by the tornado.
8. What is your (brother) shoe size?
9. The (children) dog was afraid of the fireworks.
10. A skeleton supports an (animal) body.

2.4 RECOGNIZING PLURALS, POSSESSIVES, AND CONTRACTIONS

Most plural nouns, all possessive nouns, and certain contractions end with the sound of *s*. These words may sound alike, but their spellings and meanings are different.

NOUN FORMS AND CONTRACTIONS

	EXAMPLE	MEANING
Plural Noun	The **students** wrote a play.	more than one student
Plural Possessive Noun	The **students'** play is good.	the play by several students
Singular Possessive Noun	I saw the **student's** performance.	the performance of one student
Contraction	This **student's** the author. This **student's** written other plays.	This student is the author. This student has written other plays.

A **contraction** is a word made by combining two words and leaving out one or more letters. An apostrophe shows where the letters have been omitted.

Plural nouns don't have an apostrophe. Contractions and singular possessive nouns look exactly alike. Some plural possessive nouns end with *'s*, and some end with just an apostrophe. You can tell these words apart by the way they're used in a sentence.

NOUN FORMS AND CONTRACTIONS

PLURAL NOUNS	CONTRACTIONS	SINGULAR POSSESSIVE NOUNS	PLURAL POSSESSIVE NOUNS
speakers	speaker's	speaker's	speakers'
women	woman's	woman's	women's
echoes	echo's	echo's	echoes'
countries	country's	country's	countries'

Identify the italicized word in each sentence by writing plural noun, singular possessive noun, plural possessive noun, *or* contraction.

1. The bank *teller's* hours began at 8:30 A.M.
2. *August's* paintings are becoming very popular.
3. The *donkeys* walked right up to our window.
4. *Peter's* not going to join the swim team.
5. The *chefs'* secret recipes will be available at the fair.
6. *Andy's* been waiting for a long time.
7. A *squid's* body has a cavity that takes in and ejects water.
8. The *schools'* classrooms were too cold for the students.
9. Put the toys in the *children's* playroom.
10. I am going to the hockey tournament with my *brothers*.

2.5 APPOSITIVES

An **appositive** is a noun that is placed next to another noun to identify it or add information about it.

EXAMPLE   James Madison's wife, **Dolley,** was a famous first lady.

The noun *Dolley* identifies the noun next to it, *wife.* In this sentence, *Dolley* is an appositive.

An **appositive phrase** is a group of words that includes an appositive and other words that modify the appositive.

EXAMPLE   Madison, **our fourth president,** held many other offices.

The words *our* and *fourth* modify the appositive *president.* The phrase *our fourth president* is an appositive phrase. It identifies the noun *Madison.*

An appositive or an appositive phrase can appear anywhere in a sentence as long as it appears next to the noun it identifies.

EXAMPLE   **Our fourth president,** Madison held many other offices.

EXAMPLE   Many historians have studied the life of Madison, **our fourth president.**

Appositives and appositive phrases are usually set off with commas. If the appositive is essential to the meaning of the sentence, however, commas are not used.

EXAMPLE   Madison's friend **Thomas Jefferson** was president before Madison.

EXAMPLE   Madison's father, **James Madison,** was a plantation owner.

Obviously, Madison had more than one friend, so the appositive, *Thomas Jefferson,* is needed to identify this particular friend. No commas are needed. However, Madison had only one father. The father's name is not needed to identify him. Therefore, commas are needed.

PRACTICE   Identifying Appositives

Write each sentence. Underline the appositive or appositive phrase and add appropriate commas. Circle the noun the appositive identifies.

1. In 1926, John Logie Baird a Scottish television pioneer demonstrated the first television system.
2. My new puppy a golden retriever is learning to swim.
3. Mt. Whitney the highest peak in the lower forty-eight states is on the east side of the Great Western Divide.
4. The speaker a good friend of mine is inspiring.
5. A true sportsman Uncle Bill never keeps the fish he catches.
6. My sister's friend Ellie has a pet iguana.
7. He was five when he caught his first fish a rainbow trout.
8. The author a Tibetan monk lived to be 106 years old.
9. His father the dean of students is retiring next year.
10. The Russian cosmonaut Aleksei Leonov was the first person to walk in outer space.

Rewrite the following passage, correcting errors in spelling, capitalization, grammar, and usage. Add any missing punctuation. Write legibly to be sure one letter is not mistaken for another. There are ten mistakes.

Helen Beatrix Potter

[1]Helen Beatrix Potter a popular childrens writer wrote and illustrated about twenty-five books. [2]All her books contain animals as characters. [3]*The Tale of Peter Rabbit* the most famous of her storys was written for her ex-governesses sick son.

[4]The success of *Peter Rabbit* inspired *The Tale of benjamin Bunny* another popular book. [5]The original illustrations for all of her works are now on display in the Tate Gallery in London.

[6]Potters childhood was lonely and restrictive. [7]She spent her summers painting and drawing in scotland. [8]She returned to England as an adult. [9]There she bought several farms and became a sheep farmer. [10]Upon her death, potter willed more than four thousand acres of her land to the National Trust.

Write each noun. Label the common nouns C and the proper nouns P.

1. Hannah and her sister swam in Lake Michigan on their vacation.
2. Kate pulled her little brother around the yard in their little red wagon.
3. The train ride from San Francisco to Los Angeles took us on a scenic route.
4. The band will be performing at the Circle Star Theater for two weeks.
5. Magellan was the first explorer to circumnavigate the globe.

Possessive Nouns

Write the possessive form of the noun in parentheses.

6. My (grandmother) piano needs to be tuned.
7. Wendy Mass wrote the book *(Women) Rights.*
8. The water in the (cows) watering trough is frozen.
9. (Vicky) nephew won a blue ribbon at the fair.
10. The (Turners) letter carrier lives next door to me.
11. The sequins on the (skaters) costumes were all sewn on by hand.
12. That (dish) recipe is in the newspaper today.
13. The (employees) picnic was canceled because of thunderstorms.
14. The (neighbor) tree fell on our fence.
15. Last year the adventure group climbed two of (North America) highest peaks.

POSTTEST **Recognizing Plurals, Possessives, and Contractions**

Identify the italicized word in each sentence by writing plural noun, singular possessive noun, plural possessive noun, *or* contraction.

16. What are you going to give your dad for *Father's* Day?
17. *Jonas's* mother joined the community watch group.
18. *Mary's* not going to the movie with us.
19. The baseball *players'* strike lasted three months.
20. My *sister's* never been to a concert before.
21. The *Beatles'* last concert was held at Candlestick Park in San Francisco.
22. Are there any more *tickets* for sale?
23. The *carpenter's* taking a long time to finish this job.
24. *Will's* parents were the first to congratulate him.
25. Where is the key to your *parents'* car?

Write the appositive or appositive phrase in each sentence.

26. Mrs. Nash, the principal of our school, was not at the football game.

27. Christopher Columbus, a European explorer, arrived in the Americas in 1492.

28. Fifi, my cousin's toy poodle, only weighs about five pounds.

29. Jackie Young, the star of the football team, signs autographs for his fans after every game.

30. His sister Kris will be home for the holidays.

31. The composer Leonard Bernstein worked with Stephen Sondheim, who wrote lyrics.

32. We are meeting the rest of the group in Denver, the mile-high city.

33. Her math teacher, Mr. Winston, is our coach.

34. Give this letter to that young woman, one of our attorneys.

35. Caroline's friend Tara helped establish the recycling program at our school.

Chapter 3

Verbs

● ● ● ● ● ● ● ● ● ● ● ● ● ● ● ● ●

PRETEST **Action Verbs and Linking Verbs**

Write each verb. Label the action verbs A *and the linking verbs* L.

1. Football in the United States started as a college sport.
2. The game was brand new in 1875.
3. Twenty-five players played on a team.
4. Walter Camp introduced the idea of "downs."
5. He also lined the field with chalk.
6. College football is exciting.
7. College bowl games are a tradition.
8. The Hall of Fame honors outstanding players.
9. Who can nominate a player for this honor?
10. A football weighs about fifteen ounces.

Identify the italicized word in each sentence by writing direct object, indirect object, predicate noun, *or* predicate adjective.

11. The photos in the album are *small*.
12. The White House tour guide showed *visitors* the Green and Red Rooms.
13. The whistle sounds *shrill*.
14. The dog carried its *puppies* to the basket.
15. A triangle has three *sides*.
16. The painting was *breathtaking*.
17. I showed *Sarah* the letter.
18. Read the package *directions* carefully.
19. The blues is a *form* of music.
20. Billie Holiday was a famous blues *singer*.

PRETEST **Present and Past Tenses and Progressive Forms**

Write the verb. Then write present tense, past tense, present progressive, *or* past progressive *to identify it.*

21. Anwar was doing research about the history of money.
22. People use money to trade.
23. Long ago farmers used cattle for money.
24. Money tells a story.
25. At one time, Fijians used whales' teeth as money.
26. Throughout the Revolutionary War, the Continental Congress was issuing large amounts of paper money.
27. Emma is collecting the new quarters with symbols for various states on the backs of the coins.
28. The United States Mint is printing quarters with a design for each of the fifty states.
29. A government agency protects the users of banks.
30. This agency guarantees the safety of bank deposits.

Write the verb. Then write present perfect, past perfect, future, *or* future perfect *to identify it.*

31. By noon we had completed the project.
32. We shall read the play at the first rehearsal.
33. Robert will grow vegetables in his garden this year.
34. Students have earned money to take the trip.
35. Who will set the table tonight?
36. By tonight I shall have completed the assignment.
37. The players will have left the park after the final game.
38. We have organized all of the books this week.
39. The key has disappeared from the drawer.
40. The staff had prepared all year for the camping trip.

PRETEST **Irregular Verbs**

Write the correct verb form from the choices in parentheses.

41. The baby ducks (swum, swam) in a row behind their mother.
42. Paul (find, found) the long-missing document in an old file cabinet.
43. The play (began, begun) promptly at 8:00 P.M.
44. These jeans (cost, costed) more than I expected.
45. The candidate has (spoke, spoken) at campaign rallies in five communities today.
46. The kitten had (grew, grown) quickly.
47. The news about the discovery of gold (spread, spreaded) throughout California and the United States.
48. Hashim and Terry (went, gone) to the baseball game together.
49. Katlyn (threw, thrown) the winning pitches in the last two games.
50. I (telled, told) the story about the tortoise and the hare.

3.1 ACTION VERBS

You may have heard the movie director's call for "lights, camera, *action!*" The actions in movies and plays can be expressed by verbs. If a word expresses action and tells what a subject does, it's an action verb.

An **action verb** is a word that expresses action. An action verb may be made up of more than one word.

Notice the action verbs in the following sentences.

EXAMPLE   The director **shouts** at the members of the cast.

EXAMPLE   The lights **are flashing** above the stage.

EXAMPLE   The audience **arrived** in time for the performance.

EXAMPLE   Several singers **have memorized** the lyrics of a song.

Action verbs can express physical actions, such as *shout* and *arrive*. They can also express mental activities, such as *memorize* and *forget*.

ACTION VERBS	
PHYSICAL	shout, flash, arrive, talk, applaud, act, sing, dance
MENTAL	remember, forget, think, memorize, read, dream, appreciate

Frank and Ernest

YOU'RE A TURTLE, ERNIE --- YOU CAN HIDE, BUT YOU CAN'T RUN.

THAVES

© 1999 Thaves/Reprinted with permission.
Newspaper dist. NEA, Inc.

Have, has, and *had* are often used before other verbs. They can also be used as action verbs when they tell that the subject owns or holds something.

EXAMPLE The actors already **have** their costumes.

EXAMPLE The director **has** a script in her back pocket.

EXAMPLE Rosa **had** a theater program from 1920.

PRACTICE **Identifying Action Verbs**

Write the action verbs.

1. Spanish conquerors brought horses to the Americas.
2. American wild horses may have descended from them.
3. In 1872 everyone on the ship *Mary Celeste* vanished.
4. This ship had set sail from New York harbor.
5. It was later found at sea with no one aboard.
6. Cattails grow in wetlands throughout the country.
7. Many birds and amphibians live in the wetlands.
8. In 1855 Walt Whitman published *Leaves of Grass*.
9. Whitman wrote the poem "O Captain! My Captain!"
10. It honored the assassinated president Abraham Lincoln.

3.2 TRANSITIVE AND INTRANSITIVE VERBS

In some sentences, the predicate consists of only an action verb.

EXAMPLE The actor **rehearsed.**

Most sentences provide more information. The predicate often names who or what receives the action of the verb.

EXAMPLE The actor rehearsed his **lines** from the play.

The word *lines* tells what the actor rehearsed. *Lines* is a direct object.

A **direct object** receives the action of a verb. It answers the question *whom?* or *what?* after an action verb.

A sentence may have a compound direct object. That is, a sentence may have more than one direct object.

EXAMPLE   We saw **Maurice** and **Inez** in the audience.

When an action verb transfers action to a direct object, the verb is transitive. When an action verb has no direct object, the verb is intransitive.

> A **transitive verb** has a direct object.
> An **intransitive verb** does not have a direct object.

Most action verbs can be transitive or intransitive. A verb can be labeled transitive or intransitive only by examining its use in a particular sentence.

EXAMPLE   The audience **applauds** the actors. [transitive]

EXAMPLE   The audience **applauds** loudly. [intransitive]

PRACTICE Recognizing Transitive and Intransitive Verbs

For each sentence, write the action verb. Then write T *if the verb is transitive or* I *if the verb is intransitive. If the verb is transitive, write the direct object or objects.*

1. The Sun provides energy in the form of light.
2. All plants grow toward the sun.
3. Flowers in a field face in the same direction.
4. Plants use sunlight in photosynthesis, a food-making process.
5. Plants absorb water and carbon dioxide.
6. With the help of light energy, these change into sugar and oxygen.
7. The sugar stays in the plant as food for plants.
8. The plant releases oxygen into the air.
9. Some seedlings grow into tall plants.
10. We will do some experiments with sunlight.

3.3 INDIRECT OBJECTS

A direct object answers the question *whom?* or *what?* after an action verb.

EXAMPLE   Friends sent **flowers.**

In some sentences, an indirect object also follows an action verb.

An **indirect object** answers the question *to whom?* or *for whom?* or *to what?* or *for what?* an action is done.

EXAMPLE   Friends sent the **actors** flowers.

The direct object in the sentence is *flowers.* The indirect object is *actors. Actors* answers the question *to whom?* after the action verb *sent.*

A sentence may have a compound indirect object. In the sentence below, *cast* and *orchestra* are indirect objects. The direct object is *thanks.*

EXAMPLE   Ms. Ortiz gave the **cast** and the **orchestra** her thanks.

An indirect object appears only in a sentence that has a direct object. Two clues can help you recognize an indirect object. First, an indirect object always comes between the verb and the direct object. Second, you can put the word *to* or *for* before an indirect object and change its position. The sentence will still have the same meaning, but it will no longer have an indirect object.

EXAMPLE   Friends **sent** the **director flowers.** [*Director* is an indirect object.]

EXAMPLE   Friends sent flowers **to the director.** [*Director* is not an indirect object.]

You know that in the first sentence *director* is the indirect object because it comes between the verb and the direct object and because it can be placed after the word *to,* as in the second sentence.

Write the indirect objects and underline them. Then write the direct objects.

1. The bus driver gave the passengers transfers.
2. The storyteller told the audience tales about growing up in North Carolina.
3. The catalog promises customers delivery within one week.
4. The president awarded Rosa Parks the Presidential Medal of Freedom in 1996.
5. Tenissa sent her friends picture postcards.
6. Ms. Jamison offered her co-worker assistance.
7. Val tossed the dog a small ball.
8. David and Tony served the firefighters pasta and salad for dinner.
9. Jordan drew his sister a picture of her dog.
10. Carol made her family a scrapbook.

3.4 LINKING VERBS AND PREDICATE WORDS

A **linking verb** connects the subject of a sentence with a noun or an adjective in the predicate.

EXAMPLE   Juana Ortiz **was** the **director.**

EXAMPLE   Ms. Ortiz **is imaginative.**

In the first sentence, the verb *was* links the noun *director* to the subject. *Director* identifies the subject. In the second sentence, the verb *is* links the adjective *imaginative* to the subject. *Imaginative* describes the subject.

A **predicate noun** is a noun that follows a linking verb. It renames or identifies the subject.

A **predicate adjective** is an adjective that follows a linking verb. It describes, or modifies, the subject.

A sentence may contain a compound predicate noun or a compound predicate adjective.

EXAMPLE   Ms. Ortiz is a **teacher** and a **musician.** [compound predicate noun]

EXAMPLE   Ms. Ortiz is **stern** but **fair.** [compound predicate adjective]

COMMON LINKING VERBS			
be (am, is, are, was, were) become	seem appear look	taste feel smell	sound grow turn

Most of these verbs can also be used as action verbs.

EXAMPLE   The director **sounded** angry. [linking verb]

EXAMPLE   The director **sounded** the alarm. [action verb]

NOTE   Two other linking verbs are *remain* and *stay.*

PRACTICE   Identifying Verbs, Predicate Nouns, and Predicate Adjectives

For each sentence, write the verb. Label the verb A if it's an action verb or L if it's a linking verb. If it's a linking verb, write the predicate noun or the predicate adjective. Label a predicate noun PN. Label a predicate adjective PA.

1. All insects are invertebrates.
2. Their outer skeletons feel hard and brittle.
3. Their three pairs of legs are jointed.
4. Insects live all over the world.
5. They eat many kinds of food.
6. Young insects often look different from their parents.

7. Some young insects hardly change in looks.
8. Their bodies are smaller versions of adult bodies.
9. A silverfish is an example of one such insect.
10. The goliath beetle may be the heaviest flying insect.

3.5 PRESENT AND PAST TENSES

The verb in a sentence expresses action. It also tells when the action takes place. The form of a verb that shows the time of the action is called the **tense** of the verb.

The **present tense** of a verb expresses action that happens regularly. It can also express a general truth.

EXAMPLE A great actor **wins** awards.

In the present tense, the base form of a verb is used with all plural subjects and the pronouns *I* and *you*. For singular subjects other than *I* and *you*, *-s* or *-es* is usually added to the base form of the verb. Remember that a verb must agree in number with its subject.

PRESENT TENSE FORMS	
SINGULAR	**PLURAL**
I **walk.**	We **walk.**
You **walk.**	You **walk.**
He, she, *or* it **walks.**	They **walk.**

The **past tense** of a verb expresses action that already happened.

The past tense of many verbs is formed by adding *-d* or *-ed* to the base form of the verb.

EXAMPLE The actors **rehearsed.** Ms. Ortiz **directed.**

For each sentence, write the verb. Then write present *or* past *to identify its tense.*

1. Some ideas become fads.
2. Fad items sell during a short period of time.
3. Fads sometimes make their inventors rich.
4. Peter Hodgson invested $150 in Silly Putty.
5. He produced millions of Silly Putty eggs.
6. In Australia, students exercised with bamboo hoops.
7. The idea of the hoops led to the Hula Hoop craze.
8. In the 1970s, more than a million people bought Pet Rocks.
9. The rocks came with a funny manual about pet care.
10. Americans enjoy fads.

3.6 MAIN VERBS AND HELPING VERBS

Verbs have four principal parts that are used to form all tenses. Notice how the principal parts of a verb are formed.

PRINCIPAL PARTS OF VERBS			
BASE FORM	**PRESENT PARTICIPLE**	**PAST**	**PAST PARTICIPLE**
act	acting	acted	acted

You can use the base form and the past alone to form the present and past tenses. The present participle and the past participle can be combined with helping verbs to form other tenses.

A **helping verb** helps the main verb express action or make a statement.

A **verb phrase** consists of one or more helping verbs followed by a main verb.

EXAMPLE Telma **is acting** in another play today.

The word *is* is the helping verb, and the present participle *acting* is the main verb. Together they form a verb phrase.

The most common helping verbs are *be, have,* and *do.* Forms of the helping verb *be* are *am, is,* and *are* in the present and *was* and *were* in the past. These helping verbs often combine with the present participle of the main verb.

BE AND THE PRESENT PARTICIPLE

SINGULAR	PLURAL	SINGULAR	PLURAL
I **am** learning.	We **are** learning.	I **was** learning.	We **were** learning.
You **are** learning.	You **are** learning.	You **were** learning.	You **were** learning.
She **is** learning.	They **are** learning.	He **was** learning.	They **were** learning.

The helping verb *have* combines with the past participle of the main verb. Forms of the helping verb *have* are *have* and *has* in the present and *had* in the past.

HAVE AND THE PAST PARTICIPLE

SINGULAR	PLURAL	SINGULAR	PLURAL
I **have** learned.	We **have** learned.	I **had** learned.	We **had** learned.
You **have** learned.	You **have** learned.	You **had** learned.	You **had** learned.
She **has** learned.	They **have** learned.	He **had** learned.	They **had** learned.

Forms of the helping verb *do* are *do* and *does* in the present and *did* in the past. The helping verb *do* combines with the base form of a verb: *I do believe you. She does believe you. They did believe you.*

NOTE Other helping verbs are *can, could, may, might, must, should,* and *would.*

PRACTICE **Identifying Main Verbs and Helping Verbs**

Write each verb phrase. Underline the helping verb. Write base form, present participle, *or* past participle *to identify the main verb.*

1. Many children have written books.
2. We are learning about these authors in our reading classes this year.
3. Anne Frank's diary was published in the United States in 1952.
4. She was hiding from the Nazis because she was Jewish.
5. We had read about her life last year in English class.
6. We are looking for a book by Dorothy Straight.
7. She had written her book as a four-year-old.
8. Some books do offer advice or ideas to others.
9. In his book, Jason Gaes has shared his experiences with cancer.
10. Did you read about his life?

3.7 PROGRESSIVE FORMS

You know that the present tense of a verb can express action that occurs repeatedly. To express action that is taking place at the present time, use the present progressive form of the verb.

The **present progressive form** of a verb expresses action or a condition that is continuing in the present.

EXAMPLE Althea **is finishing** her song.

The present progressive form of a verb consists of the helping verb *am, are,* or *is* and the present participle of the main verb.

PRESENT PROGRESSIVE FORMS	
SINGULAR	**PLURAL**
I **am watching.**	We **are watching.**
You **are watching.**	You **are watching.**
He, she, *or* it **is watching.**	They **are watching.**

The **past progressive form** of a verb expresses action or a condition that was continuing at some time in the past.

EXAMPLE We **were watching** a scary show.

The past progressive form of a verb consists of the helping verb *was* or *were* and the present participle of the main verb.

PAST PROGRESSIVE FORMS	
SINGULAR	**PLURAL**
I **was working.**	We **were working.**
You **were working.**	You **were working.**
He, she, *or* it **was working.**	They **were working.**

Rewrite the sentence using the progressive form of the verb. If the verb is in the present tense, change it to the present progressive form. If the verb is in the past tense, change it to the past progressive form.

1. George reads a book every week.
2. We picked all of the corn.
3. The singers practiced for the concert yesterday.
4. Alicia weeded the garden.
5. Will and Molly mowed the lawn every weekend.
6. The Moores plan a summer family reunion.
7. Aiko and Kasem walk the dogs twice a day.
8. Jill learned Spanish by using tapes.
9. I clean my closet every three months.
10. Bruce copied his files onto a disk.

3.8 PRESENT PERFECT AND PAST PERFECT TENSES

The **present perfect tense** of a verb expresses action that happened at an indefinite time in the past.

EXAMPLE   The actor **has rehearsed** for many hours.

EXAMPLE   Lori and Pam **have watched** *Grease* five times.

The present perfect tense consists of the helping verb *have* or *has* and the past participle of the main verb.

PRESENT PERFECT TENSE	
SINGULAR	**PLURAL**
I **have watched.**	We **have watched.**
You **have watched.**	You **have watched.**
He, she, *or* it **has watched.**	They **have watched.**

The **past perfect tense** of a verb expresses action that happened before another action or event in the past.

The past perfect tense is often used in sentences that contain a past-tense verb in another part of the sentence.

EXAMPLE   The actors **had rehearsed** for many weeks.

EXAMPLE   We **had** just **arrived** when the play **started.**

The past perfect tense of a verb consists of the helping verb *had* and the past participle of the main verb.

PAST PERFECT TENSE

SINGULAR	PLURAL
I **had started.**	We **had started.**
You **had started.**	You **had started.**
He, she, *or* it **had started.**	They **had started.**

PRACTICE   Identifying Perfect Tenses

Write the verb. Then write present perfect *or* past perfect *to identify the tense.*

1. Lynne has prepared pizzas and other snacks for the school party.
2. We had planned the party for months.
3. I have watched educational programs on television for many years.
4. My older sister had sent out over 220 questionnaires.
5. Claude has offered CDs as prizes.
6. I had bought groceries and laundry products on sale at the discount store.
7. Jeanne and Pedro have organized marathons and other events for charity.
8. Dad had set up the sound system earlier in the day.

9. The teachers have prepared their classrooms for the first day of school.

10. My friends had decided on a 1960s theme for the party.

3.9 EXPRESSING FUTURE TIME

The **future tense** of a verb expresses action that will take place in the future.

EXAMPLE   We **shall attend** the performance.

EXAMPLE   The actors **will show** their talents.

The future tense of a verb is formed by using the helping verb *will* before the base form of a verb. The helping verb *shall* is sometimes used when the subject is *I* or *we*.

There are other ways to show that an action will happen in the future. *Tomorrow, next year,* and *later* are all words that indicate a future time. These words are called **time words,** and they may be used with the present tense to express future time.

EXAMPLE   Our show **opens next week.**

EXAMPLE   **Tomorrow** we **start** rehearsals.

The present progressive form can also be used with time words to express future actions.

EXAMPLE   Our show **is opening next week.**

EXAMPLE   **Tomorrow** we **are starting** rehearsals.

Another way to talk about the future is with the future perfect tense.

The **future perfect tense** of a verb expresses action that will be completed before another future event begins.

EXAMPLE   By Thursday I **shall have performed** six times.

EXAMPLE   The production **will have closed** by next week.

The future perfect tense is formed by using *will have* or *shall have* before the past participle of a verb.

Write the verb. Then write present, future, present progressive, *or* future perfect *to identify the verb tense.*

1. The candidates for class president will debate at 2:30 P.M. next Friday.
2. That movie is playing throughout the Miami area this week.
3. We shall reach Nashville in three days.
4. I will have finished the quilt by the time of the shower.
5. I am driving to New York.
6. By next week, I shall have trained the dog.
7. I go to soccer practice every afternoon.
8. Jeremiah and Leanne will lead the nature hike through Ryerson Woods this week.
9. Meredith and other members of the team run one mile every afternoon.
10. You will have visited the Washington Monument and other landmarks by the end of the trip.

3.10 ACTIVE AND PASSIVE VOICE

A verb is in the **active voice** when the subject performs the action of the verb.

EXAMPLE Thornton Wilder **composed** that play.

A verb is in the **passive voice** when the subject receives the action of the verb.

EXAMPLE That play **was composed** by Thornton Wilder.

In the first example, the author, Thorton Wilder, seems more important because *Thornton Wilder* is the subject of the sentence. In the second example, the play seems more important because *play* is the subject of the sentence.

Notice that verbs in the passive voice consist of a form of *be* and the past participle. Often a phrase beginning with *by* follows the verb in the passive voice.

EXAMPLE   I am puzzled **by your question. [passive voice]**

EXAMPLE   Your question puzzles me. **[active voice]**

EXAMPLE   The puppy is frightened **by loud noises. [passive voice]**

EXAMPLE   Loud noises frighten the puppy. **[active voice]**

EXAMPLE   Plays are performed **by actors. [passive voice]**

EXAMPLE   Actors perform plays. **[active voice]**

EXAMPLE   This painting was purchased **by Ms. Jones. [passive voice]**

EXAMPLE   Ms. Jones purchased this painting. **[active voice]**

The active voice is usually a stronger, more direct way to express ideas. Use the passive voice if you want to stress the receiver of the action or if you don't know who performed the action.

EXAMPLE   *Our Town* **was performed. [You may want to stress the play.]**

EXAMPLE   The actors **were fired. [You may not know who fired the actors.]**

PRACTICE   **Using Active and Passive Voice**

Rewrite each sentence, changing the verb from active to passive or from passive to active.

 1. Many people break world records.
 2. Contestants must follow the rules.
 3. One record was broken by a famous chef.
 4. This chef made the largest apple pie.
 5. Hundreds of bushels of apples were used by the chef.
 6. A huge popcorn ball was made by scouts.
 7. One woman collected thousands of refrigerator magnets.
 8. Carole read a book about world records.
 9. Some of the categories include sports, games, and food.
 10. Facts about their culture can be learned by readers.

3.11 IRREGULAR VERBS

The irregular verbs listed here are grouped according to the way their past and past participle are formed.

IRREGULAR VERBS

PATTERN	BASE FORM	PAST	PAST PARTICIPLE
One vowel changes to form the past and the past participle.	begin	began	begun
	drink	drank	drunk
	ring	rang	rung
	shrink	shrank *or* shrunk	shrunk
	sing	sang	sung
	sink	sank	sunk
	spring	sprang *or* sprung	sprung
	swim	swam	swum
The past and the past participle are the same.	bring	brought	brought
	build	built	built
	buy	bought	bought
	catch	caught	caught
	creep	crept	crept
	feel	felt	felt
	fight	fought	fought
	find	found	found
	get	got	got *or* gotten
	have	had	had
	hold	held	held
	keep	kept	kept
	lay	laid	laid
	lead	led	led
	leave	left	left
	lend	lent	lent
	lose	lost	lost
	make	made	made
	meet	met	met
	pay	paid	paid
	say	said	said

PATTERN	BASE FORM	PAST	PAST PARTICIPLE
The past and the past participle are the same.	seek	sought	sought
	sell	sold	sold
	send	sent	sent
	sit	sat	sat
	sleep	slept	slept
	spend	spent	spent
	spin	spun	spun
	stand	stood	stood
	sting	stung	stung
	swing	swung	swung
	teach	taught	taught
	tell	told	told
	think	thought	thought
	win	won	won

PRACTICE Using Irregular Verbs I

Write the correct verb form from the choices in parentheses.

1. The horse (drank, drunk) a bucket of water.
2. I (send, sent) the package to my brother last week.
3. The shirt will (shrink, shrunk) if it is put in the dryer.
4. He (creep, crept) past the window.
5. My grandfather (teached, taught) American history for over thirty years.
6. Early European settlers (bringed, brought) wheat to the Americas.
7. Kesia (leaved, left) the library at nine o'clock.
8. James Marshall (finded, found) gold at Sutter's Mill in California in 1848.
9. I was (payed, paid) $6 an hour to wash dishes.
10. According to the story by Washington Irving, Rip Van Winkle (sleeped, slept) for twenty years.

3.12 MORE IRREGULAR VERBS

Here are some more irregular verbs.

IRREGULAR VERBS

PATTERN	BASE FORM	PAST	PAST PARTICIPLE
The base form and the past participle are the same.	become	became	become
	come	came	come
	run	ran	run
The past ends in *ew*, and the past participle ends in *wn*.	blow	blew	blown
	draw	drew	drawn
	fly	flew	flown
	grow	grew	grown
	know	knew	known
	throw	threw	thrown
The past participle ends in *en*.	bite	bit	bitten *or* bit
	break	broke	broken
	choose	chose	chosen
	drive	drove	driven
	eat	ate	eaten
	fall	fell	fallen
	freeze	froze	frozen
	give	gave	given
	ride	rode	ridden
	rise	rose	risen
	see	saw	seen
	shake	shook	shaken
	speak	spoke	spoken
	steal	stole	stolen
	take	took	taken
	write	wrote	written

PATTERN	BASE FORM	PAST	PAST PARTICIPLE
The past and the past participle don't follow any pattern.	be	was, were	been
	do	did	done
	go	went	gone
	lie	lay	lain
	tear	tore	torn
	wear	wore	worn
The base form, the past, and the past participle are the same.	burst	burst	burst
	cost	cost	cost
	cut	cut	cut
	hit	hit	hit
	hurt	hurt	hurt
	let	let	let
	put	put	put
	read	read	read
	set	set	set
	spread	spread	spread

Bizarro © by Dan Piraro. Reprinted with permission of Universal Press Syndicate. All rights reserved.

PRACTICE Using Irregular Verbs II

Write the correct verb form from the choices in parentheses.

1. The bus (come, came) right on schedule.

2. I have (chose, chosen) three songs to perform.

3. I (did, done) my homework right after school.
4. Both Jack and Jill had (fell, fallen) down the hill.
5. Caterpillars (become, became) butterflies after going through the pupal stage.
6. He (gave, given) me a program for the play.
7. I have (spoke, spoken) to my coach about the game.
8. Shereen (tore, torn) the ad for baby-sitters off the board.
9. Once farmers (spread, spreaded) seeds by hand.
10. Has Caroline (took, taken) her backpack to school?

PRACTICE Proofreading

Rewrite the following passage, correcting errors in spelling, capitalization, grammar, and usage. Add any missing punctuation. Write legibly to be sure one letter is not mistaken for another. There are ten mistakes.

Amelia Earhart

[1]Amelia Earhart setted speed and distance records as a female airplane pilot. [2]Earhart had volunteer as a nurse during World War I and later worked as a social worker. [3]However, she was most interested in flying airplains.

[4]in the 1920s, she flew in air shows. [5]Earhart married in 1931, and her husband become her manager. [6]In 1932 she was the first woman to fly alone across the Atlantic Ocean [7]In 1935 she flew alone from Hawaii to California.

[8]In June 1937, Earhart and her copilot had began a trip around the world. [9]On July 2, their plane disappeared. [10]No one ever seen or heard from them again. [11]Earhart left a letter for her husband in case she was in an accident? [12]In it she had wrote, "Women must try to do things as men have tried."

Write each verb. Label the action verbs A *and the linking verbs* L.

1. Look at the Moon with binoculars.
2. I have a powerful telescope.
3. Early astronomers gave the dark areas names.
4. These areas were probably water, according to the astronomers.
5. Galileo made drawings of the Moon in 1609.
6. The drawings show the cratered surface of the Moon.
7. Telescopes improved in size and quality.
8. They are useful tools for astronomers.
9. NASA sent space probes to the Moon.
10. Senator John Glenn was an astronaut.

POSTTEST **Direct Objects, Indirect Objects, Predicate Nouns, and Predicate Adjectives**

Identify the italicized word in each sentence by writing direct object, indirect object, predicate noun, *or* predicate adjective.

11. The dogs in the yard are *noisy*.
12. The charity fund-raiser reached its *goal*.
13. The roads look *icy*.
14. Mali never feeds her *dog* table scraps.
15. The new exhibit was *interesting*.
16. We built a *birdhouse* from a kit.
17. Use the *diagram* in the instructions.
18. The principal gave the *parents* school brochures.
19. The tree over there is a *maple*.
20. Mario is *editor* of the school newspaper.

Write the verb. Then write present tense, past tense, present progressive, *or* past progressive *to identify it.*

21. Some animals in colder climates hibernate during the winter.
22. They look asleep.
23. In the cave, bats were hanging upside down.
24. Dew formed on their bodies.
25. Bears are looking for shelters.
26. Frogs sleep at the bottom of ponds.
27. Dormice were making special winter nests of leaves and bark.
28. Badgers sleep most of the winter.
29. The groundhog remained asleep in its den most of the winter.
30. People are hoping for no groundhog's shadow on Groundhog Day.

POSTTEST **Perfect and Future Tenses**

Write the verb. Then write present perfect, past perfect, future, *or* future perfect *to identify it.*

31. Andrew Jackson had favored state-chartered banks over a federal bank.
32. The subscription will end next month.
33. By the end of February, I will have read the entire series.
34. Erin had located all the resources available from the library on the research topic.
35. The boat has disappeared from view.
36. She will have seen that movie four times.
37. I had copied the files onto the hard drive of my computer.

38. By next week, we will have confirmed your class schedule for this semester.
39. I have studied the history and geography of Africa in my social studies class.
40. My family will visit Sequoia and Yosemite National Parks next summer.

Write the correct verb form from the choices in parentheses.

41. I (bit, bitten) into the apple.
42. As an eight-year-old child, Wolfgang Amadeus Mozart had (wrote, written) a symphony.
43. Lou (left, leaved) a message on the answering machine about when he would be home.
44. The horse (hurt, hurted) its leg.
45. My brother and Luis (did, done) his math assignment during study hall.
46. Have you (saw, seen) the new color for the school crossing signs?
47. The water for the outdoor ice rink had (froze, frozen) during the night.
48. The eagle (flew, flown) to its aerie, or nest, high in a treetop.
49. Sasha has (grew, grown) several inches during this summer.
50. During the ice dance, the skaters (spun, spinned) in circles.

Pronouns

● ● ● ● ● ● ● ● ● ● ● ● ● ● ●

PRETEST Personal Pronouns

Write each personal pronoun. Then write one of the following phrases to identify the pronoun: subject pronoun as subject, subject pronoun as predicate pronoun, object pronoun as direct object, object pronoun as indirect object.

1. She was teaching the course.
2. We offered him the job.
3. The only boy on the team is I.
4. The teacher gave her the results of the test, and he congratulated her.
5. You gave her the newsmagazine yesterday, but she has not read it yet.

Write the correct word or phrase from the choices in parentheses.

6. Dad asked Harry and (she, her) about the article in the school newspaper.

7. The announcer for tonight's big basketball game is (he, him).

8. (We, Us) cousins go to the same day camp every summer.

9. Nathan and (he, him) are getting summer jobs with the city's park district.

10. (Kristen and I, I and Kristen, Kristen and me, me and Kristen) are switching lockers.

11. The first presenter in the eighth-grade speech contest was (she, her).

12. The coach gave (they, them) this month's practice schedule.

13. (I and you, You and I, Me and you, You and me) can ride to practice together.

14. The teacher gave (she and I, she and me, her and I, her and me) a copy of the report.

15. Mom and (she, her) are opening a savings account at the new bank in town.

PRETEST **Pronouns and Antecedents**

Write each personal pronoun and its antecedent. If a pronoun doesn't have a clear antecedent, rewrite the numbered item to make the meaning clear.

16. Europe has been home to many explorers. It has also been home to many scientists.

17. Alexander von Humboldt and Aime Bonpland sailed to South America. They explored the Orinoco River.

18. The explorers crossed dry, dusty plains. They stretched to the south.

19. Later Humboldt studied the cold current off the South American coast. It was later named the Humboldt Current.

20. Humboldt returned to Germany. He then wrote books.

PRETEST **Identifying Pronouns**

Write each pronoun. Then write possessive, indefinite, reflexive, intensive, interrogative, *or* demonstrative *to identify it.*

21. What did the campers bring?

22. The Mekins bought themselves a new tent and camping supplies.

23. The tent had a rip in its window.

24. No one noticed the rip until rain began pouring in through the tear.

25. Aunt Ingrid wrote in her diary about the hike through the national forest.

26. Michael packed the cooler and then loaded the cooler and other gear into the car himself.

27. Few of the campers slept outside.

28. That is the picnic table closest to the hiking trail.

29. These are beautiful rocks.

30. Which is the campsite assigned to the Mekins?

PRETEST **Indefinite Pronouns**

Write the subjects and the correct words from the choices in parentheses.

31. Many of the students in the junior high school (becomes, become) band members.

32. At first, everyone (experiments, experiment) with various instruments.

33. Then some of the students (chooses, choose) an instrument.
34. Several of the band members (is, are) playing woodwind instruments such as the flute.
35. Both of my brothers (has, have) decided to play the saxophone.
36. Someone (wants, want) to play a percussion instrument such as the bass drum.
37. Everyone (decides, decide) what music will be played.
38. Everybody in the concert band (wears, wear) a blue and white uniform.
39. All of the parents (is, are) coming to the concert.
40. (Does, Do) either of the band directors audition the students?

PRETEST **Personal, Reflexive, Intensive, Interrogative, and Demonstrative Pronouns**

Write the correct word from the choices in parentheses.

41. (Whose, Who's) taking driver's education during the summer school session?
42. Allie and (me, I) have signed up for the course.
43. (This, Those) is the state's rules-of-the-road manual.
44. Do (those, that) cars have new tires?
45. The instructor showed Allie and (me, myself) how to parallel park.
46. The students (theirselves, themselves) log their driving hours.
47. (Who, Whom) did the teacher choose for the first behind-the-wheel driving experience?
48. Do (those, that) belong to Janna?
49. Here is a book. (Who's, Whose) is it?
50. Allie and (I, myself) drove on the highway today.

4.1 PERSONAL PRONOUNS

A **pronoun** is a word that takes the place of one or more nouns.

EXAMPLE   Max likes books. **He** particularly enjoys novels.

EXAMPLE   Max and Irma like books. **They** particularly enjoy novels.

In the first example, the pronoun *He* replaces the noun *Max* as the subject of the sentence. In the second example, *They* replaces *Max and Irma*.

Pronouns that refer to people or things are called **personal pronouns.**

Some personal pronouns are used as the subjects of sentences. Others are used as the objects of verbs.

A **subject pronoun** is used as the subject of a sentence. It may also be used like a predicate noun, in which case it's called a predicate pronoun.

EXAMPLE   **I** enjoy a good book in my spare time. [subject]

EXAMPLE   **We** belong to a book club. [subject]

EXAMPLE   **She** gave a good book report. [subject]

EXAMPLE   **It** was about Andrew Jackson. [subject]

EXAMPLE   **They** especially like adventure stories. [subject]

EXAMPLE   The most popular author was **he.** [predicate pronoun]

An **object pronoun** may be a direct object or an indirect object.

EXAMPLE   The teacher praised **us.** [direct object]

EXAMPLE   Tell **me** a story. [indirect object]

EXAMPLE   The movie frightened **them.** [direct object]

EXAMPLE   The class wrote **her** a letter. [indirect object]

EXAMPLE   The story amuses **you.** [direct object]

EXAMPLE   The plot gives **him** an idea. [indirect object]

PERSONAL PRONOUNS

	SINGULAR	PLURAL
Subject Pronouns	I	we
	you	you
	he, she, it	they
Object Pronouns	me	us
	you	you
	him, her, it	them

PRACTICE **Identifying Personal Pronouns**

Write each personal pronoun. Then write one of the following phrases to identify the pronoun: subject pronoun as subject, subject pronoun as predicate pronoun, object pronoun as direct object, object pronoun as indirect object.

1. I asked her the question.
2. Alicia bought me a beautiful gift from Mexico.
3. The player in the uniform was you!
4. I saw you and her in the parade.
5. Max saw you at the museum.
6. Jude asked me the question.
7. The best athlete on the team was she.
8. He gave me the discount coupon.
9. You are coming to usher at 7:00 P.M.
10. She and he put it into the suitcase.

4.2 USING PRONOUNS

Use subject pronouns in compound subjects. Use object pronouns in compound objects.

EXAMPLE **He** and Carmen wrote the report. [not *Him and Carmen*]

EXAMPLE Tell John and **me** about the report. [not *John and I*]

If you're not sure which form of the pronoun to use, read the sentence with only the pronoun as the subject or the object. Your ear will tell you which form is correct.

When the pronoun *I, we, me,* or *us* is part of a compound subject or object, *I, we, me,* or *us* should come last. (It's simply courteous to name yourself or the group of which you are a part last.)

EXAMPLE   Lee and **I** played some new tunes. [not *I and Lee*]

EXAMPLE   Country music interests Lee and **me.** [not *me and Lee*]

In formal writing and speech, use a subject pronoun after a linking verb.

EXAMPLE   The writer of this report was **she.**

EXAMPLE   It is **I.**

A pronoun and a noun may be used together. The form of the pronoun depends on its use in the sentence.

EXAMPLE   **We** students read the book. [*We* is the subject.]

EXAMPLE   The book delighted **us** readers. [*Us* is a direct object.]

Some sentences make incomplete comparisons. The form of the pronoun can affect the meaning of such sentences. In any incomplete comparison, use the form of the pronoun that would be correct if the comparison were complete.

EXAMPLE   You like pizza better than **I** [like pizza].

EXAMPLE   You like pizza better than [you like] **me.**

PRACTICE Using Subject and Object Pronouns

Write the correct word or phrase from the choices in parentheses.

1. The teacher assigned Janine and (we, us) a cooperative research project.
2. (Sam and I, I and Sam, Me and Sam, Sam and me) decided where to pitch the tent.
3. Ask Mom and (I, me) about the movie's plot and surprise ending.

4. The organizers of the race gave (we, us) participants t-shirts.

5. The camp director told (I and Monica, Monica and I, me and Monica, Monica and me) which cabin to take.

6. The librarian read Mary and (they, them) a story.

7. (We, Us) baby-sitters know how to play many games to entertain children.

8. (Them and us, They and us, Them and we, They and we) can help each other with the job.

9. The job is challenging for (her and me, me and her, her and I, I and her).

10. The first students to complete the project were (them and us, they and us, them and we, they and we).

4.3 PRONOUNS AND ANTECEDENTS

Read the following sentences. Can you tell to whom the pronoun *She* refers?

EXAMPLE   Louisa May Alcott wrote a novel about a young woman.
She had three sisters.

The sentence is not clear because the word *She* could refer to either *Louisa May Alcott* or *a young woman*. Sometimes you must repeat a noun or rewrite a sentence to avoid confusion.

EXAMPLE   Louisa May Alcott wrote a novel about a young woman.
The young woman had three sisters.

The word a pronoun refers to is called its **antecedent.** The word *antecedent* means "going before."

EXAMPLE   **Jo March** is the main character in *Little Women*. **She** writes stories. [*Jo March* **is the antecedent of the pronoun** *She*.]

EXAMPLE   **Meg, Beth,** and **Amy** are Jo's sisters. Jo writes **them** stories. [*Meg, Beth,* **and** *Amy* **are the antecedents of** *them*.]

When you use a pronoun, be sure it refers to its antecedent clearly. Be especially careful when you use the pronoun *they*. Read the following sentence.

EXAMPLE   **They** have five books by Alcott at the school library.

The meaning of *They* is unclear. The sentence can be improved by rewriting it in the following way.

EXAMPLE   The school library has five books by Alcott.

PEANUTS reprinted by permission of United
Feature Syndicate, Inc.

GRAMMAR/USAGE/MECHANICS

When you use pronouns, be sure they agree with their antecedents in **number** (singular or plural) and **gender.** The gender of a noun may be masculine (male), feminine (female), or neuter (referring to things).

EXAMPLE   The Marches must face a death in the family. **They** face **it** with courage.

They is plural; it agrees with the plural antecedent *Marches. It* is singular and agrees with the singular antecedent *death.*

PRACTICE   **Identifying Pronouns and Antecedents**

Write each personal pronoun and its antecedent. If a pronoun doesn't have a clear antecedent, rewrite the numbered item to make the meaning clear.

1. Mr. Cannon talked to Marc about journalism. He likes to write human-interest stories.
2. Marc did a report about Katherine Graham. For many years, she headed the Washington Post Company.
3. In 1939, Katherine joined the staff of the *Washington Post.* It was a well-known newspaper owned by Katherine's father.
4. In 1940, Katherine married Philip Graham. He became publisher of the *Post* in 1948; he died in 1963.
5. Then Katherine became publisher. She wanted to make the *Post* an important newspaper.
6. Katherine worked hard. She increased the paper's budget.
7. In the 1970s, the *Post* published a series of stories about Watergate. It won the Pulitzer Prize in journalism.
8. The *Post* got information about the Watergate scandal from an anonymous source. They wrote about it without identifying the source.
9. The report said the president and his aides were involved in the scandal. They denied being involved.
10. Katherine's son replaced her as publisher in 1978.

4.4 POSSESSIVE PRONOUNS

You often use personal pronouns to replace nouns that are subjects or objects in sentences. You can use pronouns in place of possessive nouns, too.

A **possessive pronoun** is a pronoun that shows who or what has something. A possessive pronoun may take the place of a possessive noun.

Read the following sentences. Notice the possessive nouns and the possessive pronouns that replace them.

EXAMPLE   Lisa's class put on a play. **Her** class put on a play.

EXAMPLE   The idea was Lisa's. The idea was **hers.**

Possessive pronouns have two forms. One form is used before a noun. The other form is used alone.

POSSESSIVE PRONOUNS		
	SINGULAR	**PLURAL**
Used Before Nouns	my	our
	your	your
	her, his, its	their
Used Alone	mine	ours
	yours	yours
	hers, his, its	theirs

Possessive pronouns are not written with apostrophes. Don't confuse the possessive pronoun *its* with the word *it's*. *It's* is a contraction, or shortened form, of *it is* or *it has*.

EXAMPLE   **Its** popularity is growing. **[possessive pronoun]**

EXAMPLE   **It's** popular with many students. **[contraction of *It is*]**

EXAMPLE   **It's** succeeded on the stage. **[contraction of *It has*]**

Write the possessive pronouns.

1. Which equipment is yours, and which equipment is hers?
2. These are our costumes for the class play.
3. Jackson asked for her e-mail address.
4. Their ficus tree has lost its leaves.
5. Some of the school supplies are ours.
6. His backpack is lighter than yours.
7. My sister is staying overnight at their house.
8. Is the camera hers or mine?
9. Is your brother coming to our concert?
10. It's easy to follow their directions.

4.5 INDEFINITE PRONOUNS

An **indefinite pronoun** is a pronoun that does not refer to a particular person, place, or thing.

EXAMPLE **Everybody** thinks about the plot.

Some indefinite pronouns are always singular. Others are always plural. A few may be either singular or plural.

SOME INDEFINITE PRONOUNS			
ALWAYS SINGULAR			**ALWAYS PLURAL**
another	everybody	no one	both
anybody	everyone	nothing	few
anyone	everything	one	many
anything	much	somebody	others
each	neither	someone	several
either	nobody	something	

The indefinite pronouns *all, any, most, none,* and *some* may be singular or plural, depending on the phrase that follows them.

When an indefinite pronoun is used as the subject of a sentence, the verb must agree with it in number.

EXAMPLE **Everyone reads** part of the novel. **[singular]**

EXAMPLE **Several enjoy** it very much. **[plural]**

EXAMPLE **Most** of the story **happens** in England. **[singular]**

EXAMPLE **Most** of the characters **seem** real. **[plural]**

Possessive pronouns often have indefinite pronouns as their antecedents. In such cases, the pronouns must agree in number. Note that in the first example below the words that come between the subject and the verb don't affect the agreement.

EXAMPLE **Each** of the actors memorizes **his** or **her** lines.

EXAMPLE **Many** are enjoying **their** roles in the play.

PRACTICE Using Indefinite Pronouns

Write the indefinite pronouns and the correct words from the choices in parentheses.

1. Some of my friends (has, have) scooters.
2. Each (is, are) lightweight.
3. Most (has, have) an aluminum finish.
4. Everything about a scooter (is, are) compact.
5. Everybody (wants, want) to try riding a scooter.
6. Many ride (his or her, their) scooters to school.
7. One of my friends (ride, rides) a scooter to school in three minutes.
8. Many of the riders (wears, wear) helmets and knee and elbow pads.
9. No one (has, have) fallen.
10. Someone left (her or his, their) scooter in the hallway.

4.6 REFLEXIVE AND INTENSIVE PRONOUNS

A **reflexive pronoun** ends with -*self* or -*selves* and refers to the subject of a sentence. In a sentence with a reflexive pronoun, the action of the verb returns to the subject.

EXAMPLE   Yolanda bought **herself** a book on engine repair.
Reflexive Pronoun

Don't use a reflexive pronoun in place of a personal pronoun.

EXAMPLE   Yolanda asked Pat and **me** for help. [**not** *Pat and myself*]

EXAMPLE   Yolanda and **I** read the book. [**not** *Yolanda and myself*]

An **intensive pronoun** ends with -*self* or -*selves* and is used to draw special attention to a noun or a pronoun already named.

EXAMPLE   Yolanda **herself** repaired the engine.
Intensive Pronoun

EXAMPLE   Yolanda repaired the engine **herself.**
Intensive Pronoun

Reflexive and intensive pronouns are formed by adding -*self* or -*selves* to certain personal and possessive pronouns.

REFLEXIVE AND INTENSIVE PRONOUNS

SINGULAR	PLURAL
myself	ourselves
yourself	yourselves
himself, herself, itself	themselves

Don't use *hisself* or *theirselves* in place of *himself* and *themselves.*

Write the correct word from the choices in parentheses.
Then write personal, reflexive, *or* intensive *to identify the*
word you chose.

1. The students in the school play taped (theirselves, themselves) during the performance.
2. The camera (it, itself) was new.
3. Our teacher, Ms. Hanson, taught (herself, himself) and us how to use it.
4. Ms. Hanson gave Ira and (me, myself) instructions.
5. We found (us, ourselves) teaching the others.
6. Ms. Hanson asked Ira and (me, myself) to make the tape.
7. I taped the show (me, myself).
8. Ira made (himself, hisself) an extra tape.
9. The actors wanted to see the tape (theirselves, themselves).
10. I prepared (me, myself) for their review of the taped results.

4.7 INTERROGATIVE AND DEMONSTRATIVE PRONOUNS

An **interrogative pronoun** is a pronoun used to introduce an interrogative sentence.

The interrogative pronouns *who* and *whom* refer to people. *Who* is used when the interrogative pronoun is the subject of the sentence. *Whom* is used when the interrogative pronoun is an object.

EXAMPLE **Who** borrowed the book? **[subject]**

EXAMPLE **Whom** did the librarian call? **[direct object]**

Which and *what* refer to things and ideas.

EXAMPLES **Which** is it? **What** interests you?

Whose shows possession.

EXAMPLE   I found a copy of the play. **Whose** is it?

Don't confuse *whose* with *who's*. *Who's* is a contraction of *who is* or *who has*.

> A **demonstrative pronoun** is a pronoun that points out something.

The demonstrative pronouns are *this, that, these,* and *those. This* (singular) and *these* (plural) refer to things nearby. *That* (singular) and *those* (plural) refer to things at a distance.

EXAMPLE   **This** is an interesting book. [singular, nearby]

EXAMPLE   **These** are interesting books. [plural, nearby]

EXAMPLE   **That** was a good movie. [singular, at a distance]

EXAMPLE   **Those** were good movies. [plural, at a distance]

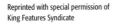

Reprinted with special permission of King Features Syndicate

PRACTICE   **Using Interrogative and Demonstrative Pronouns**

Write the correct word from the choices in parentheses.

1. (Whom, Who) will volunteer for the after-school tutoring program?
2. (Who's, Whose) going on the first bus?

3. (This, These) are the museum's floor plans.

4. (Who's, Whose) arranging the trip?

5. (Those, That) is not the picture I took.

6. (Who, Whom) is going to work at the school fair?

7. (What, Which) of the two science fiction movies did you like best?

8. (These, Those) over there are for the students.

9. Several backpacks were left in the bus. (Who's, Whose) are they?

10. She is not the woman (who, whom) we saw leaving the theater.

PRACTICE Proofreading

Rewrite the following passage, correcting errors in spelling, capitalization, grammar, and usage. Add any missing punctuation. Write legibly to be sure one letter is not mistaken for another. There are ten mistakes.

Maria Montessori

¹Some of us was students at a Montessori school. ²The school used teaching methods developed by Maria Montessori. ³Whom was Montessori. ⁴Whom was this woman changing education?

⁵In 1894 Montessori became the first Italian woman medical docter. ⁶She also was a teacher. ⁷Her developed new methods and styles for teaching the children. ⁸They focused on using the senses as a means of learning. ⁹With help, students theirselves learned by exploring their surroundings.

¹⁰The Italian government asked she to run a school for poor children. ¹¹The children progressed quickly. ¹²Today Montessori schools still use methods developed by herself.

POSTTEST **Personal Pronouns**

Write each personal pronoun. Then write one of the following phrases to identify the pronoun: subject pronoun as subject, subject pronoun as predicate pronoun, object pronoun as direct object, object pronoun as indirect object.

1. We read a story by Virginia Hamilton.
2. We saw you at the zoo Saturday afternoon.
3. The subjects of the article were we.
4. He and she brought us the latest news from town.
5. She asked him a question about the report.

POSTTEST **Using Pronouns**

Write the correct word or phrase from the choices in parentheses.

6. (We, Us) runners meet at 6:00 A.M. every morning except on Sundays.
7. The oldest members of the club are (she and I, I and she, her and me, me and her).
8. The news of the accident saddened (we, us) as well as other members.
9. The hiker told (she and he, she and him, her and him, her and he) about an alternative route.
10. (You and me, You and I, Me and you, You and me) could study together for the quiz.
11. Robin and (him, he) are washing cars as part of a class fund-raising project.
12. The people in the photograph were (they, them).
13. Adam gave Lisa and (she, her) the extra set of keys for the cabin.
14. (She and I, She and me) are auditioning for the same role in the play *Our Town*.
15. The director called (Sandra and we, we and Sandra, Sandra and us, us and Sandra) into her office.

Write each personal pronoun and its antecedent. If a pronoun doesn't have a clear antecedent, rewrite the numbered item to make the meaning clear.

16. Cattails grow in wetlands and near the edges of streams and ponds. They have narrow leaves and a tall stem.

17. They have various kinds of birds in the sanctuary.

18. Muskrats eat cattails and also use them to build homes.

19. Some types of seaweed live in shallow water, where they can get sunlight.

20. Sheila is reading about underwater plants. She wants to become a marine biologist.

POSTTEST **Identifying Pronouns**

Write each pronoun. Then write possessive, indefinite, reflexive, intensive, interrogative, *or* demonstrative *to identify it.*

21. Which of the toys are on sale?

22. Adam introduced himself to the new members in the science club.

23. Ms. Spencer conducted the experiment three times herself.

24. These are my gloves and those are yours.

25. "Whose are these?" Alejandro asked his classmates in the hallway.

26. My report is about monarch butterflies, and hers is about yucca moths.

27. Whom did Robert want to see?

28. Everyone wants front-row seats, but none are available at this time.

29. Both wanted to go skating, but neither had a ride to the rink.

30. Emily saw that and changed her mind.

GRAMMAR/USAGE/MECHANICS

Write the subjects and the correct words from the choices in parentheses.

31. Many of us (believes, believe) urban legends.

32. (Is, Are) either of you giving your report today?

33. All of the thirteen original colonies except Georgia (was, were) represented at the First Continental Congress.

34. Everyone (has, have) an opportunity to be in the yearbook.

35. Some of the space shuttle's missions (involves, involve) the new space station.

36. Much of that story (seems, seem) unbelievable.

37. Each of the friends (buys, buy) his or her own movie ticket.

38. Many of my friends ride their bikes to school, but others (takes, take) the bus.

39. (Are, Is) any of the library's new books available for checkout today?

40. Everybody (participate, participates) in Field Day activities at school.

Write the correct word from the choices in parentheses.

41. (Whose, Who's) signing up for the bus trip to Washington, D.C.?

42. Suzanne and (myself, I) joined the library's summer reading club.

43. (Who, Whom) did you ask for directions to the restaurant?

44. Is (these, that) the only writing assignment due next week?

45. (Whose, Who's) dog is in the yard?

46. (That, Those) is the last muffin.

47. I had given (me, myself) an hour for travel time to the concert.

48. The staff made (theirselves, themselves) lunch.

49. (Which, What) is taller, Ribbon Falls in California or Sutherland Falls in New Zealand?

50. (Who, Whom) reported the accident to the police?

Chapter 5

Adjectives

• • • • • • • • • • • • • • • • •

PRETEST Identifying Adjectives

Write each adjective. Beside the adjective, write the noun it modifies.

1. I remembered that the barn had always smelled of motor oil, wood chips, and cut grass.
2. The American team took the field wearing new blue and white uniforms.
3. Posters would look colorful on the walls of the college dorm.
4. Some people feel sad when the skies are gray.
5. Nomar Garciaparra, a great ball player, kept pennant hopes alive with outstanding offensive and defensive play.
6. Life in the tiny village came to a complete halt during the unexpected April storm.
7. A lingering odor of make-up remained in the reception room after the cast party.
8. Tereese wrote the entertaining eyewitness articles for the neighborhood newspaper.

9. One thousand years is a long time in human history, but in the vast sweep of geologic time it is a mere instant.

10. The astonished expression on his face convinced us that Jefferson had not known about the surprise party.

Write the correct word or phrase from the choices in parentheses.

11. Is (this, this here) the only universe, or is there (a, an) universe other than ours?

12. Pass (those, them) sandwiches around the circle.

13. I really like that work by (a, the) painter Peter Paul Rubens hanging to the right of (a, the) entrance.

14. (A, The) little paint will finish (a, the) job.

15. Hand me (this, that) pencil over there.

16. (This, These) ships do not look very seaworthy.

17. (A, The) only working wood-burning stove heated the entire room.

18. We typed our papers on (a, an) word processor.

19. Karim enjoyed (them, those) peaches.

20. (This, That) building down the street was once a church.

Write the correct comparative or superlative form of the adjective in parentheses.

21. This will be the (important) game of the season.

22. I would like a (small) serving than that.

23. Out of the ten problems, number four was (easy).

24. Which would be (quick), the coastal route or the inter-state highway?

25. The (ugly) insect Tanya had ever seen was on the screen door.

26. You can't grow pumpkins (big) than that.

27. Although the tortoise was (slow) than the hare, the tortoise won the race.

28. She has the (high) grade-point average in the class.

29. It is (sensible) to talk than to fight.

30. The decathlon may be the (demanding) of all Olympic events.

PRETEST **Irregular Comparative and Superlative Adjectives**

Write the correct word or phrase from the choices in parentheses.

31. Sam completed the laps around the track in the (less, least) amount of time.

32. There won't be a (worse, worst) blizzard than this all winter.

33. Couldn't you think of a (more good, better) solution than this?

34. (Little, Less) effort has been made to repair the damage.

35. I have the (better, best) solution of all.

36. (More, Most) people in the United States speak English.

37. The (less, least) talk I hear about it, the happier I will be.

38. Fergus did not think he had ever seen a (worse, worser) movie than *Lizards from Outer Space II.*

39. Can you come up with a (better, best) idea than mine for raising funds?

40. We learned (much, more) facts from reading the book than we did from watching the television series.

5.1 ADJECTIVES

The words we use to describe people, places, and things are called adjectives.

An **adjective** is a word that describes, or modifies, a noun or a pronoun.

Adjectives modify nouns in three ways.

HOW ADJECTIVES MODIFY NOUNS	
WHAT KIND?	We studied **ancient** history.
HOW MANY?	I read **four** chapters.
WHICH ONE?	**That** invention changed history.

Most adjectives come before the nouns they modify. Some adjectives follow linking verbs and modify the noun or pronoun that is the subject of the sentence.

EXAMPLE **Some** architects are **skillful** and **imaginative.**

The adjective *some* precedes and modifies the subject *architects*. The adjectives *skillful* and *imaginative* follow the linking verb, *are,* and modify the subject, *architects*. They are called predicate adjectives.

A **predicate adjective** follows a linking verb and modifies the subject of a sentence.

FoxTrot
by Bill Amend

Foxtrot © 1998 & 1993 Bill Amend. Reprinted with permission of Universal Press Syndicate. All rights reserved.

Two verb forms are often used as adjectives and predicate adjectives. They are the present participle and the past participle.

EXAMPLE The architect drew a **surprising** design. **[present participle]**

EXAMPLE Visitors seem **impressed. [past participle]**

Some adjectives are formed from proper nouns and begin with a capital letter. They are called proper adjectives.

Proper adjectives are adjectives formed from proper nouns.

Some proper adjectives have the same form as the noun. Others are formed by adding an ending to the noun form.

FORMING PROPER ADJECTIVES	
PROPER NOUN	**PROPER ADJECTIVE**
oranges from **Florida**	**Florida** oranges
the history of **America**	**American** history

More than one adjective may modify the same noun.

EXAMPLE **These new frozen** dinners are **tasty** and **nutritious.**

These, new, frozen, tasty, and *nutritious* all modify *dinners.*

NOTE   Many words that are usually nouns can also be used as adjectives: *stone wall,* **band** *uniform,* **baseball** *game.*

PRACTICE Identifying Adjectives

Write each adjective. Beside the adjective, write the noun it modifies.

1. Chinese foods are popular in many countries.
2. Snowy crystals fell softly on the dead leaves.
3. What amazing luck it was to win the grand prize.
4. The old stone cottage is now a pizza shop.
5. After the terrible four-alarm fire, people looked stunned and helpless.
6. The Siamese cat tore up the Persian carpet.
7. Our motel room had twin beds.
8. Every year I visit the family farm.
9. The frightened bear retreated with surprising speed.
10. Jaelyn knew that summer camp would be fun.

5.2 ARTICLES AND DEMONSTRATIVES

The words *a, an,* and *the* make up a special group of adjectives called **articles.**

A and *an* are called **indefinite articles** because they refer to one of a general group of people, places, things, or ideas. *A* is used before words beginning with a consonant sound. *An* is used before words beginning with a vowel sound. Don't confuse sounds with spellings. In speaking, you would say *a university* but *an uncle, a hospital* but *an honor.*

EXAMPLES   **a** union   **a** picture   **an** hour   **an** easel

The is called the **definite article** because it identifies specific people, places, things, or ideas.

EXAMPLE   **The** picture beside **the** fireplace is **the** best one.

The words *this, that, these,* and *those* are called **demonstrative adjectives.** They are used to point out something.

DEMONSTRATIVE ADJECTIVES	
Take **this** umbrella with you.	**That** store is closed.
Take **these** boots too.	**Those** clouds are lovely.

Demonstrative adjectives point out something and modify nouns by answering the question *which one?* or *which ones?*

Use *this* and *that* with singular nouns. Use *these* and *those* with plural nouns. Use *this* and *these* to point out something close to you. Use *that* and *those* to point out something at a distance.

DEMONSTRATIVES		
	SINGULAR	**PLURAL**
NEAR	this	these
FAR	that	those

Demonstratives can be used with nouns or without them. When they're used without nouns, they're called **demonstrative pronouns.**

DEMONSTRATIVE PRONOUNS	
This is mine.	**These** are his.
That is hers.	**Those** are yours.

The words *here* and *there* should not be used with demonstrative adjectives or demonstrative pronouns. The words *this, these, that,* and *those* already point out the locations *here* and *there.*

EXAMPLE   Look at **this** photograph. [**not** *this here photograph*]

Don't use the object pronoun *them* in place of the demonstrative adjective *those.*

EXAMPLE   I took a photo of **those** buildings. [**not** *them buildings*]

PRACTICE   Using Articles and Demonstratives

Write the correct word from the choices in parentheses.

1. I prefer (this, that) ring on my finger to (this, that) one in the store.
2. (That, That there) is (a, an) unkind remark.
3. Evening was (a, the) time of day Myles liked best.
4. I have never seen (a, the) thousand dollar bill.
5. Hers is (a, an) unique talent on (a, the) guitar.
6. Give (those, them) lollipops to (that, that there) girl.
7. (This, That) team of ours is just as good as (this, that) one from the city.
8. (This, These) children should have (a, an) equal opportunity to get a good education.
9. Please give him (a, the) break.
10. (That, That there) was certainly one long movie!

5.3 COMPARATIVE AND SUPERLATIVE ADJECTIVES

The **comparative form** of an adjective compares one person or thing with another.

The **superlative form** of an adjective compares one person or thing with several others.

For most adjectives with one syllable and for some with two syllables, add *-er* to form the comparative and *-est* to form the superlative.

EXAMPLE   Is Venezuela **larger** than Peru?

EXAMPLE   Is Brazil the **richest** country in South America?

For most adjectives with two or more syllables, form the comparative by using *more* before the adjective. Form the superlative by using *most* before the adjective.

EXAMPLE   Is Chile **more mountainous** than Bolivia?

EXAMPLE   Was Simón Bolívar South America's **most successful** general?

COMPARATIVE AND SUPERLATIVE FORMS		
BASE FORM	**COMPARATIVE**	**SUPERLATIVE**
small	small**er**	small**est**
big	big**ger**	big**gest**
pretty	prett**ier**	prett**iest**
fabulous	**more** fabulous	**most** fabulous

The words *less* and *least* are used before both short and long adjectives to form the negative comparative and superlative.

NEGATIVE COMPARATIVE AND SUPERLATIVE FORMS	
BASE FORM	The first dancer was **graceful.**
COMPARATIVE	The second dancer was **less graceful** than the first.
SUPERLATIVE	The third dancer was the **least graceful** one.

Don't use *more, most, less,* or *least* before adjectives that already end with *-er* or *-est.* This is called a double comparison.

PRACTICE Using Comparative and Superlative Adjectives I

Write the correct comparative or superlative form of the adjective in parentheses.

1. No one makes (tasty) stew than my mom.
2. The twin with the (long) hair is Seth.
3. Mr. Harris is the (talkative) of my five teachers.
4. She told me the (funny) story yesterday.
5. Could you make the brownies (sweet) than that?
6. I've never heard (complicated) directions.
7. Which do you find (interesting), math or science?
8. Mornings are (busy) than afternoons in the office.
9. That is the (majestic) tree in the forest.
10. I think Dopey was the (amusing) of the seven dwarfs.

PRACTICE Using Comparative and Superlative Adjectives II

Write the correct word or phrase from the choices in parentheses.

1. That story sounds (stranger, more strange) each time I hear it.
2. The *Russ T. Bottom* was the (rustier, rustiest) boat in the harbor.

3. Is tennis (less popular, least popular) than golf?

4. Raji's last serve was by far the (weaker, weakest) of his five attempts.

5. Putting a person on the Moon might be the (more ambitious, most ambitious) of human accomplishments.

6. Would you like a (smaller, more small) serving?

7. A baby human being is (helplesser, more helpless) than a newborn calf.

8. You seem (less committed, least committed) than before.

9. Bella was the (less excitable, least excitable) dog in her puppy training class.

10. It's (faster, more fast) to walk than to drive to the park.

5.4 IRREGULAR COMPARATIVE AND SUPERLATIVE ADJECTIVES

The comparative and superlative forms of some adjectives are not formed in the regular way.

EXAMPLE Harriet Tubman believed in a **good** cause.

EXAMPLE She knew that freedom was **better** than slavery.

EXAMPLE The Underground Railroad was the **best** route to freedom.

Better is the comparative form of the adjective *good*. *Best* is the superlative form of *good*.

IRREGULAR COMPARATIVE AND SUPERLATIVE FORMS		
BASE FORM	**COMPARATIVE**	**SUPERLATIVE**
good, well	better	best
bad	worse	worst
many, much	more	most
little	less	least

Don't use *more* or *most* before irregular adjectives that are already in the comparative or superlative form.

EXAMPLE Tubman felt **better** at the end of the day. [**not *more better***]

PRACTICE Using Irregular Adjectives

Write the correct word or phrase from the choices in parentheses.

1. I had the (worse, worst) dream last night.
2. Sylvia had by far the (best, most best) costume of anyone on stage.
3. We had (littler, less) snow this year than last.
4. Can't you find a (gooder, better) place to eat?
5. Hank Aaron hit the (most, mostest) home runs of anyone in professional baseball.
6. Is it true that (more, most) children than adults access the Internet today?
7. Nan's fever is (worse, worser) than it was yesterday.
8. That triple was Bill's (best, bestest) hit of the season.
9. There is (less, least) light in January than in June.
10. The (best, bestest) mousetrap will catch the (much, most) mice.

PRACTICE Proofreading

Rewrite the following passage, correcting errors in spelling, capitalization, grammar, and usage. Add any missing punctuation. Write legibly to be sure one letter is not mistaken for another. There are ten mistakes.

P. T. Barnum

[1]P. T. Barnum believed that people loved to be entertained. [2]He spent his life proving this here point.

[3]Barnum was one of the most famous promoters in these country. [4]In 1841 he founded the american Museum. [5]One of his most popular

museum displays was an hoax called the Feejee Mermaid. ⁶This consisted of the body of a monkey sewed to the tail of a fish. ⁷Of course, Barnum's bearded lady turned out to be a man!

⁸General Tom Thumb was one of Barnum's bestest discoveries. ⁹He was a tiny individual, who was also a talinted singer and comedian. ¹⁰Tom Thumb and Barnum went to England together. ¹¹They entertained the queen and her family.

¹²In 1871 Barnum opened a three-ring circus. ¹³Later this became known as "the Greater Show on Earth." ¹⁴One of the star circus attractions was a elephant named Jumbo. ¹⁵Barnum bought Jumbo from the London Zoo. ¹⁶Many English people, including a queen, were very unhappy about this. ¹⁷Barnum wasn't the most least bit sorry. ¹⁸Jumbo helped make him a lot of money!

POSTTEST Identifying Adjectives

Write each adjective. Beside the adjective, write the noun it modifies.

1. In a final effort to save the damaged airplane, the desperate pilot attempted a water landing.
2. Shirlee has a cheerful personality.
3. At the bottom of the shallow hole lay a bulky chest containing the treasure.
4. The friendly puppy had been brought to the animal shelter as an unwanted pet.
5. Do you want the large room painted with bold or pastel colors?
6. According to the video guide, *The China Syndrome* is an exciting movie.
7. Acid rain can result in dismal forests of dead trees and quiet brooks without fish.
8. We waited in line for two hours to get concert tickets.

9. Uncle Harry loved to tell endless stories about his long-ago high school days.

10. During the 1940s, the first nylon stockings were introduced.

POSTTEST **Articles and Demonstratives**

Write the correct word or phrase from the choices in parentheses.

11. (These, That) is (a, an) interesting idea for a research paper.

12. (These, These here) crackers are the ones I like best.

13. Will (a, an) universal remote work with this TV?

14. He wants to assemble (a, the) first-rate team before climbing (those, them) mountains.

15. (These, That) are the ruby slippers from (the, a) movie *The Wizard of Oz*.

16. Jesse Owens, (a, an) African American athlete, won four gold medals at (an, the) Olympics in 1936.

17. (That, That there) geranium needs repotting.

18. Shahid had (a, an) good time while on (a, an) apple-picking trip with his youth group.

19. Give the coach (a, an) hour with (that, those) kids, and he'll know who can play (a, the) game.

20. In (that, that there) movie, (a, the) U.S. Army defeats (the, them) Martians.

POSTTEST **Comparative and Superlative Adjectives**

Write the correct comparative or superlative form of the adjective in parentheses.

21. A deer's hearing is (sensitive) than ours.

22. She always selects the (juicy) oranges she can find.

23. A (wide) vehicle than this couldn't fit through the gate.

24. Cats and dogs are two of the (common) pets people own.

25. (Experienced) guides than he had failed to reach the summit.

26. Visiting India was the (memorable) trip of his life.

27. The cabin is (run-down) than I expected it to be.

28. The *Cullinan* was the (large) diamond ever found.

29. Dolphins are considered one of the (intelligent) animals.

30. Erin is (young) than her brothers.

POSTTEST Irregular Comparative and Superlative Adjectives

Write the correct word or phrase from the choices in parentheses.

31. The (best, bestest) rivers for trout fishing are cool and clear.

32. My car has (much, more) legroom than yours.

33. Which of that pair has sustained (more, most) damage?

34. That's the (least, most least) of my worries.

35. I trust that we will have a (better, more better) experience traveling by train than we had traveling by car.

36. The traffic on that road is (worse, worst) than that on any other road in town.

37. That's a (good, gooder) route to take home.

38. This year's weather is (worse, worst) than last year's.

39. Describe the (most, mostest) fun you've ever had.

40. I've never known anyone with (less, least) patience than Isabelle has.

Chapter 6

Adverbs

● ● ● ● ● ● ● ● ● ● ● ● ● ● ●

PRETEST Identifying Adverbs

Write each adverb and the word it modifies. Then write whether the modified word is a verb, *an* adjective, *or an* adverb.

1. The sun disappeared gradually behind the forest of oaks.
2. They often camp for weeks in the mountains of New Hampshire.
3. Peter quickly snatched his lunch bag from the kitchen counter.
4. Most people speak fondly of him.
5. He was sleeping peacefully when I saw him last.
6. Elinor played the cello so beautifully that the audience gave her a standing ovation.
7. I will have a second helping now.
8. When I play Monopoly, I'm always going directly to jail and never collecting $200.
9. First go straight for one hundred yards; then turn right and continue for another mile.
10. Just yesterday she was looking so well.

Write the correct word or phrase from the choices in parentheses.

11. Maura got to the ball (sooner, more sooner) than I did.

12. Which of those three infielders hits (more, most) consistently?

13. Pursued by the yellow jackets, Sarah ran (faster, more faster, fastest) than an Olympic sprinter.

14. On his third attempt, Rafael jumped (more far, farther, further) than on the first two.

15. I feel as if I am the (less, least) productive person in this group.

16. Clearly, Charlyn danced (better, best) of all.

17. Ivan is here (oftener, more often) than he would like.

18. You have worked (littler, less) than I have today.

19. He performed (more well, better, more better) than anyone else in the competition.

20. No one could have felt (worse, worser, more worse, worst) than Juanita when the letter carrier tripped over her skateboard.

PRETEST Using Adjectives and Adverbs

Write the correct word from the choices in parentheses.

21. How (good, well) you perform depends upon how much you practiced.

22. Red Riding Hood noticed that her grandmother's teeth seemed (real, really) sharp.

23. I woke up with a (sure, surely) sense that something was wrong.

24. He (sure, surely) looked funny in that green wig.

25. (Real, Really) friends don't spread rumors.

26. Why are you driving so (slow, slowly)?

GRAMMAR/USAGE/MECHANICS

27. He (most, almost) always arrives late.

28. Those answers look (good, well) to me.

29. They seemed (happy, happily) as they played in the back yard.

30. I'm afraid I did (bad, badly) on the quiz.

Rewrite each sentence so it correctly expresses a negative idea.

31. I couldn't see nothing in the dark.

32. Won't nobody come to say good night?

33. According to legend, there wasn't no American president more honest than Abe Lincoln.

34. Don't never cross the street when the Don't Walk sign is lit.

35. The frightened rabbit couldn't find nowhere to hide from the fox.

36. Hardly none of those birds fly south in the winter.

37. "No one never leaves my castle alive!" bellowed the giant.

38. One of the survivors wasn't barely six years old.

39. "I don't want no trouble from any of you!" the sergeant shouted at the new recruits.

40. There isn't no such thing as a free lunch.

6.1 ADVERBS THAT MODIFY VERBS

Adjectives are words that modify nouns and pronouns. Adverbs are another type of modifier. They modify verbs, adjectives, and other adverbs.

An **adverb** is a word that modifies a verb, an adjective, or another adverb.

WHAT ADVERBS MODIFY	
VERBS	People *handle* old violins **carefully.**
ADJECTIVES	**Very** *old* violins are valuable.
ADVERBS	Orchestras **almost** *always* include violins.

An adverb may tell *how* or *in what manner* an action is done. It may tell *when* or *how often* an action is done. It may also tell *where* or *in what direction* an action is done.

WAYS ADVERBS MODIFY VERBS	
ADVERBS TELL	**EXAMPLES**
HOW	grandly, easily, completely, neatly, gratefully, sadly
WHEN	soon, now, immediately, often, never, usually, early
WHERE	here, there, everywhere, inside, downstairs, above, far

When an adverb modifies an adjective or another adverb, the adverb usually comes before the word it modifies. When an adverb modifies a verb, the adverb can occupy different positions in a sentence.

POSITION OF ADVERBS MODIFYING VERBS	
BEFORE THE VERB	Guests **often** dine at the White House.
AFTER THE VERB	Guests dine **often** at the White House.
AT THE BEGINNING	**Often** guests dine at the White House.
AT THE END	Guests dine at the White House **often.**

Many adverbs are formed by adding *-ly* to adjectives. However, not all words that end in *-ly* are adverbs. The words *friendly, lively, kindly, lovely,* and *lonely* are usually adjectives. On the other hand, not all adverbs end in *-ly.*

SOME ADVERBS NOT ENDING IN *-LY*			
afterward	everywhere	near	short
already	fast	never	sometimes
always	forever	not	somewhere
anywhere	hard	now	soon
away	here	nowhere	straight
below	home	often	then
even	late	outside	there
ever	long	seldom	well

PRACTICE Identifying Adverbs I

Write each adverb. Beside the adverb, write the verb it modifies.

1. He silently paddled the canoe from the lake into the river.
2. I always meet her here.
3. A fierce wind sprang up suddenly and tore shingles from the roof.
4. Are you staying long at the Anderson's party?
5. Often you can see a deer near that road.
6. All this rubbish must be thrown away.
7. We walked home quickly.
8. He stood outside in the chilly night and stared wonderingly at the stars.
9. Mr. Reynolds claims that an alien spacecraft sometimes makes an emergency landing in his backyard.
10. John Hancock boldly signed the Declaration of Independence.

6.2 ADVERBS THAT MODIFY ADJECTIVES AND OTHER ADVERBS

Adverbs are often used to modify adjectives and other adverbs. Notice how adverbs affect the meaning of the adjectives in the following sentences. Most often they tell *how* or *to what extent.*

EXAMPLE   Harry Truman used **extremely** direct language.

EXAMPLE   He became a **very** popular president.

In the first sentence, the adverb *extremely* modifies the adjective *direct. Extremely* tells to what extent Truman's language was direct. In the second sentence, the adverb *very* modifies the adjective *popular. Very* tells to what extent Truman was popular.

PEANUTS reprinted by permission of United
Feature Syndicate, Inc.

In the following sentences, adverbs modify other adverbs.

EXAMPLE   Truman entered politics **unusually** late in life.

EXAMPLE   He moved through the political ranks **quite** quickly.

In the first sentence, the adverb *unusually* modifies the adverb *late. Unusually* tells how late Truman entered politics. In the second sentence, the adverb *quite* modifies the adverb *quickly. Quite* tells how quickly Truman moved through the ranks.

When an adverb modifies an adjective or another adverb, the adverb almost always comes directly before the word it modifies. On the following page is a list of some adverbs that are often used to modify adjectives and other adverbs.

Chapter 6 Adverbs   **161**

ADVERBS OFTEN USED TO MODIFY ADJECTIVES AND OTHER ADVERBS			
almost	just	rather	too
barely	nearly	really	totally
extremely	partly	so	unusually
hardly	quite	somewhat	very

PRACTICE Identifying Adverbs II

Write each adverb and the word it modifies. Then write whether the modified word is a verb, an *adjective,* or an adverb.

1. She could barely keep a straight face.
2. Jose dribbled so skillfully that several defenders just stood there and helplessly watched him.
3. He will be returning unusually late tomorrow.
4. The winner raced hard to the finish line, very red in the face from all his exertion.
5. Her car radio blared music really loudly.
6. The antelope stopped short and listened intently.
7. I am extremely grateful for your help.
8. They seemed quite ready for the nearly Arctic weather.
9. Nina sometimes awakens too early.
10. Somewhere in the woods, a huge beast growled menacingly.

6.3 COMPARATIVE AND SUPERLATIVE ADVERBS

The **comparative form** of an adverb compares one action with another.

The **superlative form** of an adverb compares one action with several others.

Most short adverbs add *-er* to form the comparative and *-est* to form the superlative.

COMPARING ADVERBS WITH *-ER* AND *-EST*	
COMPARATIVE	The pianist arrived **earlier** than the violinist.
SUPERLATIVE	The drummer arrived **earliest** of all the players.

Long adverbs and a few short ones require the use of *more* or *most*.

COMPARING ADVERBS WITH *MORE* AND *MOST*	
COMPARATIVE	The violinist plays **more often** than the harpist.
SUPERLATIVE	Which musicians play **most often?**

Some adverbs have irregular comparative and superlative forms.

IRREGULAR COMPARATIVE AND SUPERLATIVE FORMS

BASE FORM	COMPARATIVE	SUPERLATIVE
well	better	best
badly	worse	worst
little	less	least
far (distance)	farther	farthest
far (degree)	further	furthest

The words *less* and *least* are used before adverbs to form the negative comparative and superlative.

EXAMPLES I play **less well.** I play **least accurately.**

Don't use *more, most, less,* or *least* before adverbs that already end in *-er* or *-est.*

PRACTICE Using Comparative and Superlative Adverbs

Write the correct word or phrase from the choices in parentheses.

1. Jill sings (sweeter, sweetlier, more sweetly) than any bird.
2. Who on the team jumps (higher, highest, most high)?
3. Never before had the team played (more badly, worse, worst).
4. I think (better, best) of all on a full stomach.
5. She double faults (oftener, more often) than her partner.
6. He is (less, least) likely to be on time than his friends are.
7. Mary gets up (later, more lately) in the summer than during the school year.
8. Which of the museum's pictures do you like (better, best)?
9. "Push (harder, more hard, more hardly)," the child on the swing urged.
10. Late arrivals are sitting (more far, farther, further) from the stage.

6.4 USING ADJECTIVES AND ADVERBS

Sometimes it's hard to decide whether a sentence needs an adjective or an adverb. Think carefully about how the word is used.

EXAMPLE He was (**careful, carefully**) with the antique clock.

EXAMPLE He worked (**careful, carefully**) on the antique clock.

In the first sentence, the missing word follows a linking verb and modifies the subject, *He.* Therefore, an adjective is needed. *Careful* is the correct choice. In the second sentence, the missing word modifies the verb, *worked.* Thus, an adverb is needed, and *carefully* is the correct choice.

The words *good* and *well* and the words *bad* and *badly* are sometimes confused. *Good* and *bad* are adjectives. Use them before nouns and after linking verbs. *Well* and *badly* are adverbs. Use them to modify verbs. *Well* may also be used as an adjective to mean "healthy": *You look well today.*

TELLING ADJECTIVES FROM ADVERBS

ADJECTIVE	ADVERB
The band sounds **good.**	The band plays **well.**
The band sounds **bad.**	The band plays **badly.**
The soloist is **well.**	The soloist sings **well.**

Use these modifiers correctly: *real* and *really, sure* and *surely, most* and *almost. Real* and *sure* are adjectives. *Really, surely,* and *almost* are adverbs. *Most* can be an adjective or an adverb.

TELLING ADJECTIVES FROM ADVERBS

ADJECTIVE	ADVERB
Music is a **real** art.	This music is **really** popular.
A pianist needs **sure** hands.	Piano music is **surely** popular.
Most pianos have eighty-eight keys.	Piano strings **almost** never break.

PRACTICE Using Adjectives and Adverbs

Write the correct word from the choices in parentheses.

1. Often a movie's villain looks (bad, badly).
2. With its new coat of paint, the porch looked (good, well).

3. How (bad, badly) do you want the part?
4. That fish is (sure, surely) going to make a good meal.
5. He ran (real, really) fast to catch up with his sister.
6. She'll have to play (good, well) to make the team.
7. Come here (quick, quickly).
8. At last he made a (real, really) commitment to join the club.
9. The show is (most, almost) over when the actor says that line.
10. Those gray clouds are a (sure, surely) sign of rain.

6.5 CORRECTING DOUBLE NEGATIVES

The adverb *not* is a **negative word,** expressing the idea of "no." *Not* often appears in a short form as part of a contraction. When *not* is part of a contraction, as in the words in the chart below, *n't* is an adverb.

CONTRACTIONS WITH *NOT*		
are not = aren't	does not = doesn't	should not = shouldn't
cannot = can't	had not = hadn't	was not = wasn't
could not = couldn't	has not = hasn't	were not = weren't
did not = didn't	have not = haven't	will not = won't
do not = don't	is not = isn't	would not = wouldn't

In all but two of these words, the apostrophe replaces the *o* in *not.* In *can't* both an *n* and the *o* are omitted. *Will not* becomes *won't.*

Other negative words are listed in the following chart. Each negative word has several opposites. These are **affirmative words,** or words that show the idea of "yes."

SOME NEGATIVE AND AFFIRMATIVE WORDS

NEGATIVE	AFFIRMATIVE
never, scarcely, hardly, barely	always, ever
nobody	anybody, everybody, somebody
no, none	all, any, one, some
no one	anyone, everyone, one, someone
nothing	anything, something
nowhere	anywhere, somewhere

Don't use two negative words to express the same idea. This is called a **double negative.** Only one negative word is necessary to express a negative idea. You can correct a double negative by removing one of the negative words or by replacing one of the negative words with an affirmative word.

EXAMPLE **INCORRECT** I **don't** have **no** homework.

EXAMPLE **CORRECT** I have **no** homework.

EXAMPLE **CORRECT** I **don't** have **any** homework.

PRACTICE Expressing Negative Ideas

Rewrite each sentence so it correctly expresses a negative idea.

1. We can't do nothing about the broken window now.
2. Jim hasn't got nowhere to stay on Saturday.
3. Weren't none of you signing up for baseball this summer?
4. You shouldn't never use language like that.
5. It isn't barely seven o'clock yet.

Chapter 6 Adverbs **167**

6. I wouldn't ask no one to wear a shirt like that.
7. Losing this game doesn't make no difference.
8. She was so nervous that she couldn't eat nothing.
9. Won't nobody come to the movie with me?
10. It was so foggy that Ms. Suarez couldn't hardly see the car in front of hers.

PRACTICE Proofreading

Rewrite the following passage, correcting errors in spelling, capitalization, grammar, and usage. Add any missing punctuation. Write legibly to be sure one letter is not mistaken for another. There are ten mistakes.

Pocahontas

[1]Pocahontas was a Native American girl, the daughter of Chief Powhatan. [2]She wasn't barely eleven years old when English settlers first arrived in Virginia. [3]She became a real important figure in the history of the United States.

[4]One famous story about Pocahontas is told more oftener than any other. [5]Powhatan's people had taken John Smith prisoner. [6]The chief wanted to kill Smith. [7]Pocahontas jumped quick to Smith's defense. [8]She persuaded her father not to kill him. [9]Most people know this story bestest. [10]However, some historians believe that this didn't never happen.

[11]Pocahontas was kidnapped by the English in 1613. [12]She learned to speak English good and wore European clothes. [13]Later she married John Rolfe and had a son.

[14]In 1616 Pocahontas traveled more farther from home than she ever had before. [15]She sailed with her family to England where she was sure treated like royalty. [16]Her life ended sad. [17]She got sick and died in England.

Write each adverb and the word it modifies. Then write whether the modified word is a verb, *an* adjective, *or an* adverb.

1. The dog barked loudly as I passed the gate.
2. Sometimes I exercise early in the morning.
3. Work hard and you will never fail.
4. Knock very gently three times and enter.
5. They finished eating extremely quickly.
6. Lightning suddenly lit the night sky with an almost white light.
7. These granola bars are too chewy for me.
8. Bill never practices piano very cheerfully.
9. They played rather well together.
10. The puppy looked so silly with its very big feet and short legs.

POSTTEST Comparative and Superlative Adverbs

Write the correct word or phrase from the choices in parentheses.

11. She is now serving the ball (more well, better, more better) than ever before.
12. The test pilot flew (more fast, fastest, most fast) on the second of his three flights.
13. The black bear eats (less, least) in winter than in autumn.
14. I would not take that idea any (more far, further).
15. Of all the days of the week, the cafeteria food is (worse, worst) on Friday.
16. You can do no (more well, better) than that.
17. They slept (sounder, more soundly) in the motel than they had in the tent.
18. Of all the towns hit by the storm, Jefferson suffered the (worse, most badly, worst) damage.

GRAMMAR/USAGE/MECHANICS

19. The foal always stands (more nearly, nearer, most nearly) to its mother than to any other horse.

20. Can you hit the (farther, farthest, fartherest) of those six targets?

Write the correct word from the choices in parentheses.

21. The expedition was a (real, really) test of character.

22. I think I did (good, well) on the math test.

23. Fumbling that pass made him look (bad, badly) in front of ten million people.

24. She is (sure, surely) playing a practical joke.

25. I wanted to finish the job (real, really) (bad, badly).

26. There has been no (sure, surely) sighting of Bigfoot.

27. She was very (good, well) for the baby-sitter.

28. She is (most, almost) always right.

29. Look at how (good, well) you did.

30. Get help as (quick, quickly) as you can.

Rewrite each sentence so it correctly expresses a negative idea.

31. I wouldn't tell nobody what you've just heard.

32. The police couldn't find no evidence of theft.

33. That wasn't none of their business.

34. When they closed the youth club, a lot of kids didn't have nowhere to go.

35. You can't never predict what Sal's going to say next.

36. They can't do nothing about the report today.

37. The baby isn't hardly walking yet.

38. Ben doesn't take advice from no one.

39. It wasn't barely light when we arrived at the camp.

40. My opinion doesn't make no difference.

Chapter 7

Prepositions, Conjunctions, and Interjections

• • • • • • • • • • • • • • •

PRETEST **Prepositions and Prepositional Phrases**

Write each prepositional phrase. Underline the preposition and circle the object of the preposition. Then write the word the prepositional phrase modifies. Finally, write adjective *or* adverb *to tell how the prepositional phrase is used.*

   1. Approximately 30 percent of Earth is covered by land.
   2. Water covers the other 70 percent of Earth's surface.
   3. Coasts along the oceans may be beaches or cliffs.
   4. There are actually mountains under the ocean.
   5. Mount Everest is 29,028 feet above sea level.
   6. It is the highest mountain on Earth.
   7. People have climbed to the mountaintop.
   8. There they stood at the top of Earth.

171

9. Many climbers proved to themselves that they could make the difficult climb.
10. Are cave explorers the opposite of mountain climbers?

PRETEST Pronouns as Objects of Prepositions

Write the correct word or phrase from the choices in parentheses.

11. Kathy and Lawanda went to the show with my friend Sean and (I, me).
12. The usher gave programs to (them and me, they and I, them and I, they and me).
13. The people in front of Kathy, Lawanda, Sean, and (I, me) talked during the show.
14. We didn't know to (who, whom) we should complain.
15. Finally, the usher came toward Sean and (I, me).
16. The usher reached across (him and me, he and I).
17. He asked the talkers to be more considerate of (we, us).
18. They sent surprised looks toward the girls and (we, us).
19. The woman apologized to Lawanda and (she, her).
20. Without the noise from (he and she, him and her), the four of (we, us) enjoyed the show more.

PRETEST Conjunctions

Write each conjunction. Then write compound subject, compound object, compound predicate, *or* compound sentence *to tell what parts the conjunction joins.*

21. Both Sammy Sosa and Mark McGwire are great home-run hitters.
22. Neither they nor Tiger Woods was the most popular sports hero during the last decade, though.
23. That and many other honors go to Michael Jordan.
24. Jordan played spectacularly and led his team well.
25. Top basketball honors went to Jordan and his team.

26. Jordan helped the Chicago Bulls win six national championships, and he became known around the world.

27. McGwire and Sosa have not led their teams to championships, but they are still heroes to many fans.

28. Jordan no longer plays basketball, but he does like to play golf.

29. Tiger Woods plays golf and wins many championships.

30. Woods and Jordan are both champion athletes.

PRETEST **Making Compound Subjects and Verbs Agree**

Write the correct word from the choices in parentheses.

31. Paintings and ceramics (is, are) shown at the art fair.

32. Neither Tim nor his aunt (like, likes) modern art.

33. The woodworker or his assistant (carve, carves) small figurines.

34. The jewelry or handmade hats in that display (do, does) not interest them.

35. A band and dancers (appear, appears) on stage.

36. The heat and humidity of an August day (slow, slows) some people down.

37. Neither lemonade nor other soft drinks (quench, quenches) my thirst.

38. Ice and water (refresh, refreshes) me after a run.

39. Either an oak or a maple tree (have, has) been planted in the park.

40. Dark clouds and lightning (serve, serves) as warnings of an approaching storm.

PRETEST **Conjunctive Adverbs**

Write each sentence. Underline the conjunctive adverb. Add appropriate punctuation.

41. A library is an excellent source of information likewise you can find fiction and poetry there.

42. Of course, many of a library's resources are in books however many are on computers and videos, too.

43. You can search for books with a computer moreover you can search the Internet with a librarian's help.

44. A library offers other services as well thus you might find a community meeting or a story hour there.

45. You can use a library in many ways besides you can have fun there.

7.1 PREPOSITIONS AND PREPOSITIONAL PHRASES

A **preposition** is a word that relates a noun or a pronoun to another word in a sentence.

EXAMPLE The boy **near** the window is French.

The word *near* is a preposition. It shows the relationship between the noun *window* and the word *boy*.

COMMON PREPOSITIONS				
aboard	at	down	off	to
about	before	during	on	toward
above	behind	except	onto	under
across	below	for	opposite	underneath
after	beneath	from	out	until
against	beside	in	outside	up
along	besides	inside	over	upon
among	between	into	past	with
around	beyond	like	since	within
as	but (except)	near	through	without
	by	of	throughout	

A preposition may consist of more than one word.

EXAMPLE   Yasmin will visit Trinidad **instead of** Jamaica.

SOME PREPOSITIONS OF MORE THAN ONE WORD			
according to	aside from	in front of	instead of
across from	because of	in place of	on account of
along with	except for	in spite of	on top of

A **prepositional phrase** is a group of words that begins with a preposition and ends with a noun or a pronoun, which is called the **object of the preposition.**

EXAMPLE   Hang the painting **outside the new auditorium.**

A preposition may have a compound object.

EXAMPLE   Between the **chair** and the **table** was a window.

PRACTICE Identifying Prepositional Phrases

Write each prepositional phrase. Underline the preposition and draw a circle around the object of the preposition.

1. Throughout the world, people have similar wants and needs for themselves and for their children.
2. People have in common their needs for food, shelter, clothing, and love.
3. The kinds of food, shelter, and clothing people have are different in various climates.
4. Yet, people across all cultures share love of family, love of country, and love for each other.
5. In spite of our differences, we all feel affection toward others.
6. There are a number of us who also share a love of animals.

Chapter 7 Prepositions, Conjunctions, and Interjections   **175**

7. Many families in the United States are crazy about their cats, dogs, or even fish.
8. Some people in other parts of the world keep crickets or pigs as pets.
9. On a shelf or tabletop in some homes, you might see pictures of pets displayed beside the pictures of family members.
10. Underneath it all is the universal emotion of love.

7.2 PRONOUNS AS OBJECTS OF PREPOSITIONS

When a pronoun is the object of a preposition, use an object pronoun, not a subject pronoun.

EXAMPLE Dan handed the tickets to Natalie.

EXAMPLE Dan handed the tickets to **her.**

In the example, the object pronoun *her* replaces *Natalie* as the object of the preposition *to.*

A preposition may have a compound object: two or more nouns, two or more pronouns, or a combination of nouns and pronouns. Use object pronouns in compound objects.

EXAMPLE I borrowed the suitcase from Ivan and Vera.

EXAMPLE I borrowed the suitcase from Ivan and **her.**

EXAMPLE I borrowed the suitcase from **him** and Vera.

EXAMPLE I borrowed the suitcase from **him** and **her.**

Object pronouns are used in the second, third, and fourth sentences. In the second sentence, *Ivan and her* is the compound object of the preposition *from.* In the third sentence, *him and Vera* is the compound object of the preposition *from.* In the fourth sentence, *him and her* is the compound object of the preposition *from.*

If you're not sure whether to use a subject pronoun or an object pronoun, read the sentence aloud with only the pronoun.

EXAMPLE   I borrowed the suitcase from **her.**

EXAMPLE   I borrowed the suitcase from **him.**

Who is a subject pronoun. *Whom* is an object pronoun.

EXAMPLE   **Who** lent you the suitcase?

EXAMPLE   From **whom** did you borrow the suitcase?

Frank and Ernest

© 2000 Thaves. Reprinted with permission.
Newspaper dist. by NEA, Inc.

PRACTICE Using Pronouns as Objects of Prepositions

Write the correct word or phrase from the choices in parentheses.

1. There were six of (we, us) first-time sailors aboard Roy's boat.
2. Roy gave life jackets to (them and me, they and I, them and I, they and me).
3. According to (he, him), a life jacket is an essential piece of equipment for all boats.
4. The boat's motor and rudder were behind (we, us).
5. From (who, whom) came that uncomfortable squeal?
6. Someone's feet were up against Sam and (she, her).
7. Those feet were pushing them into the side of the boat and (he, him).
8. As the wind rushed toward Sam and (I, me), we almost fell backward into Roy and (they, them).
9. We got up and sat near Sandra and (she, her).
10. We don't know for (who, whom) that boat ride was more fun, those in back or those across from Roy and (I, me).

7.3 PREPOSITIONAL PHRASES AS ADJECTIVES AND ADVERBS

A prepositional phrase is an **adjective phrase** when it modifies, or describes, a noun or a pronoun.

EXAMPLE   The servers **at the new restaurant** are courteous.

EXAMPLE   The atmosphere includes photographs **from old movies.**

In the first sentence, the prepositional phrase *at the new restaurant* modifies the subject of the sentence, *servers.* In the second sentence, the prepositional phrase *from old movies* modifies the direct object, *photographs.*

Notice that, unlike most adjectives, an adjective phrase usually comes after the word it modifies.

A prepositional phrase is an **adverb phrase** when it modifies a verb, an adjective, or another adverb.

ADVERB PHRASES	
USE	**EXAMPLES**
Modifies a Verb	The servers *dress* **like movie characters.**
Modifies an Adjective	The restaurant is *popular* **with young people.**
Modifies an Adverb	The restaurant opens *early* **in the morning.**

Most adverb phrases tell *when, where,* or *how* an action takes place. More than one prepositional phrase may modify the same word.

HOW ADVERB PHRASES MODIFY VERBS	
WHEN?	Many people eat a light meal **during the lunch hour.**
WHERE?	Some eat lunch **on the covered patio.**
HOW?	Others eat their meals **in a hurry.**

Write each prepositional phrase. Then write the word it modifies. Finally, write adjective *or* adverb *to tell how it's used.*

1. Put the books on the top shelf.
2. The plants can be displayed along the windowsill.
3. The one in the pink vase should go in the middle.
4. I'll put the souvenirs from my trip here.
5. CDs go in the special holder beside the sound system.
6. Videotapes in their cases should be placed under the TV.
7. The dictionary is between the bookends on the desk.
8. Let's put the small lamp next to the books on the desk too.
9. We can hang more shelves on the wall by the window.
10. Move the clothes on hangers into the closet.

7.4 TELLING PREPOSITIONS AND ADVERBS APART

Sometimes it can be difficult to tell whether a particular word is being used as a preposition or as an adverb. Both prepositions and adverbs can answer the questions *where?* and *when?* The chart below shows fifteen words that can be used as either prepositions or adverbs. Whether any one of these words is a preposition or an adverb depends on its use in a particular sentence.

SOME WORDS THAT CAN BE USED AS PREPOSITIONS OR ADVERBS		
about	below	out
above	down	outside
around	in	over
before	inside	through
behind	near	up

If you have trouble deciding whether a word is being used as a preposition or as an adverb, look at the other words in the sentence. If the word is followed closely by a noun or a pronoun, the word is probably a preposition, and the noun or pronoun is the object of the preposition.

EXAMPLE   We ate our lunch **outside** the **library.**

EXAMPLE   We walked **around** the **park** for an hour.

In the first example, *outside* is followed closely by the noun *library. Outside* is a preposition, and *library* is the object of the preposition. In the second example, *around* is a preposition, and *park* is the object of the preposition.

If the word is not followed closely by a noun or a pronoun, the word is probably an adverb.

EXAMPLE   We ate our lunch **outside.**

EXAMPLE   We walked **around** for an hour.

In the first sentence, *outside* answers the question *where?* but is not followed by a noun or a pronoun. In this sentence, *outside* is an adverb. In the second sentence, *around* is an adverb. *For an hour* is a prepositional phrase.

PRACTICE **Identifying Prepositions and Adverbs**

Write preposition *or* adverb *to identify each underlined word.*

   1. What is the movie <u>about</u>?
   2. I think it is <u>about</u> people in a circus.
   3. Mike has a brother who lives <u>up</u> the street.
   4. Will you give <u>up</u> or are you ready to continue?
   5. There are drinking glasses <u>behind</u> that cupboard door.
   6. The last bicyclist is falling <u>behind</u> in the race.
   7. Will the show be <u>over</u> soon?
   8. The gas station is just <u>over</u> the next hill.
   9. Don't look <u>down</u> when you are mountain climbing.
   10. Both Jack and Jill tumbled <u>down</u> the hill.

7.5 CONJUNCTIONS

A **coordinating conjunction** is a word used to connect compound parts of a sentence. *And, but, or, nor,* and *for* are coordinating conjunctions. *So* and *yet* are also sometimes used as coordinating conjunctions.

USING COORDINATING CONJUNCTIONS TO FORM COMPOUNDS	
COMPOUND SUBJECT	Allison **and** Rosita have lived in Mexico City.
COMPOUND OBJECTS	Give your suitcases **and** packages to Ben **or** Bill.
COMPOUND PREDICATE	Tourists shop **or** relax on the beaches.
COMPOUND SENTENCE	Tillie shopped every day, **but** we toured the city.

To make the relationship between words or groups of words especially strong, use correlative conjunctions.

Correlative conjunctions are pairs of words used to connect compound parts of a sentence. Correlative conjunctions include *both . . . and, either . . . or, neither . . . nor,* and *not only . . . but also.*

EXAMPLE   Examples of great architecture exist in **both** New York **and** Paris.

EXAMPLE   **Neither** Luis **nor** I have visited those cities.

When a compound subject is joined by *and,* the subject is usually plural. The verb must agree with the plural subject.

EXAMPLE   Winnie **and** Sumi **are** in Madrid this week.

When a compound subject is joined by *or* or *nor,* the verb must agree with the nearer subject.

EXAMPLE   **Neither** Rhondelle **nor** the twins **speak** Spanish.

EXAMPLE   **Neither** the twins **nor** Rhondelle **speaks** Spanish.

Write each conjunction. Then write compound subject, compound object, compound predicate, *or* compound sentence *to tell what parts the conjunction joins.*

1. People in the United States benefit from both the Bill of Rights and the Constitution every day.
2. The first ten amendments to the Constitution are called the Bill of Rights, and together they identify basic rights.
3. They protect our rights and freedoms.
4. This Bill of Rights lists the rights of the individual and the limitations of the federal government.
5. England and France have their own systems for protecting civil liberties.
6. In the United States, any act contrary to the Bill of Rights is illegal and can be brought to court.
7. Under the First Amendment, Congress cannot establish a national religion or exclude any religion.
8. Not only these documents but also others such as the Declaration of Independence define our rights.
9. Neither Congress nor the courts can contradict them.
10. We all must respect and honor these documents.

PRACTICE Making Compound Subjects and Verbs Agree

Write the correct word from the choices in parentheses.

1. Both the Peralta and the Johnson families (own, owns) home computers.
2. Neither Mr. Peralta nor the Johnsons (know, knows) much about computers.
3. Ms. Peralta and her daughter (is, are) very knowledgable.
4. Either Ms. Peralta or Nadine (fix, fixes) computers.

5. Nadine and her mother (install, installs) extra memory in their computer.

6. Nadine and Tony Johnson (do, does) homework on computers.

7. Neither Nadine nor Tony (log, logs) onto the Internet without a parent's approval.

8. However, Nadine, Tony, and his parents (is, are) learning how to use the Internet wisely.

9. The Internet and its resources (have, has) great assets.

10. Nadine and her mother (show, shows) Tony how to set up computers.

7.6 CONJUNCTIVE ADVERBS

You can use a special kind of adverb instead of a conjunction to join the simple sentences in a compound sentence. This special kind of adverb is called a **conjunctive adverb.**

EXAMPLE Many Asians use chopsticks, but some use forks.

EXAMPLE Many Asians use chopsticks; **however,** some use forks.

A conjunctive adverb, such as *however,* is usually stronger and more exact than a coordinating conjunction like *and* or *but.*

USING CONJUNCTIVE ADVERBS	
TO REPLACE *AND*	besides, furthermore, moreover
TO REPLACE *BUT*	however, nevertheless, still, otherwise
TO STATE A RESULT	consequently, therefore, thus
TO STATE EQUALITY	equally, likewise, similarly

A **conjunctive adverb** may be used to join the simple sentences in a compound sentence.

When two simple sentences are joined with a conjunctive adverb, use a semicolon at the end of the first sentence. Place a comma after a conjunctive adverb that begins the second part of a compound sentence. If a conjunctive adverb is used in the middle of a simple sentence, set it off with commas.

EXAMPLE   The school cafeteria sometimes serves Chinese food; **however,** these meals are not very tasty.

EXAMPLE   The school cafeteria sometimes serves Chinese food; these meals, **however,** are not very tasty.

PRACTICE **Identifying Conjunctive Adverbs**

Write each sentence. Underline the conjunctive adverb. Add appropriate punctuation.

1. Many people in the United States go to restaurants frequently moreover some do it almost every day.
2. Some restaurants are very expensive however many popular ones are inexpensive and serve fast food.
3. It is easy to go for a quick hamburger for lunch nevertheless that's not the best way to eat.
4. It's permissible once in a while still it's not a good or healthful habit to have.
5. Order a salad otherwise select something else low in fat.
6. Many restaurants serve food from different countries consequently people are exposed to international cuisine.
7. Asian restaurants often provide chopsticks however they also provide knives and forks.
8. Restaurants offer different combinations of foods and spices thus Americans have many food choices.
9. Some dishes are too complicated for amateur cooks besides many people would rather eat out.
10. It is a treat to go to a restaurant nevertheless I would rather eat at home.

7.7 INTERJECTIONS

You can express emotions in short exclamations that aren't complete sentences. These exclamations are called interjections.

An **interjection** is a word or group of words that expresses emotion. It has no grammatical connection to other words in a sentence.

Interjections are used to express emotion, such as surprise or disbelief. They're also used to attract attention.

SOME COMMON INTERJECTIONS			
aha	great	my	ouch
alas	ha	no	well
gee	hey	oh	wow
good grief	hooray	oops	yes

An interjection that expresses strong emotion may stand alone. It begins with a capital letter and ends with an exclamation point.

EXAMPLE **Good grief!** My favorite restaurant has closed.

When an interjection expresses mild feeling, it is written as part of the sentence. In that case, the interjection is set off with commas.

EXAMPLE **Oh, well,** I'll just eat at home.

NOTE Most words may be more than one part of speech. A word's part of speech depends on its use in a sentence.

EXAMPLE A duck has soft **down** on its body. **[noun]**

EXAMPLE The hungry boy **downed** the hamburger in three bites. **[verb]**

EXAMPLE Libby felt **down** all day. **[adjective]**

EXAMPLE   The baby often falls **down.** [adverb]

EXAMPLE   A car drove **down** the street. [preposition]

EXAMPLE   **"Down!"** I shouted to the dog. [interjection]

PRACTICE   Writing Sentences with Interjections

Write ten sentences, using a different interjection with each. Punctuate correctly.

PRACTICE   Proofreading

Rewrite the following passage, correcting errors in spelling, capitalization, grammar, and usage. Add any missing punctuation. Write legibly to be sure one letter is not mistaken for another. There are ten mistakes.

Colin Powell

[1]General Colin L. Powell is an American hero. [2]He was Chairman of the Joint Chiefs of Staff under both President George Bush and President Bill Clinton. [3]He served as the chief military advisor to both of they. [4]Earlier, President Ronald Reagan had appointed General Powell as the Assistant to the President for National Security Affairs. [5]Now retried from the military, Powell has written his autobiography, titled *my American Journey*. [6]He actively works for the improvement of children's lives. [7]Hooray for General Powell.

[8]General Powell have received many military awards and honors furthermore he also has been recognized with civilian awards for public service. [9]These include the Presidential Medal of Freedom, given to he and others who have served our country especially well.

[10]Powell was born in New York City [11]He and his wife has three children.

Write each prepositional phrase. Underline the preposition and circle the object of the preposition. Then write the word the prepositional phrase modifies. Finally, write adjective *or* adverb *to tell how the prepositional phrase is used.*

1. Summer vacation is fun for most students.
2. If you live near a beach, you are especially lucky.
3. You can be among the crowd of people on the sand or in the water.
4. Just remember that you will also be in the sun, which can be dangerous to your skin.
5. Silly as you may think it sounds, you should hide under a hat and put lots of protectant lotion on your skin.
6. Doctors now believe that people with some skin cancers spent too much time under the sun without protection.
7. Many people with skin cancer reported sunburns throughout their youth.
8. With enough protection, you can have a safe swim.
9. You should put sunblock lotion on your skin whenever you will be in the sun.
10. You can avoid being among those who end up with severe sunburn!

POSTTEST **Pronouns as Objects of Prepositions**

Write the correct word from the choices in parentheses.

11. Jorge wants to make a movie with Laura and (I, me).
12. It will be about (she and I, her and me, she and me, her and I) and our adventures in a treehouse.
13. I went with (he and she, him and her, he and her, him and she) to find a good place to shoot the story.
14. Behind Jorge and (she, her), I saw a large tree.
15. According to Laura and (he, him), the tree was too small.
16. Besides Laura and (I, me), two others will be in the film.
17. Some kids walked toward Laura and (we, us).
18. They want to make the movie with Jorge and (we, us).

19. We saw a huge tree in an empty lot across from Jorge and (she, her).

20. Jorge will make the movie with us and (they, them) there.

Write each conjunction. Then write compound subject, compound object, compound predicate, *or* compound sentence *to tell what parts the conjunction joins.*

21. The bad storm last night knocked out power and blew some trees down.

22. Thunder and lightning began about dinnertime.

23. Then the sky got very dark, and the wind started to blow very hard.

24. Either driving rain or hail battered the house all night.

25. Some people ran out to close their car windows, but it was dangerous for them to be out in the storm.

26. Lightning can strike people, trees, cars, or houses.

27. Sometimes you see lightning and hear thunder at the same time.

28. The storm is very close, and you should seek shelter.

29. City workers will clean up tree branches this morning, but the electric company is fixing the power lines.

30. Neither doors nor windows should remain open.

Write the correct word from the choices in parentheses.

31. Neither Joan nor her sister (want, wants) to move to the new neighborhood.

32. Both their mother and their father (talk, talks) to them about the move.

33. Neither the parents nor their daughters (look, looks) forward to packing.

34. Before long, the girls and their parents (move, moves) into their new apartment.

35. In the kitchen, cabinets and a pantry (provide, provides) plenty of space for dishes, utensils, and groceries.

36. Wallpaper or fresh paint (adorn, adorns) every wall.

37. Large closets and three bedrooms (make, makes) the apartment appealing.

38. Either the den room or master bedroom (have, has) high ceilings.

39. Several boxes or a large crate (is, are) in every room and hallway of the apartment.

40. Soon books and knickknacks (fill, fills) the shelves.

POSTTEST Conjunctive Adverbs

Write each sentence. Underline the conjunctive adverb. Add appropriate punctuation.

41. It is fun to go on a trip nevertheless it is always nice to return home too.

42. The national parks are great vacation spots however it is important to always follow the parks' rules.

43. A trip to a different country is often fun besides it enables you to explore other cultures.

44. You find out how people there live similarly you can enjoy the foods they eat.

45. Perhaps a vacation isn't in your plans still you can visit places by reading books about them.

Chapter 8

Clauses and Complex Sentences

●●●●●●●●●●●●●●●

PRETEST **Simple, Compound, and Complex Sentences**

Write simple, compound, *or* complex *to identify each sentence.*

1. It can be fun to write in a diary or a journal.
2. Keep your diary or journal in a safe place, and you can enjoy reading it a year or more from now.
3. Both famous people and everyday people have kept diaries.
4. Samuel Pepys was a British official who kept a diary during the 1600s.
5. He wrote the diary in shorthand; the diary was decoded over one hundred years later.
6. He wrote about the Great Plague that killed thousands of people in London during the 1660s.

7. His diary gave an account of the Great Fire of London, which raged through the city in 1666.

8. According to reports, the fire caused only six deaths, but it did destroy most of London.

9. Pepys also wrote about many other things, including his own ideas and gossip about other people.

10. Like Pepys, you can write a diary about the world around you and about yourself, or you may just want to keep a simple record of your own life.

PRETEST Adjective, Adverb, and Noun Clauses

Identify each italicized clause by writing adjective, adverb, *or* noun.

11. Road maps, *which show roadways,* can be fascinating.

12. *When you travel by car,* take a road atlas with you.

13. It has maps for all states *that are in the United States.*

14. You can find a road map for *wherever you want to go.*

15. Maps *that have other purposes* have different keys.

16. Maps *that you see on TV* may show the weather.

17. Most maps include a compass rose, *which indicates north, south, east, and west.*

18. A political map labels *whatever countries and cities are located in the area.*

19. Political maps show places *that people have established.*

20. *Before you use a map,* read its title and its legend.

21. They show *what a map's purpose is.*

22. Some maps provide information *that others do not.*

23. *If you want to know about the natural resources of a state,* you would use a thematic map on that subject.

24. A topographic map shows *which are the highest mountains.*

25. You can find out *where most people live* by reading a population-density map.

8.1 SENTENCES AND CLAUSES

A **sentence** is a group of words that has a subject and a predicate and expresses a complete thought.

A **simple sentence** has one complete subject and one complete predicate.

The **complete subject** names whom or what the sentence is about. The **complete predicate** tells what the subject does or has. Sometimes the complete predicate tells what the subject is or is like. The complete subject or the complete predicate or both may be compound.

COMPLETE SUBJECT	COMPLETE PREDICATE
People	travel.
Neither automobiles nor airplanes	are completely safe.
Travelers	meet new people and see new sights.
Trains and buses	carry passengers and transport goods.

A **compound sentence** contains two or more simple sentences. Each simple sentence is called a main clause.

A **main clause** has a subject and a predicate and can stand alone as a sentence.

Main clauses can be connected by a comma and a conjunction, by a semicolon, or by a semicolon and a conjunctive adverb. The conjunctive adverb is followed by a comma. In the following examples, each main clause is in black. The connecting elements are in blue type.

EXAMPLE   Many people live in cities, **but** others build houses in the suburbs. [comma and coordinating conjunction]

EXAMPLE   Most people travel to their jobs; others work at home. [semicolon]

EXAMPLE   Companies relocate to the suburbs; **therefore,** more people leave the city. [semicolon and conjunctive adverb]

Write each sentence. Underline each main clause. Add commas or semicolons where they're needed. Write simple *or* compound *to identify the sentence.*

1. Roads and highways seem especially crowded today.
2. New highways are being built however each new high-way becomes quickly clogged with traffic too.
3. Even cities with good public transportation systems have too much traffic on their roads and highways.
4. One solution is for people to carpool nevertheless people seem reluctant to do this.
5. Another solution is to install or expand public transportation but this is expensive.
6. Not only is building public transportation expensive but many people just won't use it.
7. People use cars to go to school or work or to run errands.
8. People avoid carpools and public transportation they want to be independent.
9. They prefer using their own vehicles.
10. In the United States, more than 1.5 trillion miles are traveled by automobiles each year.

8.2 COMPLEX SENTENCES

A **main clause** has a subject and a predicate and can stand alone as a sentence. Some sentences have a main clause and a subordinate clause.

A **subordinate clause** is a group of words that has a subject and a predicate but does not express a complete thought and cannot stand alone as a sentence. A subordinate clause is always combined with a main clause in a sentence.

A **complex sentence** has one main clause and one or more subordinate clauses.

In each complex sentence that follows, the subordinate clause is in blue type.

EXAMPLE   Mariah, **who moved here from Montana,** is very popular.

EXAMPLE   **Since Mariah moved to Springfield,** she has made many new friends.

EXAMPLE   Everyone says **that Mariah is friendly.**

Subordinate clauses can function in three ways: as adjectives, as adverbs, or as nouns. In the examples, the first sentence has an adjective clause that modifies the noun *Mariah.* The second sentence has an adverb clause that modifies the verb *has made.* The third sentence has a noun clause that is the direct object of the verb *says.* Adjective, adverb, and noun clauses are used in the same ways one-word adjectives, adverbs, and nouns are used.

NOTE   A **compound-complex sentence** has two or more main clauses and one or more subordinate clauses.

PRACTICE	Identifying Simple and Complex Sentences

Write each sentence. Underline each main clause once and each subordinate clause twice. Write simple *or* complex *to identify the sentence.*

1. It can be fun to stay in a big hotel, even though it is often expensive.
2. Hotels that have swimming pools are common.
3. Many hotels also have workout rooms, which are like small gymnasiums.
4. Of course, large hotels have at least one restaurant.
5. You can get room service so you can eat in your room.
6. In some hotels, someone turns your bed down in the evening and leaves candy on your pillow.
7. You don't even have to carry your own luggage.

8. When you check in or out, a hotel employee will carry your bags for you.
9. That person also shows you everything in your room.
10. Give the person a tip because he or she works hard.

8.3 ADJECTIVE CLAUSES

An **adjective clause** is a subordinate clause that modifies a noun or a pronoun in the main clause of a complex sentence.

EXAMPLE The Aqua-Lung, **which divers strap on,** holds oxygen.

EXAMPLE The divers breathe through a tube **that attaches to the tank.**

Each subordinate clause in blue type is an adjective clause that adds information about a noun in the main clause. An adjective clause is usually introduced by a relative pronoun. The relative pronoun *that* may refer to people or things. *Which* refers only to things.

RELATIVE PRONOUNS				
that	which	who	whom	whose

An adjective clause can also begin with *where* or *when*.

EXAMPLE Divers search for reefs **where much sea life exists.**

EXAMPLE Herb remembers the day **when he had his first diving experience.**

A relative pronoun that begins an adjective clause is often the subject of the clause.

EXAMPLE Some divers prefer equipment **that is lightweight.**

EXAMPLE Willa is a new diver **who is taking lessons.**

In the first sentence, *that* is the subject of the adjective clause. In the second sentence, *who* is the subject of the adjective clause.

Write each adjective clause. Underline the subject of the adjective clause. Then write the word the adjective clause modifies.

1. Scientists who specialize in ancient history continue to discover new information.
2. Ancient Egypt, Greece, and Rome, which thrived at different times, had complex societies.
3. Recently some archaeologists have changed their opinions about the people who built Egypt's pyramids.
4. They may have been ordinary people who lived nearby rather than slaves.
5. The pyramids, which took years to build, were tombs.
6. These structures that stand near the Nile are imposing.
7. Imhotep, who was a great architect, was the designer and builder of the first pyramid.
8. It was a step pyramid, which was built about 4,600 years ago in Memphis, an ancient Egyptian city.
9. The builders used no wheels, which were invented later.
10. Workers dragged the huge stones that were put on sleds.

"I realize that those of you who are planning to go into psychiatry may find this dull."

8.4 ESSENTIAL AND NONESSENTIAL CLAUSES

Read the example sentence. Is the adjective clause in blue type needed to make the meaning of the sentence clear?

EXAMPLE   The girl **who is standing beside the coach** is our best swimmer.

The adjective clause in blue type is essential to the meaning of the sentence. The clause tells *which* girl is the best swimmer.

An **essential clause** is a clause that is necessary to make the meaning of a sentence clear. Don't use commas to set off essential clauses.

Now look at the adjective clause in this sentence.

EXAMPLE   Janice, **who is standing beside the coach,** is our best swimmer.

In the example, the adjective clause is set off with commas. The clause is nonessential, or not necessary to identify which swimmer the writer means. The clause simply gives additional information about the noun it modifies.

A **nonessential clause** is a clause that is not necessary to make the meaning of a sentence clear. Use commas to set off nonessential clauses.

In this book, adjective clauses that begin with *that* are always essential, and adjective clauses that begin with *which* are always nonessential.

EXAMPLE   Were you at the meet **that** our team won yesterday?
[essential]

EXAMPLE   That meet, **which** began late, ended after dark.
[nonessential]

Write each sentence. Underline the adjective clause. Add commas where they're needed. Write essential *or* nonessential *to identify each adjective clause.*

1. Dinosaurs were huge creatures that lived on Earth millions of years ago and then disappeared.
2. The word *dinosaur* is from Greek words that mean "terrifying lizard."
3. A fearsome dinosaur was *Tyrannosaurus rex* which was a huge meat-eater.
4. Sue Hendrickson who is an amateur fossil hunter found an almost-complete skeleton of a tyrannosaur.
5. Today those bones are displayed at the Field Museum of Natural History which is in Chicago.
6. The dinosaur that many people once called a brontosaurus is now known as an apatosaurus.
7. This dinosaur which had a long neck was a plant eater.
8. Scientists who have studied dinosaurs do not always agree about the reasons for their disappearance.
9. Scientists who visit fossil sites learn about dinosaurs.
10. Some dinosaurs may have traveled in herds that roamed vast areas.

8.5 ADVERB CLAUSES

An **adverb clause** is a subordinate clause that often modifies the verb in the main clause of a complex sentence.

An adverb clause tells *how, when, where, why,* or *under what conditions* the action occurs.

EXAMPLE **After we won the meet,** we shook hands with our opponents.

EXAMPLE We won the meet **because we practiced hard.**

In the first sentence, the adverb clause *After we won the meet* modifies the verb *shook.* The adverb clause tells *when* we shook hands. In the second sentence, the adverb clause *because we practiced hard* modifies the verb *won*. The adverb clause tells *why* we won the meet.

An adverb clause is introduced by a subordinating conjunction. A subordinating conjunction signals that a clause is a subordinate clause and cannot stand alone.

SUBORDINATING CONJUNCTIONS			
after	because	though	whenever
although	before	till	where
as	if	unless	whereas
as if	since	until	wherever
as though	than	when	while

Use a comma after an adverb clause that begins a sentence. You usually don't use a comma before an adverb clause that comes at the end of a sentence.

NOTE   Adverb clauses can also modify adjectives and adverbs.

PRACTICE **Identifying Adverb Clauses**

Write each adverb clause. Underline the subordinating conjunction. Then write the verb the adverb clause modifies.

1. Tim sometimes baby-sits for a neighbor's children after he comes home from school.
2. Although he has homework to do, he can earn some money and have fun by taking kids to the park.
3. He does his homework after he returns home.
4. He is usually available to baby-sit whenever Mrs. Anderson calls him.

5. The children like Tim because he plays with them.
6. They stay at the park until Mrs. Anderson comes home.
7. If it rains, they play in the Andersons' apartment.
8. The children feel as though Tim is their older brother.
9. Since Tim has been baby-sitting for them, he and the children have invented several new games.
10. Tim has more money since he has been baby-sitting.

8.6 NOUN CLAUSES

A **noun clause** is a subordinate clause used as a noun.

Notice how the subject in blue type in the following sentence can be replaced by a clause.

EXAMPLE **A hockey player** wears protective equipment.

EXAMPLE **Whoever plays hockey** wears protective equipment.

The clause in blue type, like the words it replaces, is the subject of the sentence. Because this kind of clause acts as a noun, it's called a noun clause.

You can use a noun clause in the same ways you use a noun—as a subject, a direct object, an indirect object, an object of a preposition, and a predicate noun. In most sentences containing noun clauses, you can replace the noun clause with the word *it*, and the sentence will still make sense.

HOW NOUN CLAUSES ARE USED	
SUBJECT	**Whoever plays hockey** wears protective equipment.
DIRECT OBJECT	Suzi knows **that ice hockey is a rough game.**
INDIRECT OBJECT	She tells **whoever will listen** her opinions.
OBJECT OF A PREPOSITION	Victory goes to **whoever makes more goals.**
PREDICATE NOUN	This rink is **where the teams play.**

Here are some words that can introduce noun clauses.

WORDS THAT INTRODUCE NOUN CLAUSES		
how, however	when	who, whom
if	where	whoever, whomever
that	whether	whose
what, whatever	which, whichever	why

EXAMPLE **Whichever you choose** will look fine.

EXAMPLE **What I wonder** is **why she said that.**

EXAMPLE I don't know **who left this package here.**

EXAMPLE Ask the teacher **if this is the right answer.**

EXAMPLE Promise **whoever calls first** a special bonus.

EXAMPLE He worried about **what he had done.**

PRACTICE Identifying Noun Clauses

Write each noun clause. Then write subject, direct object, indirect object, object of a preposition, *or* predicate noun *to tell how the noun clause is used.*

1. Whoever signs up can go on the eighth-grade trip to Washington, D.C.
2. Most kids know that Washington is a fascinating city.
3. Washington is where Congress meets.
4. Here the Supreme Court justices listen to whatever case is before them.
5. The tour guide gave whoever wanted one a map of the city's sites.
6. I can tell you which documents are exhibited in the National Archives Building.
7. Do you know whether we are touring the White House?
8. Find out when the National Gallery of Art opens today.
9. We learned about how the British burned the White House.
10. Museums for whatever interests you are located here.

Rewrite the following passage, correcting errors in spelling, capitalization, grammar, and usage. Add any missing punctuation. Write legibly to be sure one letter is not mistaken for another. There are ten mistakes.

Jackie Joyner-Kersee

[1]Many people think that Jackie Joyner-Kersee is the best female athelete in the world. [2]In the Olympics, she have won two gold, one silver, and two bronze medals? [3]She was the first woman to score more than seven thousand points in the heptathlon which is made up of seven events.

[4]Joyner-Kersee's career began, when she won her first National Junior Pentathlon Championship at the age of sixteen. [5]She played several sports in high school but she won a basketball scholarship to the University of California at los angeles. [6]Her coach there, Bob Kersee, encouraged her to compete in various events he eventually married her.

[7]Joyner-Kersee's brother, Al Joyner, was also an Olympian [8]He was married to Olympic champion Florence Griffith Joyner who was called "Flo-Jo" by fans.

POSTTEST **Simple, Compound, and Complex Sentences**

Write simple, compound, *or* complex *to identify each sentence.*

1. Zebras seem to be small striped horses, but they are quite different from horses.
2. Although some people—including animal handlers—have tried to tame zebras, they are almost impossible to tame.

GRAMMAR/USAGE/MECHANICS

3. Zebras remain wild, as do many other animals in the world.
4. Stripes help hide zebras from human hunters and other predators.
5. Zebras are found wild in Africa; they don't exist naturally on any other continent.
6. Like horses and some other animals, zebras graze on grasses.
7. Zebras can be vicious; they are tough fighters.
8. Other than human hunters, the zebra's main enemy is the lion, which stalks the zebra on the grassy plains.
9. The small family groups in which zebras live are comprised of stallions, mares, and their foals.
10. Although zebras are beautiful animals, people should avoid approaching them under any circumstance.

POSTTEST Adjective, Adverb, and Noun Clauses

Identify each italicized clause by writing adjective, adverb, *or* noun.

11. Most people *who like animals* like zoo animals and house pets.
12. *Whichever pet they choose* is likely to become their favorite.
13. People *who have big yards* can choose big dogs.
14. Someone *who lives in a condominium* must obey the rules of the condo's governing association.
15. *Although Samuel Tilden won the popular vote in 1876,* he did not become president.
16. The Alamo, *which is an old mission,* was a battle site during the Mexico-Texas conflict in 1836.
17. Do most people know *who their congressperson is?*

18. In 2000, Sydney, Australia, was *where the Summer Olympics were held.*

19. Misty Hyman is an American swimmer *who won the gold medal in the women's 200-meter butterfly event.*

20. *Before the city will issue dog licenses,* the animals must have had their rabies shots.

21. *Although the candidates debated,* their stances on the issues were still unclear.

22. *Whatever you want* can be found on the Web.

23. The coach and players reviewed *what the team did right to win the game.*

24. Oregon, *which is on the Pacific Coast,* became a state in 1859.

25. Napoleon served as the emperor of France *until he was exiled to Elba in 1814.*

Chapter 9

Verbals

● ● ● ● ● ● ● ● ● ● ● ● ● ● ●

PRETEST Verbal Phrases

Identify each italicized phrase by writing participial, gerund, *or* infinitive.

1. *Roaming the outback,* camels are not an uncommon sight in Australia.
2. Many people *thinking about Australia* might picture kangaroos and koala bears.
3. Camels, *introduced in the 1800s,* are now common.
4. Explorers of Australia's desert first brought the camels from India and Pakistan *to provide transportation.*
5. Camels also were used in *mining and cattle farming.*
6. Camel drivers, *called cameleers,* also came.
7. *Coming mostly from Pakistan and Afghanistan,* the cameleers lived together in small groups.
8. Many Australians *living in the 1800s* thought of the cameleers as Afghans.
9. Australians, *making a false assumption,* thought that all cameleers were from Afghanistan.
10. *Carrying heavy loads,* the camels could go days without water.
11. They were perfect for *carrying supplies* into the desert.
12. Long camel trains, *plodding along,* made regular trips.
13. Camels were used to *carry construction supplies.*
14. The *railroad building* took place in the late nineteenth century.
15. *Hauling food and supplies,* camels did heavy work.

16. People began *to travel by train.*
17. Camel trains, *losing their usefulness,* were unnecessary.
18. Australians, *shortening the word Afghan,* gave the name "Ghan towns" to cameleer groups.
19. The railroad "The Ghan" is named *to honor camel trains.*
20. The cameleers released the camels *to live in the wild.*
21. Now, *living in the wild,* Australian camels number about 100,000 to 150,000.
22. Some camels, *owned by individuals,* live on farms.
23. There are special farms *to provide for others.*
24. Some people *talking about camels* say that they are mean.
25. Other people say it is unfair *to give camels a bad name.*

9.1 PARTICIPLES AND PARTICIPIAL PHRASES

A present participle is formed by adding -*ing* to a verb. A past participle is usually formed by adding -*d* or -*ed* to a verb. A participle can act as the main verb in a verb phrase or as an adjective to modify a noun or a pronoun.

EXAMPLE Erik is **taking** piano lessons. [present participle used as main verb in a verb phrase]

EXAMPLE His talent has **impressed** his teacher. [past participle used as main verb in a verb phrase]

EXAMPLE His **playing** skill improves daily. [present participle used as adjective modifying *skill*]

EXAMPLE He practices at home on a **rented** piano. [past participle used as adjective modifying *piano*]

A participle that is used as an adjective may be modified by a single adverb or by a prepositional phrase. It may also have a direct object.

EXAMPLE **Sitting quietly,** Erik loses himself in the music.

EXAMPLE **Sitting at the piano,** Erik loses himself in the music.

EXAMPLE **Playing the piano,** Erik loses himself in the music.

A **participial phrase** is a group of words that includes a participle and other words that complete its meaning.

A participial phrase that begins a sentence is always set off with a comma. Participial phrases in other places in a sentence may or may not need commas. If the phrase is necessary to identify the modified word, it is an essential phrase and should not be set off with commas. If the phrase simply gives additional information about the modified word, it is a nonessential phrase. Use commas to set off nonessential phrases.

EXAMPLE   The musician **seated at the piano** is Erik. [essential]

EXAMPLE   Erik, **dreaming of fame,** sits at the piano. [nonessential]

EXAMPLE   **Dreaming of fame,** Erik sits at the piano. [nonessential]

An essential participial phrase must follow the noun it modifies. A nonessential participial phrase can appear before or after the word it modifies. Place the phrase as close as possible to the modified word to make the meaning of the sentence clear.

PRACTICE Identifying Participles

Write each participle. Then write main verb *or* adjective *to tell how the participle is used.*

1. Outdoor concerts are becoming very popular.
2. Audiences sitting outside can be a bit noisy.
3. Some people are enjoying picnic lunches.
4. Many have been coming to these concerts for many years.
5. Some places even provide rented chairs and tables for the audiences.
6. These outdoor concerts are often profitable for sponsoring organizations.
7. However, performers sometimes are distracted by rain, thunder, trains, and planes.

8. Often the parking lots are packed with cars.

9. At times, cars leaving the lots have been delayed for almost an hour because of the volume of traffic.

10. Many people are now taking public transportation.

PRACTICE **Identifying Participial Phrases**

Write each sentence. Underline the participial phrase once. Draw two lines under the word the participial phrase modifies. Add commas where they're needed.

1. Obviously enjoying themselves many adults participate in unusual contests every summer.

2. Giving up all attempts at seriousness they look forward to summertime fun.

3. A race pushing beds down a road is a most unusual competition.

4. There is a contest challenging competitors to spit watermelon seeds as far as they can.

5. Jan, joining in the annual Mackinac Island contest, skips stones every July fourth.

6. Digging fence postholes some people in Oklahoma compete in the World Championship Posthole Contest.

7. A competitive event skinning muskrats is held in Maryland.

8. There is even a contest for adults riding tricycles.

9. People participating in the contest use borrowed trikes.

10. Lining the streets the audience cheers the cyclists on.

9.2 GERUNDS AND GERUND PHRASES

When a verb form ending in *-ing* is used as a noun, it's called a gerund.

EXAMPLE   The **skating** rink is near my house. **[adjective]**

EXAMPLE   **Skating** is a favorite winter pastime in my neighborhood. **[noun, gerund]**

A **gerund** is a verb form that ends in *-ing* and is used as a noun.

Like other nouns, a gerund may be used as a subject, a predicate noun, a direct object, or the object of a preposition.

EXAMPLE **Exercising** builds strength and endurance. **[subject]**

EXAMPLE My favorite activity is **exercising.** **[predicate noun]**

EXAMPLE Some people enjoy **exercising.** **[direct object]**

EXAMPLE What are the benefits of **exercising?** **[object of a preposition]**

A gerund may be modified by a single adverb or by a prepositional phrase. It may also have a direct object.

EXAMPLE **Exercising daily** is a good habit.

EXAMPLE Many people enjoy **exercising on a bike.**

EXAMPLE Tell me something about **exercising the body.**

A **gerund phrase** is a group of words that includes a gerund and other words that complete its meaning.

You can identify the three uses of *-ing* verb forms if you remember that a present participle can serve as part of a verb phrase, as an adjective, and as a noun.

EXAMPLE The young people are **bicycling** in the country. **[main verb]**

EXAMPLE The **bicycling** club travels long distances. **[adjective]**

EXAMPLE **Bicycling** is good exercise. **[noun, gerund]**

PRACTICE **Identifying Gerunds and Participles**

Write main verb, adjective, or gerund to identify each underlined word.

1. Many people enjoy <u>running</u>.
2. People are <u>running</u> in parks and streets every day.
3. Many enter <u>running</u> races.
4. <u>Exercising</u> this way can be good for your health.

5. <u>Jogging</u> may be a better word for what most runners do.
6. A <u>jogging</u> pace is somewhat slower than a <u>running</u> pace.
7. Most joggers enjoy <u>running</u> all year long.
8. They must be careful about <u>dressing</u> properly for the weather, especially in very hot or very cold weather.
9. Some carry water for a <u>refreshing</u> drink as they run.
10. A runner may be <u>carrying</u> a tiny radio too.

PRACTICE **Identifying Gerund Phrases**

Write each gerund phrase. Then write subject, predicate noun, direct object, *or* object of a preposition *to tell how it's used.*

1. Attending school for the first time can be frightening.
2. Many parents like taking their children to school.
3. Walking to school with a parent can be fun.
4. A child's biggest fear may be riding the school bus.
5. The bus drivers are often good at caring for children.
6. One of their skills is driving while maintaining order.
7. Children look forward to meeting their teachers.
8. Most teachers like seeing the children's parents.
9. The new kindergartners will start getting acquainted with each other.
10. Learning to read and making new friends are part of the school experience.

9.3 INFINITIVES AND INFINITIVE PHRASES

Another verb form that may be used as a noun is an infinitive.

EXAMPLE   **To write** is Alice's ambition.

EXAMPLE   Alice wants **to write.**

An **infinitive** is formed with the word *to* and the base form of a verb. Infinitives are often used as nouns in sentences.

How can you tell if the word *to* is a preposition or part of an infinitive? If the word *to* comes immediately before a verb, it's part of an infinitive.

EXAMPLE   Alice liked **to write.** [infinitive]

EXAMPLE   She sent a story **to a magazine.** [prepositional phrase]

In the first sentence, the words in blue type work together as a noun to name *what* Alice liked. In the second sentence, the words in blue type are a prepositional phrase used as an adverb to tell *where* she sent a story.

Because infinitives are used as nouns, they can be subjects, predicate nouns, and direct objects.

EXAMPLE   **To write** was Alice's ambition. **[subject]**

EXAMPLE   Alice's ambition was **to write.** **[predicate noun]**

EXAMPLE   Alice liked **to write.** **[direct object]**

An infinitive may be modified by a single adverb or by a prepositional phrase. It may also have a direct object.

EXAMPLE   **To write well** was Alice's ambition.

EXAMPLE   Alice's ambition was **to write for fame and money.**

EXAMPLE   Alice wanted **to write a great novel.**

An **infinitive phrase** is a group of words that includes an infinitive and other words that complete its meaning.

PRACTICE **Identifying Infinitives and Prepositional Phrases**

Write infinitive phrase *or* prepositional phrase *to identify each underlined group of words.*

1. Tina stopped <u>after school</u> <u>to buy some milk.</u>
2. Venus is the planet closest <u>to Earth.</u>
3. Are you planning <u>to ride your bike</u> <u>after school today?</u>
4. David plans <u>to give a donation</u> <u>to that charity.</u>
5. The Assad family came <u>to the United States</u> in 1999.

6. The Pilgrims agreed <u>to form a government.</u>
7. Matthew wanted <u>to sign up</u> for soccer camp.
8. The tourists went <u>to Mount Rushmore.</u>
9. A jaguar is able <u>to run seventy miles per hour.</u>
10. Take the elevator <u>to the fourth floor.</u>

PRACTICE Identifying Infinitive Phrases

Write each infinitive phrase. Then write subject, predicate noun, *or* direct object *to tell how it's used.*

1. Patrick wanted to play trumpet in the school band.
2. To carry out a search on the Internet often requires patience and time.
3. Our plan was to leave by noon.
4. The flat tire needed to be repaired.
5. Leon wanted to share his ideas with someone.
6. To find a four-leaf clover is considered good luck.
7. Lenny offered to type the report on his computer.
8. To change his opinion might be difficult.
9. Kara's assignment is to compile the survey results.
10. Olivia's dream was to act in a Broadway play.

PRACTICE Proofreading

Rewrite the following passage, correcting errors in spelling, capitalization, grammar, and usage. Add any missing punctuation. Write legibly to be sure one letter is not mistaken for another. There are ten mistakes.

Oprah Winfrey

[1]Hired as a news reader in Tennessee Oprah winfrey began her television career at the age of eighteen. [2]Winfrey having graduated from Tennessee State University later took a newscaster job in Baltimore. [3]She then became the host for a baltimore morning talk show. [4]Highlighting her engaging personality this program showed

Winfrey's potential. [5]She was soon hosting a talk show in Chicago [6]Renamed *The Oprah Winfrey Show* the program drew large audiences. [7]The show produced in Chicago has been very successful and has earned Winfrey many awards.

[8]Winfrey decided to start a book club. [9]Featuring books on her show Winfrey encouraged people to read, and the book club has had a major impact on book sales.

[10]In addition, Winfrey has become a motion picture and TV acter and producer. [11]She has also participated in many philanthropic activities.

POSTTEST **Verbal Phrases**

Identify each italicized phrase by writing participial, gerund, *or* infinitive.

1. *Creating the unusual,* Michael Westmore's work is memorable.
2. He is responsible for *making the weird faces for* Star Trek *actors.*
3. He uses makeup, foam rubber, and paint *to transform ordinary actors into monsters.*
4. *Coming from a family of makeup artists* helped Westmore learn his trade from an early age.
5. *Heading the makeup departments of major studios for three generations,* the Westmore family has abundant talent.
6. Michael began *to work in the family business* when he worked with an uncle who created faces for characters in *Planet of the Apes.*
7. Did he ever make a mistake like *gluing an actress's eyes closed?*
8. Now there are hundreds of people *creating looks for television and movie actors.*
9. The Westmore family provides advice to plastic surgeons *to aid burn victims.*

10. Disguise tricks *developed by Michael* help the government too.

11. His work includes *providing makeup for Sylvester Stallone in* Rocky.

12. Michael received an Oscar for *doing makeup for the movie* Mask.

13. He then began *to head another makeup department.*

14. This time he was *to manage the makeup department for the TV show* Star Trek: The Next Generation.

15. Westmore, *creating the look for actors on* Deep Space Nine *and* Voyager, is one of TV's favorite makeup artists.

16. In *Star Trek,* the look of all characters *being seen for the first time* will have Westmore's touch.

17. He is likely *to keep pictures of turtles and dust mites.*

18. They might be used *to inspire details for an alien's features.*

19. He might also keep boxes *holding such things as Vulcan ears, Klingon heads, and Borg pieces.*

20. A cap *embedded with electronic components* is a useful device.

21. *Dangling by a rope,* the head of a Borg is a fearsome creature.

22. For fun, Michael likes *to play pinball machines.*

23. Machines *displaying his Oscar and nine Emmys* are in his house.

24. *Building a waterfall on the grounds of the home* was Michael's latest project.

25. Michael Westmore is tops at *making wonderful illusions.*

Chapter 10

Subject-Verb Agreement

• • • • • • • • • • • • • • • • •

PRETEST   Subject-Verb Agreement

Write the correct verb from the choices in parentheses.

1. Many of Saki's short stories (ends, end) in a surprising way.
2. Neither of the athletes (practices, practice) after dinner.
3. The Mississippi River (flows, flow) into the Gulf of Mexico.
4. Each of the new quarters (has, have) its own design on the back.
5. Both Caitlyn and Corinne (takes, take) ballet.
6. The scissors (is, are) on the table over there.
7. In the desert (lives, live) many unusual creatures.
8. The committee (elects, elect) its new officers at tonight's meeting.
9. Everyone (presents, present) a science project.
10. *Walk Two Moons* (was, were) awarded the Newbery Medal for outstanding children's literature in 1995.
11. Mark (catches, catch) the bus at eight o'clock.
12. You (studies, study) plants and animals in biology.

13. On top of the tower (flashes, flash) the red beacon.
14. Exercise and sleep (is, are) two ingredients for healthful living.
15. Mathematics (includes, include) geometry and algebra.
16. Residents of Montreal (speaks, speak) either French or English.
17. Neither rain nor snow flurries (was, were) predicted.
18. The rainbow (stretches, stretch) across the sky.
19. The tracks of mud (leads, lead) into Ty's room.
20. Nothing (disappears, disappear) faster than lemonade on a hot summer afternoon.
21. There (is, are) no classes this afternoon because of parent-teacher conferences.
22. The Sanchez family (lives, live) on the corner of Western Avenue and Peterson Drive.
23. Beans (is, are) a good source of dietary fiber.
24. Most of the story (takes, take) place on a small farm.
25. (Has, Have) you seen Cerise's jacket?

10.1 MAKING SUBJECTS AND VERBS AGREE

The basic idea of subject-verb agreement is a simple one: A singular subject requires a singular verb, and a plural subject requires a plural verb. The subject and its verb are said to *agree in number.*

Notice that in the present tense the singular form of the verb usually ends in *-s* or *-es.*

SUBJECT-VERB AGREEMENT WITH NOUNS AS SUBJECTS	
SINGULAR	**PLURAL**
A **botanist studies** plant life.	**Botanists study** plant life.
A **plant requires** care.	**Plants require** care.

A verb must also agree with a subject that is a pronoun. Look at the chart that follows. Notice how the verb changes. In the present tense, the -s ending is used with the subject pronouns *he*, *she*, and *it*.

SUBJECT-VERB AGREEMENT WITH PRONOUNS AS SUBJECTS

SINGULAR	PLURAL
I **work.**	We **work.**
You **work.**	You **work.**
He, she, *or* it **works.**	They **work.**

The irregular verbs *be*, *have*, and *do* can be main verbs or helping verbs. These verbs must agree with the subject whether they're main verbs or helping verbs.

EXAMPLES   I **am** a botanist. He **is** a botanist. They **are** botanists. **[main verbs]**

EXAMPLES   She **is** working. You **are** studying. **[helping verbs]**

EXAMPLES   I **have** a job. She **has** a career. **[main verbs]**

EXAMPLES   He **has** planted a tree. They **have** planted trees. **[helping verbs]**

EXAMPLES   He **does** well. They **do** the job. **[main verbs]**

EXAMPLES   It **does** sound good. We **do** work hard. **[helping verbs]**

PRACTICE **Making Subjects and Verbs Agree I**

Write the subject. Then write the correct verb from the choices in parentheses.

1. The Galapagos Islands (is, are) in the Pacific Ocean.
2. Iguanas (lives, live) either in the sea or on land.
3. The Milky Way (is, are) a spiral galaxy.

4. It (has, have) billions of stars including our sun.
5. Kristen (enjoys, enjoy) nursery rhymes.
6. Her parents (reads, read) them to her every night.
7. Roberto (takes, take) tae kwon do classes.
8. The instructors (teaches, teach) the importance of discipline.
9. The catalog (pictures, picture) a variety of goods.
10. They (sells, sell) name brands at a discount.

10.2 PROBLEMS IN LOCATING THE SUBJECT

Making a verb agree with its subject is easy when the verb directly follows the subject. Sometimes, however, a prepositional phrase comes between the subject and the verb.

EXAMPLE This **book** of Mark Twain's stories **appeals** to people of all ages.

EXAMPLE **Stories** by Washington Irving **are** also popular.

In the first sentence, *of Mark Twain's stories* is a prepositional phrase. The singular verb *appeals* agrees with the singular subject, *book,* not with the plural noun *stories,* which is the object of the preposition *of.* In the second sentence, *by Washington Irving* is a prepositional phrase. The plural verb *are* agrees with the plural subject, *Stories,* not with the singular noun *Washington Irving,* which is the object of the preposition *by.*

An **inverted sentence** is a sentence in which the subject follows the verb.

Inverted sentences often begin with a prepositional phrase. Don't mistake the object of the preposition for the subject of the sentence.

EXAMPLE Across the ocean **sail millions** of immigrants.

In inverted sentences beginning with *Here* or *There,* look for the subject after the verb. *Here* or *there* is never the subject of a sentence.

EXAMPLE Here **is a picture** of my grandparents.

EXAMPLE There **are** many **immigrants** among my ancestors.

By rearranging the sentence so the subject comes first, you can see the agreement between the subject and the verb.

EXAMPLE **Millions** of immigrants **sail** across the ocean.

EXAMPLE A **picture** of my grandparents **is** here.

EXAMPLE Many **immigrants are** there among my ancestors.

In some interrogative sentences, a helping verb comes before the subject. Look for the subject between the helping verb and the main verb.

EXAMPLE **Do** these **stories interest** you?

You can check the subject-verb agreement by making the sentence declarative.

EXAMPLE These **stories do interest** you.

PRACTICE Making Subjects and Verbs Agree II

Write the subject. Then write the correct verb from the choices in parentheses.

1. Standing on the cliff (was, were) mountain goats.
2. There (is, are) a tomato in the refrigerator.
3. (Is, Are) their permission slips signed?
4. The workers at the construction site (wears, wear) hard hats.
5. (Has, Have) you seen today's newspaper yet?
6. Here (is, are) the best recipe for pasta sauce.
7. The number of award shows on television (increases, increase) every year.
8. (Does, Do) bees sting only when threatened?

9. The fans in that section (holds, hold) tickets to all the home games.

10. In the field (grow, grows) many kinds of wildflowers.

10.3 COLLECTIVE NOUNS AND OTHER SPECIAL SUBJECTS

A **collective noun** names a group.

Collective nouns follow special agreement rules. A collective noun has a singular meaning when it names a group that acts as a unit. A collective noun has a plural meaning when it refers to the members of the group acting as individuals. The meaning helps you decide whether to use the singular or plural form of the verb.

EXAMPLE   The **audience sits** in silence. **[a unit, singular]**

EXAMPLE   The **audience sit** on chairs and pillows. **[individuals, plural]**

Certain nouns, such as *news* and *mathematics,* end in *s* but require singular verbs. Other nouns that end in *s* and name one thing, such as *scissors* and *binoculars,* require plural verbs.

EXAMPLE   **News is** important to everyone. **[singular]**

EXAMPLE   The **scissors are** in the top drawer. **[plural]**

SPECIAL NOUNS THAT END IN *S*			
SINGULAR		**PLURAL**	
civics	physics	binoculars	scissors
Los Angeles	United Nations	jeans	sunglasses
mathematics	United States	pants	trousers
news		pliers	tweezers

A subject that refers to an amount as a single unit is singular. A subject that refers to a number of individual units is plural.

EXAMPLE **Ten years seems** a long time. **[single unit]**

EXAMPLE **Ten years pass** quickly. **[individual units]**

EXAMPLE **Three dollars is** the admission price. **[single unit]**

EXAMPLE **Three dollars are** on the table. **[individual units]**

The title of a book or a work of art is always singular, even if a noun in the title is plural.

EXAMPLE ***Snow White and the Seven Dwarfs**** is** a good Disney movie.

EXAMPLE ***The Last of the Mohicans**** was** written by James Fenimore Cooper.

PRACTICE Making Subjects and Verbs Agree III

Write the subject. Then write the correct verb from the choices in parentheses.

1. *Cats* (was, were) the longest-running show on Broadway.
2. The team (plays, play) home games on this field.
3. (Does, Do) your sunglasses have prescription lenses?
4. The United States (belongs, belong) to the North Atlantic Treaty Organization, NATO.
5. The plan commission (meets, meet) every month.
6. Six years (is, are) the length of a senator's term.
7. Physics (explores, explore) the interaction of matter and energy.
8. *Island of the Blue Dolphins* (tells, tell) the story of Karana, who spends years on an island by herself.
9. The binoculars (enables, enable) me to watch the birds from a distance.
10. Seven dollars (was, were) scattered under the desk.

10.4 INDEFINITE PRONOUNS AS SUBJECTS

An **indefinite pronoun** is a pronoun that does not refer to a particular person, place, or thing.

Some indefinite pronouns are singular. Others are plural. When an indefinite pronoun is used as a subject, the verb must agree in number with the pronoun.

SOME INDEFINITE PRONOUNS			
SINGULAR			**PLURAL**
another	everybody	no one	both
anybody	everyone	nothing	few
anyone	everything	one	many
anything	much	somebody	others
each	neither	someone	several
either	nobody	something	

The indefinite pronouns *all, any, most, none,* and *some* may be singular or plural, depending on the phrase that follows.

EXAMPLE **Most** of the forest **lies** to the east. [singular]

EXAMPLE **Most** of these scientists **study** forest growth. [plural]

Often a prepositional phrase follows an indefinite pronoun that can be either singular or plural. To decide whether the pronoun is singular or plural, look at the object of the preposition. In the first sentence, *most* refers to *forest*. Because *forest* is singular, *most* must be considered as a single unit. In the second sentence, *most* refers to *scientists*. Because *scientists* is plural, *most* should be considered as individual units.

GRAMMAR/USAGE/MECHANICS

Write the subject. Then write the correct verb from the choices in parentheses.

1. No one (lives, live) there any longer.
2. Everything (belong, belongs) in that cabinet.
3. (Does, Do) anyone need a pencil?
4. Both (earns, earn) money by baby-sitting for their neighbors.
5. Some of the paint (was, were) easy to remove.
6. Much of the story (captures, capture) the imagination.
7. Most fables (has, have) morals.
8. Everyone in the race (runs, run) through the forest preserve and the city's business district.
9. Nothing (was, were) learned from the investigation.
10. None of the issues (was, were) resolved.

10.5 AGREEMENT WITH COMPOUND SUBJECTS

A **compound subject** contains two or more simple subjects that have the same verb.

Compound subjects may require a singular or a plural verb, depending on how the subjects are joined. When two or more subjects are joined by *and* or by the correlative conjunction *both . . . and,* the plural form of the verb should be used.

EXAMPLE New York, Denver, **and** London **have** smog.

EXAMPLE **Both** automobiles **and** factories **contribute** to smog.

Sometimes *and* is used to join two words that are part of one unit or refer to a single person or thing. In these cases, the subject is singular. In the following example, *captain* and *leader* refer to the same person. Therefore, the singular form of the verb is used.

EXAMPLE The captain **and** leader of the team **is** Ms. Cho.

When two or more subjects are joined by *or* or by the correlative conjunction *either . . . or* or *neither . . . nor,* the verb agrees with the subject that is closer to it.

EXAMPLE   The cities **or** the state **responds** to pollution complaints.

EXAMPLE   **Either** smoke **or** gases **cause** the smog.

In the first sentence, *responds* is singular because the closer subject, *state,* is singular. In the second sentence, *gases* is the closer subject. The verb is plural because the closer subject is plural.

PRACTICE **Making Subjects and Verbs Agree V**

Write the complete subject. Then write the correct verb from the choices in parentheses.

1. The senator or he (addresses, address) the crowd today.
2. Tarquin and Dave (has, have) a hockey game today after school.
3. The director and star of *Braveheart* (was, were) Mel Gibson.
4. Helmets and kneepads (protects, protect) scooter riders from injuries.
5. (Is, Are) Birmingham or Montgomery the largest city in Alabama?
6. Both the Golden Globe Awards and the Academy Awards (honor, honors) motion pictures.
7. Neither Paul nor Brandon (remember, remembers) where they left the camera.
8. *Charlotte's Web* and *The Outsiders* (is, are) among the best-selling children's books.
9. Either Caroline or Sheri (sets, set) the table for dinner every night.
10. Neither the students nor their teacher (leaves, leave) the lab before cleaning the equipment.

PRACTICE Proofreading

Rewrite the following passage, correcting errors in spelling, capitalization, grammar, and usage. Add any missing punctuation. Write legibly to be sure one letter is not mistaken for another. There are ten mistakes.

Lenny Krayzelburg

[1]The Krayzelburg family immigrate to the United States in 1989. [2]Thirteen-year-old Lenny and his parents comes from Ukraine. [3]They settles in California.

[4]Eleven years later, Lenny swim the 100-meter and 200-meter backstroke events in the Olympics. [5]Everyone expect him to win the 100-meter event, and he does. [6]He says, "You measures yourself in this sport by whether you have won an Olympic gold medal."

[7]The 100-meter and the 200-meter backstroke events and a leg in the medley relay are won by him in olympic record-setting time. [8]On the gold-medal pedestal stand Lenny Krayzelburg. [9]The United States celebrate this grate champion.

POSTTEST Subject-Verb Agreement

Write the correct verb from the choices in parentheses.

1. Outside the stadium gates (waits, wait) fans hoping to see the players.
2. Neither the players nor the coach (appears, appear) however.
3. (Is, Are) your friend planning to attend the concert?
4. Alexia (visits, visit) her grandparents every summer.
5. His parents or Steve (answers, answer) the doctor's questions.
6. Everything (looks, look) large to a small child.
7. The pants (needs, need) pressing.
8. I (watch, watches) that program every week.
9. There (is, are) several ways to use that Internet site.

10. The clothes in the basket (belongs, belong) in the closet.
11. The United Nations (has, have) headquarters in New York City.
12. The Spanish class (listens, listen) to audiotapes.
13. The conductors on the train (collects, collect) the tickets.
14. Coyotes (is, are) moving into suburban areas.
15. My friends and I (meets, meet) at the library.
16. Representatives (serves, serve) two-year terms.
17. Three hours (seems, seem) like a long time for a movie.
18. Both Jay and James (collects, collect) comic books and records.
19. The band (plays, play) before the game.
20. The space shuttle (delivers, deliver) supplies to the space station.
21. None of these CDs (is, are) mine.
22. The Senate (approves, approve) the trade bill for China.
23. Megan Quann and Misty Hyman (was, were) gold medal winners in the Olympic swimming competition.
24. Some of the President's speech (is, are) quoted in today's newspaper.
25. At the museum (hangs, hang) two paintings by Monet.

Chapter 11

Diagraming Sentences

●●●●●●●●●●●●●●●

PRETEST   Diagraming Sentences

Diagram each sentence.

1. Bells rang.
2. Autumn is approaching.
3. Can penguins fly?
4. Yell!
5. Write a story.
6. Shrimp gives me a stomachache.
7. Fog concealed the mountaintop.
8. The new Japanese train travels so speedily.
9. We walked slowly through the garden of the old mansion.

10. A common adult housefly can live from nineteen to seventy days.
11. Last winter seemed warmer than usual.
12. After his illness, William became a better student.
13. Film and television became popular in the twentieth century.
14. Broadway musicals employ singers and dancers.
15. Many Germans settled in Wisconsin, and many Irish settled in New York.
16. The sun came out, but no rainbow appeared.
17. Jewels that are precious include diamonds and rubies.
18. When spring comes, farmers in New England collect maple syrup.
19. How he survived the accident is a mystery.
20. The teacher showed us how magnets work.
21. The firefighters were prepared for whatever happened.
22. Iced tea brewed in the Sun tastes delicious.
23. The candidate, waving cheerfully, spoke to the crowd.
24. Driving from Boston to New York takes about four hours.
25. To end the Great Depression was one of Roosevelt's goals.

11.1 DIAGRAMING SIMPLE SUBJECTS AND SIMPLE PREDICATES

The basic parts of a sentence are the subject and the predicate. To diagram a sentence, first draw a horizontal line. Then draw a vertical line that crosses the horizontal line.

To the left of the vertical line, write the simple subject. To the right of the vertical line, write the simple predicate. Use capital letters as they appear in the sentence, but don't include punctuation.

EXAMPLE **People are working.**

| People | are working |

In a diagram, the positions of the subject and the predicate always remain the same.

EXAMPLE **Caravans rumbled** across the prairie.

$$\text{Caravans} \mid \text{rumbled}$$

EXAMPLE Across the prairie **rumbled caravans.**

$$\text{caravans} \mid \text{rumbled}$$

PRACTICE **Diagraming Simple Subjects and Simple Predicates**

Diagram the simple subject and the simple predicate.

1. Firecrackers exploded.
2. Honeysuckle smells sweet.
3. Into the sky flew the helicopter.
4. After World War I came a short time of peace.
5. Suddenly a rock crashed through the window.
6. We had been waiting for the bus for twenty minutes.
7. Authors often sign their books for readers.
8. The waves will grow larger during the hurricane.
9. Down the aisle walked the bride.
10. Our new minivan seems quite roomy.

11.2 DIAGRAMING THE FOUR KINDS OF SENTENCES

Study the diagrams of the simple subject and the simple predicate for the four kinds of sentences. Recall that in an interrogative sentence the subject often comes between the two parts of a verb phrase. In an imperative sentence, the simple subject is the understood *you.*

Notice that the positions of the simple subject and the simple predicate in a sentence diagram are always the same, regardless of the word order in the original sentence.

DECLARATIVE

EXAMPLE **People write** letters.

$$\begin{array}{c|c} \text{People} & \text{write} \end{array}$$

INTERROGATIVE

EXAMPLE **Do** many **people write** letters?

$$\begin{array}{c|c} \text{people} & \text{Do write} \end{array}$$

IMPERATIVE

EXAMPLE **Write** a letter.

$$\begin{array}{c|c} \text{(you)} & \text{Write} \end{array}$$

EXCLAMATORY

EXAMPLE What interesting letters **you write!**

$$\begin{array}{c|c} \text{you} & \text{write} \end{array}$$

PRACTICE **Diagraming the Four Kinds of Sentences**

Diagram the simple subject and the simple predicate.

1. Have you forgotten anything?
2. Hold the tennis racket correctly.
3. Do many people get their news from the Internet?
4. What an original writer J. K. Rowling is!
5. Video games became popular in the 1980s.
6. Look at the mother elephant and her baby.
7. Did Betsy Ross really make the first American flag?
8. Land along the ocean is quite valuable.
9. Volunteer in your community.
10. How difficult the math test was!

11.3 DIAGRAMING DIRECT AND INDIRECT OBJECTS

A direct object is part of the predicate. In a sentence diagram, write the direct object to the right of the verb. Draw a vertical line to separate the verb from the direct object. This vertical line, however, does *not* cross the horizontal line.

EXAMPLE People invent **machines.**

$$\text{People} \mid \text{invent} \mid \text{machines}$$

EXAMPLE Students use **computers.**

$$\text{Students} \mid \text{use} \mid \text{computers}$$

An indirect object is also part of the predicate. It usually tells to whom or for whom the action of a verb is done. An indirect object always comes before a direct object in a sentence. In a sentence diagram, write an indirect object on a horizontal line below and to the right of the verb. Join it to the verb with a slanted line.

EXAMPLE Rosa gave the **dog** a bone.

$$\text{Rosa} \mid \text{gave} \mid \text{bone}$$
$$\diagdown \text{dog}$$

PRACTICE **Diagraming Direct and Indirect Objects**

Diagram the simple subject, the simple predicate, and the direct object. Diagram the indirect object if the sentence has one.

1. Pandas eat bamboo.
2. The college offered Jon a baseball scholarship.
3. Jane Addams helped many people at Hull House.
4. Mosquitoes can spread malaria.
5. The Inca gave the world some unique clothing syles.

6. George Lucas created several *Star Wars* movies.

7. The pilot told the passengers the arrival time.

8. Cheryl bought the old quilt online.

9. The company recalled the dangerous toys.

10. The haunted house gave us a few scares.

11.4 DIAGRAMING ADJECTIVES, ADVERBS, AND PREPOSITIONAL PHRASES

In a diagram, write adjectives and adverbs on slanted lines beneath the words they modify.

EXAMPLE **Elena's strange** dream faded **quickly.**

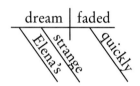

EXAMPLE **The very old** tree produced **incredibly delicious** apples **rather slowly.**

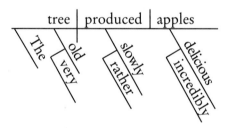

A prepositional phrase can be either an adjective phrase or an adverb phrase. Study the diagram for prepositional phrases.

EXAMPLE A woman **in a pink hat** was sitting **beside me.**

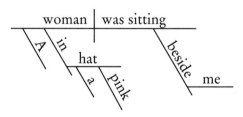

Beginning duck

PRACTICE Diagraming Adjectives, Adverbs, and Prepositional Phrases

Diagram each sentence.

1. The lovely piece of colorful glass was bought cheaply in Italy.
2. The palm trees on the sandy Hawaiian beach blew gently.
3. Tyrannosaurs had extremely short front legs.
4. We could almost see our neighborhood in the suburbs from the top of the tall building in the city.
5. A single stroke of lightning discharges millions of volts of electricity.
6. Auguste Rodin created intensely realistic bronze statues of the human figure.
7. Many scientists are studying the intelligence of apes.
8. Kangaroos have few native Australian enemies.
9. Boston had slightly more snowfall than New York City.
10. Ben created a brand new magazine for computer buffs.

11.5 DIAGRAMING PREDICATE NOUNS AND PREDICATE ADJECTIVES

In a sentence diagram, a direct object follows the verb.

EXAMPLE People use telephones.

People | use | telephones

To diagram a sentence with a predicate noun, write the predicate noun to the right of the linking verb. Draw a slanted line to separate the verb from the predicate noun.

EXAMPLE Telephones are useful **instruments.**

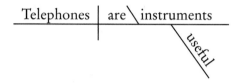

Diagram a predicate adjective in the same way.

EXAMPLE Telephones are **useful.**

Telephones | are \ useful

PRACTICE **Diagraming Predicate Nouns and Predicate Adjectives**

Diagram each sentence.

1. K2 is the world's second highest mountain.
2. The school band sounds loud in the football stadium.
3. The Morris dance is an old custom in England.
4. The wild gooseberries tasted sour.
5. The Internet was useful for my research paper.
6. Kerri Strug was an Olympic gymnast in 1996.
7. The delicate bluebell is a very pretty wildflower.

8. The forest looked mysterious in the fog.

9. My birthday present might be a scooter.

10. One of Edison's inventions was the phonograph.

11.6 DIAGRAMING COMPOUND SENTENCE PARTS

Coordinating conjunctions such as *and, but,* and *or* are used to join compound parts: words, phrases, or sentences. To diagram compound parts of a sentence, write the second part of the compound below the first. Write the coordinating conjunction on a dotted line connecting the two parts.

COMPOUND SUBJECT

EXAMPLE **Gas and oil** heat homes.

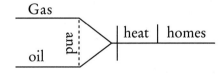

COMPOUND PREDICATE

EXAMPLE Babies **eat and sleep.**

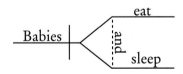

COMPOUND DIRECT OBJECT

EXAMPLE The bakery serves **sandwiches and beverages.**

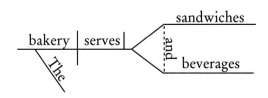

COMPOUND PREDICATE NOUN OR PREDICATE ADJECTIVE

EXAMPLE   Dogs are **loyal and friendly.**

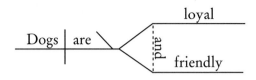

PRACTICE   Diagraming Compound Sentence Parts

Diagram each sentence.

1. We saw paintings and sculptures at the museum.
2. Books and magazines cluttered the professor's office.
3. Chicken or beef can be used for enchiladas.
4. Chinese immigrants built railroad tracks and tunnels.
5. This dog is cute but mischievous.
6. Arizona and New Mexico were home to the Anasazi.
7. Michael Jordan played basketball and baseball.
8. The tourists strolled or relaxed.
9. Plymouth and Jamestown were early colonies.
10. Audiences laughed and applauded.

11.7 DIAGRAMING COMPOUND SENTENCES

To diagram a compound sentence, diagram each main clause separately. If the main clauses are connected by a semicolon, use a vertical dotted line to connect the verbs of the clauses. If the main clauses are connected by a conjunction such as *and, but,* or *or,* write the conjunction on a solid horizontal line and connect it to the verb in each clause with a dotted line.

EXAMPLE James practices football after school, **and** on Saturdays he helps his parents at their restaurant.

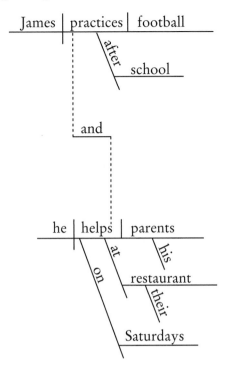

PRACTICE **Diagraming Compound Sentences**

Diagram each sentence.

1. Robins may live in cities, but owls nest in rural areas.
2. The Sopwith Camel was flown during World War I, and the Tomcat fighter was developed in the 1970s.
3. The students may travel to Washington, D.C., in the fall, or they may go to the state capital in the spring.
4. Comets orbit the Sun, and meteors fall through Earth's atmosphere.
5. Charlotte Brontë wrote *Jane Eyre*; her sister wrote *Wuthering Heights*.
6. Julia bought a dress for the party, but she returned it.
7. The boys took a Frisbee to the baseball diamond, and they invented a new game.

8. Algebra is studied around the world; it is useful in everyday life.

9. The chorus will sing, or a special guest will speak.

10. Cork comes from a tree; it is made from the bark.

11.8 DIAGRAMING COMPLEX SENTENCES WITH ADJECTIVE AND ADVERB CLAUSES

To diagram a sentence with an adjective clause, write the adjective clause below the main clause. Draw a dotted line between the relative pronoun in the adjective clause and the word the adjective clause modifies in the main clause. Position the relative pronoun according to its use in its own clause. In the first example, *who* is the subject of the verb *complete.* In the second example, *that* is the direct object of the verb *watched.*

ADJECTIVE CLAUSE

EXAMPLE Students **who complete their assignments** will surely succeed.

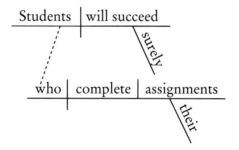

EXAMPLE The movie **that we watched** was very funny.

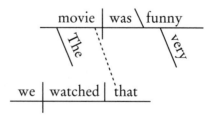

Diagram an adverb clause below the main clause. Draw a dotted line between the verb in the adverb clause and the word the adverb clause modifies in the main clause. Then write the subordinating conjunction on the dotted connecting line.

ADVERB CLAUSE

EXAMPLE   **If you complete your assignments,** you will surely succeed.

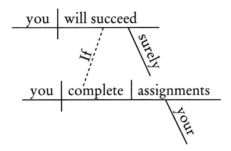

PRACTICE **Diagraming Complex Sentences with Adjective and Adverb Clauses**

Diagram each sentence.

1. People buy small cars when gasoline prices go up.
2. John Keats, who died at the age of twenty-five, was one of England's most popular poets.
3. Art deco was a style that was popular in the 1920s.
4. You can find that information if you research online.
5. The country that produces the most coffee beans is Brazil.
6. Crops often fail when a drought occurs.
7. This is the popcorn that you cook in the microwave.
8. The girl who lost her dog put an ad in the paper.
9. Before you make that dessert, check a cookbook.
10. I planted roses because I like their scent.

11.9 DIAGRAMING NOUN CLAUSES

Noun clauses can be used in sentences as subjects, direct objects, indirect objects, objects of prepositions, and predicate nouns. In the following example, the noun clause is the subject.

NOUN CLAUSE AS SUBJECT

EXAMPLE **What she told us** was the simple truth.

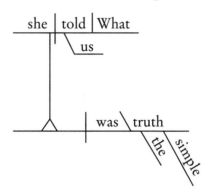

Notice that the clause is written on a "stilt" placed on the base line where the subject usually appears. The word that introduces a noun clause is diagramed according to its use within its own clause. In the noun clause in the example, the word *What* is the direct object. If the word that introduces the noun clause isn't really part of either the noun clause or the main clause, write the word on its own line.

NOUN CLAUSE AS DIRECT OBJECT

EXAMPLE Terry knows **that good grades are important.**

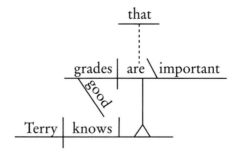

NOUN CLAUSE AS INDIRECT OBJECT

EXAMPLE   Tell **whomever you see** the news.

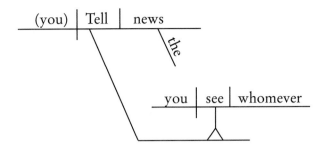

NOUN CLAUSE AS OBJECT OF A PREPOSITION

EXAMPLE   This is an example of **what I mean.**

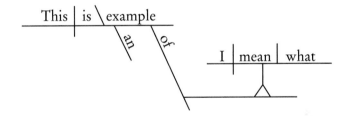

NOUN CLAUSE AS PREDICATE NOUN

EXAMPLE   The result was **that nobody believed me.**

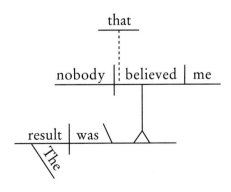

Diagram each sentence.

1. Tolstoy wrote that all happy families are alike.
2. Whoever likes that movie should read the book.
3. The campers paid attention to what their counselor said.
4. What she told them concerned snakebites.
5. Cable networks give whoever keeps up with the news the latest stories.
6. Einstein believed that the world was an orderly place.
7. What the Allies needed in World War II was help from the United States.
8. The problem is that the airplane pilots went on strike.
9. A Nobel Prize is an honor for whoever receives it.
10. Ask whoever answers the phone your question.

11.10 DIAGRAMING VERBALS

To diagram a participle or a participial phrase, draw a line that descends diagonally from the word the participle modifies and then extend it to the right horizontally. Write the participle along the angle, as shown.

EXAMPLE   The birds, **singing merrily,** splashed in the birdbath.

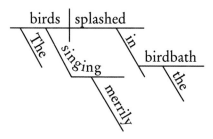

To diagram a gerund or a gerund phrase, make a "stilt," located according to the role of the gerund. (A gerund can be a subject, a direct object, or the object of a preposition.) Then write the gerund on a "step" above the stilt, as shown at the top of the next page.

EXAMPLE **Building new nests** is another job for the returning birds.

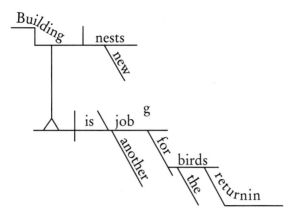

To diagram an infinitive or an infinitive phrase that is used as a noun, make a "stilt" in the appropriate position. Then diagram the phrase as you would a prepositional phrase.

EXAMPLE The purpose of a microscope is **to magnify objects.**

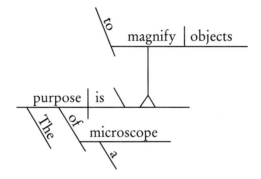

PRACTICE **Diagraming Verbals**

Diagram each sentence.

1. The Heimlich maneuver can help a choking victim.
2. The teacher taught the students to drive defensively.
3. Getting a sunburn can seriously harm your skin.
4. Gutenberg made the first printing press in the 1400s.

5. One good form of aerobic exercise is jogging.
6. The Canada geese, flying in formation, headed south.
7. Being a chef is an interesting career.
8. One of Lincoln's ambitions was to become a lawyer.
9. Tina learned about economics by investing in the stock market.
10. To survive on a desert island requires intelligence and physical strength.

POSTTEST Diagraming Sentences

Diagram each sentence.

1. Puddles formed.
2. Passengers were sleeping.
3. Jump!
4. Did violinists play?
5. Close the gate.
6. The athlete told the reporters his story.
7. The game show gave the winner a vacation.
8. The opera singers wore amazingly elaborate costumes in elegant fabrics.
9. The adventurous hikers almost fell into the deep rocky canyon.
10. The fierce crocodile in the murky swamp had tough scaly skin.
11. The old clothes from Grandma's attic smelled musty.
12. The African grasslands were a photographer's paradise.
13. Poachers and human diseases are serious threats to mountain gorillas.
14. The graceful horses trotted or galloped.
15. Some readers like books on the Internet; others prefer pages of print.
16. People formerly killed whales for oil, but whale oil is rarely used now.
17. Thomas Edison, who received numerous patents, had the help of many employees.

18. Watch out for jellyfish when you surf in Florida.

19. What I liked about the movie was the many disguises of the actors.

20. Did you know that the rose is our national flower?

21. Chad gave whomever he saw a school newspaper.

22. Students need good advice about getting into college.

23. The museum displayed beautiful gowns worn by the first ladies.

24. The goal of the biology major was to become a doctor.

25. Exploring the ocean fascinated Jacques Cousteau.

Chapter 12

Capitalization

● ● ● ● ● ● ● ● ● ● ● ● ● ● ●

PRETEST **Capitalization**

Write each sentence. Use capital letters correctly.

1. The capital of japan is tokyo.
2. I read *The view from Saturday* by e. l. Konigsburg this Summer.
3. *Cats,* which closed on Broadway in the year 2000, was the longest running broadway musical.
4. Are your mother and your Father registered as democrats, republicans, or independents?
5. About 76 million People watched the last episode of *seinfeld* in 1998.
6. Henry Hudson, an englishman, explored the Hudson bay.
7. Following my doctor's advice, I've been taking healthy teen Vitamins since december.
8. Daniel Williams, m.d., believes that many teenagers need vitamin supplements.

9. "Is english spoken in namibia?" asked Debbie, who was writing a report on the nation.
10. "I wrote a report on Namibia last year," said Warren. "it gained independence from south Africa in 1990."
11. Edgar Degas was a famous french painter, who may be best-known for his paintings of ballet dancers.
12. Larry sent me a postcard from yosemite national park in april.
13. the authors of the latest self-help book are Donald Clark, ph.d., and Abigail Morris, m.d.
14. Vincent asked his Uncle to come with us to los angeles.
15. Jamie said that She is taking algebra II next year and geometry the following year.
16. Is mt. McKinley, the highest mountain in north America, in Northern or Southern Alaska?
17. "Yankee doodle, " a familiar tune to most americans, is the state song of connecticut.
18. many mexican immigrants live in texas after they first arrive in the United states.
19. Jessica's Aunt Annie now lives on the west coast, but she grew up on a farm in kansas.
20. "Have you tried the new soft drink moxie?" asked Helen. "it is a lemon-lime soda that is popular in new england."
21. The Nurse said that i should make a follow-up appointment in july.
22. President Lincoln, our sixteenth President, wrote the gettysburg address and signed the emancipation proclamation.
23. The senate has one hundred members, two elected from each State in the nation.
24. Did you read the june issue of *sports illustrated*?
25. Check the schedule of tours of the white house before we go to Washington, d.c.

12.1 CAPITALIZING SENTENCES, QUOTATIONS, AND LETTER PARTS

A capital letter marks the beginning of a sentence. A capital letter also marks the beginning of a direct quotation and the salutation and the closing of a letter.

RULE 1 Capitalize the first word of every sentence.

EXAMPLE **M**any people worked for the independence of the colonies.

RULE 2 Capitalize the first word of a direct quotation that is a complete sentence. A direct quotation gives a speaker's exact words.

EXAMPLE Travis said, "**O**ne of those people was Paul Revere."

RULE 3 When a direct quotation is interrupted by explanatory words, such as *she said,* don't begin the second part of the direct quotation with a capital letter.

EXAMPLE "I read a famous poem," said Kim, "**a**bout Paul Revere."

When the second part of a direct quotation is a new sentence, put a period after the explanatory words and begin the second part of the quotation with a capital letter.

EXAMPLE "I know that poem," said Sarah. "**M**y class read it last week."

RULE 4 Don't capitalize an indirect quotation. An indirect quotation does not repeat a person's exact words and should not be enclosed in quotation marks. An indirect quotation is often introduced by the word *that.*

EXAMPLE The teacher said **t**he poem was written by Longfellow.

EXAMPLE The teacher said **that t**he poem was written by Longfellow.

RULE 5 Capitalize the first word in the salutation and the closing of a letter. Capitalize the title and the name of the person addressed.

EXAMPLES   **Dear Mrs. Adamson,**   **Sincerely yours,**

EXAMPLES   **My dear Abigail,**   **With love,**

NOTE   Usually, the first word in each line of a poem is capitalized, but many modern poets don't follow this style. When you copy a poem, use the style of the original version.

PRACTICE   **Capitalizing Sentences, Quotations, and Letter Parts**

Write each sentence. Use capital letters correctly. If a sentence is already correct, write correct.

1. "Oh, no," said Allen. "this bread is moldy, and we cannot eat it."
2. Chris asked, "is the bread spoiled?"
3. mold that lands on bread begins to grow.
4. "most molds spoil food," said Mom, "but some make cheese taste better."
5. the mums in the garden are beautiful in the fall.
6. Mums are classified as plants and mushrooms as fungi.
7. "have you ever seen a white pumpkin?" asked Ted.
8. Unlike plants, fungi—which include mushrooms and mold—cannot make their own food.
9. Jess said, "i hope Mr. Danke will be our science teacher."
10. *Rewrite each salutation or closing that is incorrect.*
       a. Dear mr. Danke,   c. sincerely,
       b. my dearest friend,   d. yours truly,

12.2 CAPITALIZING NAMES AND TITLES OF PEOPLE

RULE 1 Capitalize the names of people and the initials that stand for their names.

EXAMPLES　Clark Kent　　Susan **B.** Anthony　　**E. C.** Stanton

RULE 2 Capitalize a title or an abbreviation of a title when it comes before a person's name.

EXAMPLES　**P**resident Wilson　**D**r. Martin Luther King　**M**s. Ruiz

Capitalize a title when it's used instead of a name.

EXAMPLE　"Has the enemy surrendered, **G**eneral?" asked the colonel.

Don't capitalize a title that follows a name or one that is used as a common noun.

EXAMPLE　Woodrow Wilson, **p**resident of the United States during World War I, supported cooperation among nations.

EXAMPLE　Who was Wilson's **v**ice **p**resident?

RULE 3 Capitalize the names and abbreviations of academic degrees that follow a name. Capitalize *Jr.* and *Sr.*

EXAMPLES　M. Katayama, **M.D.**　Janis Stein, **Ph.D.**　Otis Ames **Jr.**

RULE 4 Capitalize words that show family relationships when they're used as titles or as substitutes for names.

EXAMPLE　Last year **F**ather and **A**unt Beth traveled to several western states.

Don't capitalize words that show family relationships when they follow possessive nouns or pronouns.

EXAMPLE　Jo's **u**ncle took photographs. My **a**unt Mary framed them.

RULE 5 Always capitalize the pronoun *I*.

EXAMPLE   American history is the subject **I** like best.

PRACTICE **Capitalizing Names and Titles of People**

Write each sentence. Use capital letters correctly. If a sentence is already correct, write correct.

1. Ross is going to see dr. Adams.
2. Lydia's homeroom teacher is ms. morris.
3. Are you going to see George's Uncle?
4. Ron made an appointment with Charles Lucas jr.
5. Dan has finished his report on president Kennedy.
6. Yesterday mom and aunt Tomeka went shopping at the new mall.
7. Jimmy Carter, former President of the United States, continues to work for the American people.
8. "The nurse made the appointment," said Dad.
9. Shawna Dickenson, Ph.d., wrote the article, which is printed in today's newspaper.
10. We toured the military base and the home of the retired Colonel.

12.3 CAPITALIZING NAMES OF PLACES

The names of specific places are proper nouns and should be capitalized. Don't capitalize articles and short prepositions that are part of geographical names.

RULE 1 Capitalize the names of cities, counties, states, countries, and continents.

EXAMPLES   San Diego   Cook County   North Carolina
           Japan   Mexico   Europe

RULE 2 Capitalize the names of bodies of water and other geographical features.

EXAMPLES Lake Michigan   Gulf of Mexico   Pacific Ocean
Mojave Desert   Napa Valley   Rocky Mountains

RULE 3 Capitalize the names of sections of a country.

EXAMPLES the Sun Belt   New England   the Great Plains

RULE 4 Capitalize direction words when they name a particular section of a country.

EXAMPLES the South   the West Coast   the Northeast

Don't capitalize direction words used in other ways.

EXAMPLES southern California   northerly winds
Kansas is west of Missouri.

RULE 5 Capitalize the names of streets and highways.

EXAMPLES Main Street   Route 66   Pennsylvania Turnpike

RULE 6 Capitalize the names of particular buildings, bridges, monuments, and other structures.

EXAMPLES the White House   Golden Gate Bridge
Lincoln Memorial   the Rose Bowl

PRACTICE Capitalizing Names of Places

Write each sentence. Use capital letters correctly.

1. Matthew is going to fly to Southern California.
2. Aunt Helen lives on Perry road.
3. I received a postcard with a picture of the golden gate Bridge in San Francisco on it.
4. Do you live in new england?
5. Take route 103 to interstate 395.
6. Does your tour include New york and boston?

7. We decided to visit the statue of liberty.

8. Texas is Southeast of arizona.

9. Is lake Michigan one of the Great Lakes?

10. The atlantic ocean and the pacific ocean have similarities and differences.

12.4 CAPITALIZING OTHER PROPER NOUNS AND ADJECTIVES

Many nouns besides the names of people and places are proper nouns and should be capitalized. Adjectives formed from proper nouns are called proper adjectives and should also be capitalized.

RULE 1 Capitalize all important words in the names of clubs, organizations, businesses, institutions, and political parties.

EXAMPLES   Girl Scouts of America   American Red Cross

Microsoft Corporation   Smithsonian Institution

University of Nebraska   Republican Party

RULE 2 Capitalize brand names but not the nouns following them.

EXAMPLES   Downhome soup   Lull-a-bye diapers   Kruncho crackers

RULE 3 Capitalize all important words in the names of particular historical events, time periods, and documents.

EXAMPLES   Revolutionary War   Iron Age   Gettysburg Address

RULE 4 Capitalize the names of days of the week, months of the year, and holidays. Don't capitalize the names of the seasons.

EXAMPLES   Sunday   April   Thanksgiving Day   spring

RULE 5 Capitalize the first word and the last word in the titles of books, chapters, plays, short stories, poems, essays, articles, movies, television series and programs, songs, magazines, and newspapers. Capitalize all other words except articles, coordinating conjunctions, and prepositions of fewer than five letters. Don't capitalize the word *the* before the title of a magazine or newspaper.

EXAMPLES   *A Wrinkle in Time*   "Mammals and Their Young"
                  "The Lady or the Tiger?" "The Truth About Dragons"
                  "Over the Rainbow"   *Seventeen*

RULE 6 Capitalize the names of languages, nationalities, and ethnic groups.

EXAMPLES   English   Japanese   Native Americans

RULE 7 Capitalize proper adjectives. A proper adjective is an adjective formed from a proper noun.

EXAMPLES   African American voters   Mexican art
                 a Broadway musical   Appalachian families

NOTE   Capitalize the names of religions and the people who practice them. Capitalize the names of holy days, sacred writings, and deities.

EXAMPLES   Islam   Muslims   Easter   the Bible   Allah

NOTE   Capitalize the names of trains, ships, airplanes, and spacecraft.

EXAMPLES   the Orient Express   *Titanic*
                 Spirit of St. Louis   *Voyager 2*

NOTE   Don't capitalize the names of school subjects, except for proper nouns and adjectives and course names followed by a number.

EXAMPLES   language arts   geography   earth science
                 American history   French   Algebra 1

Write each sentence. Use capital letters correctly.

1. Brennan is attending the university of new Hampshire in the Fall.
2. I prefer starbrite Cleaner to Glow and shine.
3. Many books have been written about the Vietnam war.
4. In december we will travel to Missouri for the christmas holidays.
5. The Heard museum in phoenix displays art by native americans.
6. Are you going to take Astronomy in the Spring?
7. Have you read *the outsiders?*
8. The movie *star wars* has been re-released.
9. The word *sugar* has arabic roots.
10. The United States constitution established three branches of government.

PRACTICE Proofreading

Rewrite the following passage, correcting errors in spelling, capitalization, grammar, and usage. Add any missing punctuation. Write legibly to be sure one letter is not mistaken for another. There are ten mistakes.

¹Dear aunt Miranda,
²I took your advice and read *ethan frome* this Summer. ³I really enjoyed it. ⁴I found out more about the author, Edith wharton.
⁵Did you know that she was born into a rich family in New York on January 24, 1862. ⁶After she married in 1885, she frequently traveled. ⁷She wrote novels, travel books, and storys, and poems for magazines, including *scribner's magazine.*

⁸Wharton published her first novel when she was forty years old. ⁹she liked to write about people's conflicts. ¹⁰She was the first woman to win a Pulitzer Prize for fiction. ¹¹I'll see you in september.

¹²Love Always,

¹³Alyssa

POSTTEST Capitalization

Write each sentence. Use capital letters correctly.

1. Diana lives in columbus, ohio, and maria elena lives in cincinnati, ohio.
2. "do you want to visit me?" she asked when she last talked to Maria elena on the telephone.
3. "are you a new york yankees fan, or do you support the mets?" Barry asked.
4. Every four years the President is elected in november and serves a four-year term, beginning on january 20.
5. In terms of land area, the smallest State in the u.s.a. is Rhode island.
6. The egyptians may have been the first people to develop a Solar calendar.
7. Twenty-four soccer teams compete for the world cup, which is an International competition held every four years.
8. My cousin invented a card came called chance.
9. A Museum in Detroit focuses on african american history.
10. I'm going to take a french class this Summer.
11. Old Sturbridge Village in massachusetts is a museum that recreates a new england farming community.
12. Dennis Peters sr. signed the letter.
13. Roger Bacon, who lived in england, was interested in Alchemy.
14. Ferdinand Magellan, from portugal, sailed around the tip of south America.

15. Albania is in eastern Europe, North of Greece.

16. Software from the art institute of Chicago has games and puzzles.

17. the Empire state building in new york city is 102 stories high.

18. Uncle Kevin and mother are planning a family reunion to be held in july at highlands Prairie Park.

19. turn east on Odlin road and then drive North until you reach route 55.

20. Are you going to ask ms. DeVries about the Algebra quiz?

21. My Father gave me a subscription to *seventeen* magazine.

22. The Columbus zoo in powell, Ohio, has a coral reef.

23. Whales can be seen in the Summer in the Atlantic ocean.

24. "I agree," said Trevor. "let's leave at six o'clock so we can get to the game about twenty minutes early."

25. Cheetahs, which are the world's fastest runners, live in africa, iran, and northwestern afghanistan.

Chapter 13

Punctuation

• • • • • • • • • • • • • • • •

PRETEST Commas, Semicolons, Colons, and End Punctuation

Write each sentence. Add commas, semicolons, colons, and end punctuation where needed.

1. Good grief Will it rain throughout our entire vacation
2. Yes George I did remember the key this time
3. "The parade will proceed up Lincoln Highway go left on First Street and then turn down Taylor Street" said Emily
4. Over a week after the fire I still felt fearful
5. Crickets were singing and birds were chirping
6. In the sky above the clouds were wispy and white
7. Will you stop and see me after you finish your lesson
8. Wherever the dog wandered it made friends quickly

9. Ms. Wong said "Tomatoes too are rich in vitamins and minerals."
10. Mail the insurance form to Jennifer McCall M.D. 351 Elm Street Stephenville TX 76901.
11. Sprinting away from the others the runner who had no registration number won the race easily
12. Mix these ingredients well two eggs a cup of sugar one-half cup of butter and a teaspoon of vanilla
13. Mrs. Baie the guidance counselor usually administers the tests however our teacher Mr. Imm is taking charge today
14. The Sandburgs lived in Flat Rock North Carolina from 1943 until Carl's death on July 22 1967.
15. Gene's old Farmall tractor which is an antique has been beautifully restored he delights in polishing it starting it up and giving children tractor rides.

PRETEST Quotation Marks, Italics, and Apostrophes

Write each sentence. Add quotation marks, underlining (for italics), apostrophes, and other punctuation marks where they're needed. If the sentence is already correct, write correct.

16. This week said Mr. Locascio we will study the civilization of ancient Egypt
17. How were the pyramids built asked Waylan What a remarkable feat of engineering!
18. Its supposed that thousands of people worked many decades moving the stone suggested Mr. Locascio.
19. The pharaohs monument was built by peasants.
20. Erics report on the pyramids is based on information from World Book encyclopedia.
21. Egyptians beliefs are known from writings, called The Book of the Dead, that had been carved on the Pyramids in the form of hieroglyphics.

22. Those beliefs are very different from yours and mine.

23. Did he say, ancient Egyptian religion had many myths

24. Did you say that the sun god Ra ruled over all the others asked Anamai.

25. A tomb included its inhabitants earthly treasures.

Write each sentence. Add hyphens, dashes, and parentheses where they're needed. Use the correct form for each number. If the sentence is already correct, write correct.

26. The emu a swift running, flightless Australian bird is smaller than the ostrich.

27. More than fifty five members of the eighth grade class had a low grade fever and upset stomach.

28. One half the population does not take a big circulation newspaper; their current events IQ isn't first rate.

29. Her great grandmother, a self confident actor, earned ten million dollars over her lifetime.

30. The shelter had 25 kittens at the beginning of last month.

31. I counted fifty people who used the stairs and 120 who used the elevator.

32. On May 22d at ten twenty A.M., the fire alarm at Eight Six Five Westbury Avenue went off, and the fire department responded.

33. Jeffrey and Lee they're our favorite cousins will be staying with us for the summer.

34. 12 old movie posters decorate the lobby of the restored theater on 3rd Avenue.

35. Our survey showed that thirty percent of the students prefer the hot lunch, fifty percent choose the a la carte line, and twenty percent bring lunches from home.

13.1 USING END PUNCTUATION

RULE 1 Use a period at the end of a declarative sentence. A declarative sentence makes a statement.

EXAMPLE Tractors perform many jobs on a farm.

EXAMPLE I worked on a farm during the summer.

RULE 2 Use a period at the end of an imperative sentence. An imperative sentence gives a command or makes a request.

EXAMPLE Turn the key. **[command]**

EXAMPLE Please start the motor. **[request]**

RULE 3 Use a question mark at the end of an interrogative sentence. An interrogative sentence asks a question.

EXAMPLE Who built the first tractor?

EXAMPLE Did you know that?

RULE 4 Use an exclamation point at the end of an exclamatory sentence. An exclamatory sentence expresses strong feeling.

EXAMPLE How powerful your tractor is!

EXAMPLE What a loud noise it makes!

RULE 5 Use an exclamation point after a strong interjection. An interjection is a word or group of words that expresses emotion.

EXAMPLES Wow! Whew! My goodness! Ouch!

Yippee! Hi! Hey! Oops!

PRACTICE Using End Punctuation

*Write each sentence. Add the correct end punctuation.
Then write* declarative, imperative, interrogative, exclamatory, *or* interjection *to show the reason for the end mark you chose.*

1. I am taking swimming lessons at the YMCA
2. Brrr That water is too cold
3. Show me how to do the butterfly stroke
4. Hey Did you see that girl's swan dive
5. Are they asking members of the class to join the swim team
6. What an exciting season they had last year
7. The coach asked all team members to practice twice a day
8. Keep your body straight and your knees together
9. I think I could be an excellent swimmer
10. Would you like to learn to dive off the highest diving board

13.2 USING COMMAS I

When you use commas to *separate* items, you place a comma between items. When you use commas to *set off* an item, you place a comma before and after the item. Of course, you never place a comma at the beginning or the end of a sentence.

RULE 1 Separate three or more words, phrases, or clauses in a series.

EXAMPLE   Cars, buses, and trucks clog city streets. **[words]**

EXAMPLE   Beside the fence, on the porch, or outside the back door is a good place for that potted plant. **[phrases]**

EXAMPLE   Call me before you leave town, while you're in Florida, or after you return home. **[clauses]**

RULE 2 Set off an introductory word such as *yes, no,* or *well.*

EXAMPLE Yes, we enjoyed your performance in the play.

EXAMPLE No, you didn't sing off key.

RULE 3 Set off names used in direct address.

EXAMPLE Claire, have you ever traveled on a ship?

EXAMPLE I traveled to Alaska, Mr. Hess, on a cruise ship.

EXAMPLE Did you enjoy your trip down the Ohio River, Dale?

RULE 4 Set off two or more prepositional phrases at the beginning of a sentence. Set off a single long prepositional phrase at the beginning of a sentence.

EXAMPLE In the fall of 1998, Frank Jordan ran for mayor. **[two prepositional phrases—*In the fall* and *of 1998*]**

EXAMPLE Beneath a dozen fluttering red and blue banners, he made his campaign speech. **[one long prepositional phrase—*Beneath a dozen fluttering red and blue banners*]**

You need not set off a single short prepositional phrase, but it's not wrong to do so.

EXAMPLE In 1998 Frank Jordan ran for mayor. **[one short prepositional phrase—*In 1998*]**

RULE 5 Set off participles and participial phrases at the beginning of a sentence.

EXAMPLE Talking, we lost track of the time.

EXAMPLE Talking on the telephone, we lost track of the time.

Set off a participial phrase that is not essential to the meaning of a sentence.

EXAMPLE The band, marching in formation, moves down the field.

EXAMPLE Independence Day, celebrated on July 4, is a national holiday.

GRAMMAR/USAGE/MECHANICS

RULE 6 Set off words that interrupt the flow of thought in a sentence.

EXAMPLE   Politicians, of course, sometimes forget their campaign promises after the election.

RULE 7 Use a comma after a conjunctive adverb, such as *however, moreover, furthermore, nevertheless,* or *therefore.*

EXAMPLE   The school district is growing; therefore, taxes will rise.

RULE 8 Set off an appositive that is not essential to the meaning of a sentence.

EXAMPLE   The *Titanic,* a luxury liner, sank on its first voyage.
[The appositive, *a luxury liner*, is not essential.]

PRACTICE   Using Commas I

Write the following sentences. Add commas where they're needed.

1. Waiting for her friends Crystal paced impatiently in the hallway.
2. Lance was determined to ride again; therefore he worked with determination to overcome his illness.
3. I assure you Dad I will be careful when I drive.
4. This building in case you're interested was built in 1850.
5. The students entered the room quietly looked around curiously and waited anxiously for the teacher.
6. The kittens playing on the living room floor looked like a furry, tangled whirlwind.
7. Can you meet us at the mall Kori?
8. No Ms. Hill we did not find your directions unclear overlong or disorganized.

9. Over a hundred eighth-graders turned out for the track team; therefore the district has had to hire two assistant coaches.

10. The baseball sailed high in the air over the fence and into the street.

13.3 USING COMMAS II

RULE 9 Use a comma before a coordinating conjunction (*and, but, or, nor,* or *for*) that connects the two parts of a compound sentence.

EXAMPLE   Steve opened the door, and the dog ran out.

EXAMPLE   Mari called her best friend, but no one answered.

EXAMPLE   They will raise money, or they will donate their time.

RULE 10 Set off an adverb clause at the beginning of a sentence. An adverb clause begins with a subordinating conjunction, such as *after, although, as, because, before, if, since, though, unless, until, when, whenever, where, wherever,* or *while.*

EXAMPLE   Whenever I feel afraid, I whistle a happy tune.

Usually, an adverb clause that falls at the end of a sentence is not set off.

EXAMPLE   I whistle a happy tune whenever I feel afraid.

RULE 11 Set off a nonessential adjective clause. A nonessential adjective clause simply gives additional information and is not necessary to the meaning of a sentence. An adjective clause usually begins with a relative pronoun, such as *who, whom, whose, which,* or *that.*

EXAMPLE   My house, which has green shutters, is at the corner of Elm and Maple.

Don't set off an essential adjective clause. An essential adjective clause is necessary to the meaning of a sentence.

EXAMPLE   The house that has green shutters is at the corner of Elm and Maple.

Write each sentence. Add commas where they're needed. If a sentence needs no commas, write correct.

1. Lettie planted lettuce and radishes in April but she waited until May to plant the other vegetables.
2. Since he has no car my brother rides his bike.
3. Should we ship your order to your home or would you like to pick it up at the store?
4. An iceberg which is nine-tenths hidden in the water is more menacing to a boat than it appears.
5. A book that no one reads is like an instrument lying unplayed and dusty on a shelf.
6. We can play cards after the dishes are done.
7. Wherever disaster strikes the Red Cross is soon there.
8. The morning was sunny and bright and I felt cheerful.
9. I'll walk with you for I need the exercise.
10. The platypus which has a bill like a duck is a mammal.

13.4 USING COMMAS III

RULE 12 In a date, set off the year when it's used with both the month and the day. Don't use a comma if only the month and the year are given.

EXAMPLE The ship struck an iceberg on April 14, 1912, and sank early the next morning.

EXAMPLE The ship sank in April 1912 on its first voyage.

RULE 13 Set off the name of a state or a country when it's used after the name of a city. Set off the name of a city when it's used after a street address. Don't use a comma after the state if it's followed by a ZIP code.

EXAMPLE The ship was sailing from Southampton, England, to New York City.

EXAMPLE You can write to Leeza at 15 College Court, Stanford, CA 94305.

RULE 14 Set off an abbreviated title or degree following a person's name.

EXAMPLE   Michelle Nakamura, Ph.D., will be the graduation speaker.

EXAMPLE   Letisha Davis, M.D., is our family physician.

RULE 15 Set off *too* when it's used in the middle of a sentence and means "also." Don't set off *too* at the end of a sentence.

EXAMPLE   Parents, too, will attend the ceremony.

EXAMPLE   Parents will attend the ceremony too.

RULE 16 Set off a direct quotation.

EXAMPLE   Mom asked, "Have you finished your homework?"

EXAMPLE   "I did it," I replied, "in study hall."

EXAMPLE   "Tell me what you learned," said Mom.

RULE 17 Use a comma after the salutation of a friendly letter and after the closing of both a friendly letter and a business letter.

EXAMPLES   Dear Dad,   Your loving daughter,   Yours truly,

RULE 18 Use a comma to prevent misreading.

EXAMPLE   Instead of two, five teachers made the trip.

EXAMPLE   In the field below, the brook gurgled merrily.

PRACTICE **Using Commas III**

Write each sentence. Add commas where they're needed.

1. "I too" remarked Ms. Pateki "have enjoyed sightseeing in Philadelphia Pennsylvania."
2. "I saw the Liberty Bell too" said Gorav.
3. A rodeo championship will be held in Cody Wyoming in September 2003.
4. "My uncle Johnny won the calf-roping event at the rodeo in Laramie Wyoming" said Peter Running Wolf.

5. This highway takes you from East St. Louis Illinois to St. Louis Missouri in twenty minutes.

6. Phia Yang M.D. delivered the commencement address at Boston University.

7. Michael reported "The United States entered World War II on December 8 1941 the day after Japan attacked Pearl Harbor."

8. Send your rebate forms and receipts to PO Box 12792 Mankato MN 56006.

9. Beneath the snow hills took on a softer cleaner look.

10. *Write the following message, adding commas where needed.*

Dear Grandpa Don

    The poster is great! I didn't know that you too liked NASCAR racing. Thanks for remembering me.

Your grandson
Joshua

13.5 USING SEMICOLONS AND COLONS

RULE 1 Use a semicolon to join the main clauses of a compound sentence if they're not joined by a conjunction such as *and, but, or, nor,* or *for.*

EXAMPLE   The electric car was once the most popular car in the United States; people liked electric cars because they were clean and quiet.

RULE 2 Use a semicolon to join the main clauses of a compound sentence if they're long and if they already contain commas. Use a semicolon even if the clauses are joined by a coordinating conjunction such as *and, but, or, nor,* or *for.*

EXAMPLE   Before the invention of the automobile, people rode horses, bicycles, or streetcars for short distances; and they used horse-drawn carriages, trains, or boats for longer trips.

RULE 3 Use a semicolon to separate main clauses joined by a conjunctive adverb, such as *consequently, furthermore, however, moreover, nevertheless,* or *therefore.*

EXAMPLE   I started my homework immediately after school; consequently, I finished before dinner.

RULE 4 Use a colon to introduce a list of items that ends a sentence. Use a word or a phrase such as *these, the following,* or *as follows* before the list.

EXAMPLE   I'll need **these** supplies for my project: newspapers, flour, water, string, and paint.

EXAMPLE   I participate in **the following** sports: softball, tennis, basketball, and swimming.

Don't use a colon immediately after a verb or a preposition.

EXAMPLE   My subjects **include** reading, math, home economics, and language arts.

EXAMPLE   I sent messages **to** Grandma, Aunt Rita, and Julie.

RULE 5 Use a colon to separate the hour and the minutes when you use numerals to write the time of day.

EXAMPLE   The train left the station at 10:17 A.M. and arrived in the city at 12:33 P.M.

RULE 6 Use a colon after the salutation of a business letter.

EXAMPLES   Dear Professor Sanchez: Dear Editor in Chief:

PRACTICE **Using Semicolons and Colons**

Write each sentence. Add semicolons and colons where they're needed. If a sentence is already correct, write correct.

1. It grew darker and darker at last the lights came on.
2. This is your menu for lunch lasagna, tossed salad, garlic bread, milk, lemonade.

3. Marco Polo was among the first Europeans to reach China he even claimed to have been governor of a Chinese city for three years.

4. The pizza should be here by 717 P.M., or it's free.

5. I sent for information on careers in oceanology, computer programming, and health care furthermore, I plan to attend Career Day at the local junior college.

6. In the next decade, there will be more senior citizens, fewer workers, and still fewer school-age children but there will be better communication, health care, and wages for workers.

7. The bus to Milwaukee leaves at 1108 A.M. and arrives at 235 P.M.

8. Her strengths are grace, agility, and a good attitude.

9. Edgar Allan Poe, Emily Dickinson, and Walt Whitman failed to achieve all the recognition they deserved in their lifetimes however, they have become justly famous for their insights, technical skill, and lyric expression.

10. *Write the following business letter, adding necessary punctuation.*

Dear Mr. Krupp

    Please send me a brochure for OSU's summer basketball camps. I hope to attend one in June.

Yours truly,
Tyana Williams

13.6 USING QUOTATION MARKS AND ITALICS

RULE 1 Use quotation marks to enclose a direct quotation.

EXAMPLE "Please return these books to the library," said Ms. Chu.

RULE 2 Use quotation marks to enclose each part of an interrupted quotation.

EXAMPLE "Spiders," explained Sean, "have eight legs."

RULE 3 Use commas to set off an explanatory phrase, such as *he said,* from the quotation itself. Place commas inside closing quotation marks.

EXAMPLE "Spiders," explained Sean, "have eight legs."

RULE 4 Place a period inside closing quotation marks.

EXAMPLE Toby said, "My aunt Susan received her degree in June."

RULE 5 Place a question mark or an exclamation point inside closing quotation marks if it's part of the quotation.

EXAMPLE Yoko asked, "Have you ever visited Florida?"

Place a question mark or an exclamation point outside closing quotation marks if it's part of the entire sentence but not part of the quotation.

EXAMPLE Did Jerry say, "Spiders have ten legs"?

When both a sentence and the direct quotation at the end of the sentence are questions (or exclamations), use only one question mark (or exclamation point). Place the mark inside the closing quotation marks.

EXAMPLE Did Yoko ask, "Have you ever visited Florida?"

NOTE When you're writing conversation, begin a new paragraph each time the speaker changes.

EXAMPLE

"You're kidding!" I exclaimed. "That sounds unbeliev-able. Did she really say that?"

"Indeed she did," Kara insisted.

RULE 6 Enclose in quotation marks titles of short stories, essays, poems, songs, articles, book chapters, and single tele-vision shows that are part of a series.

EXAMPLES "Charles" **[short story]**   "Jingle Bells" **[song]**

RULE 7 Use italics or underlining for titles of books, plays, movies, television series, magazines, newspapers, works of art, music albums, and long musical compositions. Also use italics or underlining for the names of ships, airplanes, and spacecraft. Don't italicize or underline the word *the* before the title of a magazine or newspaper.

EXAMPLE *The Adventures of Tom Sawyer* **[book]**

EXAMPLE <u>The Monsters Are Due on Maple Street</u> **[play]**

EXAMPLE *The Hunchback of Notre Dame* **[movie]**

EXAMPLE <u>Sesame Street</u> **[television series]**

EXAMPLE *Cricket* **[magazine]**

EXAMPLE the <u>New York Times</u> **[newspaper]**

EXAMPLE the *Mona Lisa* **[painting]**

EXAMPLE <u>The Best of Reba McEntire</u> **[music album]**

EXAMPLE *Rhapsody in Blue* **[long musical composition]**

EXAMPLE <u>Titanic</u> **[ship]**

EXAMPLE the *Spirit of St. Louis* **[airplane]**

EXAMPLE <u>Friendship 7</u> **[spacecraft]**

THE POWER OF FORMATTING

A WELL-FORMATTED, STUPID PROPOSAL WILL GET FARTHER THAN A GOOD IDEA WHICH IS POORLY FORMATTED.

AT FIRST, I THOUGHT YOUR PROPOSAL WAS RIDICULOUS...

Using Quotation Marks, Italics, and Other Punctuation

Write each sentence. Add quotation marks, underlining (for italics), and other punctuation marks where they're needed.

1. The sources for my report said Judy are Sports Illustrated and The Fab Five by Mitch Albom.
2. As soldiers prepared for bed, a bugler played Taps.
3. What an exhausting march that was exclaimed Stubbs.
4. Have you heard Beethoven's Fifth Symphony asked Mr. Zaslow.
5. I was there when the herd stampeded Juanita told me.
6. This book said Erin is my all-time favorite
7. I enjoyed it too Alan replied.
8. Did Hector say I prefer to wait for the movie version
9. Little Coyote observed Those wolf tracks are fresh
10. Jana's article, Forgotten Children, appeared in Time magazine.

13.7 USING APOSTROPHES

RULE 1 Use an apostrophe and *s* (*'s*) to form the possessive of a singular noun.

EXAMPLES   girl + **'s** = girl**'s**   James + **'s** = James**'s**

RULE 2 Use an apostrophe and *s* (*'s*) to form the possessive of a plural noun that does not end in *s*.

EXAMPLES   men + **'s** = men**'s**   geese + **'s** = geese**'s**

RULE 3 Use an apostrophe alone to form the possessive of a plural noun that ends in *s*.

EXAMPLES   boys + **'** = boys**'**   judges + **'** = judges**'**

RULE 4 Use an apostrophe and *s* (*'s*) to form the possessive of an indefinite pronoun, such as *everyone, everybody, anyone, no one,* or *nobody.*

EXAMPLES anybody + **'s** = anybody**'s**   someone + **'s** = someone**'s**

Don't use an apostrophe in the possessive personal pronouns *ours, yours, his, hers, its,* and *theirs.*

EXAMPLES   That car is **ours.**   Is that cat **yours**?

The bird flapped **its** wings.   These skates are **hers.**

RULE 5 Use an apostrophe to replace letters that are omitted in a contraction.

EXAMPLES   it is = it's   you are = you're

I will = I'll   is not = isn't

PRACTICE **Using Apostrophes**

Write each sentence. Add apostrophes where they're needed. If the sentence is already correct, write correct.

1. Will the boys or the girls win the match?
2. Well bring Moiras yearbook to her in the hospital.
3. Anyones misfortune quickly becomes everyones business.
4. My boom box lost its record function somehow.
5. The boys track banquet is in the teachers cafeteria.
6. The womens bowling league hasnt started its season.
7. Several horses stalls were damaged in the fire.
8. I lost my umbrella and would like to borrow your's.
9. Its hard to tell where registration is, and everyones gear is scattered around in a confusing manner.
10. Ill arrange for the girls rooms if youll get the registration packet from the coaches booth.

13.8 USING HYPHENS, DASHES, AND PARENTHESES

RULE 1 Use a hyphen to divide a word at the end of a line. Divide words only between syllables.

EXAMPLE   With her husband, Pierre, Marie Sklodowska Curie dis-covered radium and polonium.

RULE 2 Use a hyphen in compound numbers.

EXAMPLES   **thirty-two** pianos   **sixty-five** experiments

RULE 3 Use a hyphen in fractions expressed in words.

EXAMPLE   Add **one-half** cup of butter or margarine.

EXAMPLE   **Three-fourths** of the students sing in the chorus.

RULE 4 Use a hyphen or hyphens in certain compound nouns. Check a dictionary for the correct way to write a compound noun.

EXAMPLES   great-aunt   brother-in-law   attorney-at-law

editor in chief   vice president

RULE 5 Use a hyphen in a compound modifier when it comes before the word it modifies.

EXAMPLES   Fido is a **well-trained** dog.   The dog is **well trained.**

RULE 6 Use a hyphen after the prefixes *all-*, *ex-*, and *self-*. Use a hyphen to separate any prefix from a word that begins with a capital letter.

EXAMPLES   all-powerful   ex-president

self-educated   trans-Atlantic

RULE 7 Use dashes to set off a sudden break or change in thought or speech.

EXAMPLE   Billy Adams—he lives next door—is our team manager.

RULE 8 Use parentheses to set off words that define or explain a word.

EXAMPLE Simulators (devices that produce the conditions of space flight) are used in flight training for the space program.

PRACTICE Using Hyphens, Dashes, and Parentheses

Write each sentence. Add hyphens, dashes, and parentheses where they're needed.

1. Our team made forty five bookmarks while Lou's made sixty two.
2. Can you divide three fifths by one half?
3. Craig he's the goalie is our most skilled player.
4. Forty percent of the Greek population lives in Athens, and much of the country is mountainous.
5. Kay's sister in law she's an attorney in Los Angeles is going to visit next month.
6. By the time the fire chief arrived, the building was well encased in flames.
7. The coach explained that a self starter has a well documented advantage over a lazy player.
8. Several eighth grade students who are taking algebra at the high school seem well satisfied with the teacher.
9. The chrysalis a butterfly pupa is usually attached to a milkweed plant.
10. Great grandmother is ninety one; she was the first woman to serve as editor in chief of a major newspaper.

13.9 USING ABBREVIATIONS

RULE 1 Use the abbreviations *Mr., Mrs., Ms.,* and *Dr.* before a person's name. Abbreviate professional or academic degrees that follow a person's name. Abbreviate *Junior* as *Jr.* and *Senior* as *Sr.* when they follow a person's name.

EXAMPLES **Mr.** Ed Hall **Dr.** Ann Chu Juan Diaz, **Ph.D.**

Ava Danko, **D.D.S.** Amos Finley **Jr.**

RULE 2 Use capital letters and no periods for abbreviations that are pronounced letter by letter or as words. Exceptions are *U.S.* and Washington, *D.C.*, which should have periods.

EXAMPLES **MVP** most valuable player **EST** eastern standard time

NASA National Aeronautics and Space Administration

RULE 3 Use the abbreviations *A.M.* (*ante meridiem,* "before noon") and *P.M.* (*post meridiem,* "after noon") with times. For dates use *B.C.* (before Christ) and, sometimes, *A.D.* (*anno Domini,* "in the year of the Lord," after Christ).

EXAMPLES 6:22 **A.M.** 4:12 **P.M.** 33 **B.C.** **A.D.** 476

RULE 4 Abbreviate days and months only in charts and lists.

EXAMPLES **Mon. Wed. Thur. Jan. Apr. Aug. Nov.**

RULE 5 In scientific writing, abbreviate units of measure. Use periods with abbreviations of U.S. units but not with abbreviations of metric units.

EXAMPLES inch(es) **in.** foot (feet) **ft.** gram(s) **g** liter(s) **l**

RULE 6 In addressing envelopes, abbreviate words that refer to streets. Spell out these words everywhere else.

EXAMPLES **St.** (Street) **Ave.** (Avenue) **Rd.** (Road)

I live at the corner of Elm **Street** and Maple **Road.**

RULE 7 In addressing envelopes, use the two-letter postal abbreviations for states. Spell out state names everywhere else.

EXAMPLES Texas **TX** Florida **FL** California **CA**

My cousin lives in Chicago, **Illinois.**

RULE 8 When an abbreviation with a period falls at the end of a sentence, don't add another period. Add a question mark if the sentence is interrogative; add an exclamation point if the sentence is exclamatory.

EXAMPLE   I just met Francis X. Colavito Jr.

EXAMPLE   Have you met Francis X. Colavito Jr.?

For more information about abbreviations, see pages 56–61 in Part One, Ready Reference.

PRACTICE   **Using Abbreviations**

Write the abbreviation for each item described.

1. feet
2. the day after Thursday
3. the fourth month
4. Senior
5. central standard time
6. the state of Wisconsin in an address on an envelope
7. Washington Boulevard
8. grams
9. six minutes past ten in the morning
10. the abbreviation used before a woman's name

13.10 WRITING NUMBERS

In charts and tables, always write numbers as figures. In ordinary sentences, you sometimes spell out numbers and sometimes write them as numerals.

RULE 1 Spell out numbers you can write in one or two words. If the number is greater than 999,999, see Rule 4.

EXAMPLE   There are **twenty-six** students in the class.

EXAMPLE   The arena holds **fifty-five hundred** people.

RULE 2 Use numerals for numbers of more than two words.

EXAMPLE   The distance between the two cities is **150** miles.

RULE 3 Spell out any number that begins a sentence or reword the sentence so it doesn't begin with a number.

EXAMPLE   **Four thousand two hundred eighty-three** fans attended the game.

EXAMPLE   Attendance at the game was **4,283.**

RULE 4 Use figures for numbers greater than 999,999, followed by the word *million, billion*, and so on, even if the number could be written in two words.

EXAMPLES   **1 million**   **280 billion**   **3.2 trillion**

RULE 5 Numbers of the same kind should be written in the same way. If one number must be written as a numeral, write all the numbers as numerals.

EXAMPLE   On September 8, **383** students voted for the new rule, and **50** students voted against it.

RULE 6 Spell out ordinal numbers (*first, second, third,* and so on) under one hundred.

EXAMPLE   The **ninth** of June will be the couple's **twenty-fourth** wedding anniversary.

RULE 7 Use words to write the time of day unless you are using *A.M.* or *P.M.*

EXAMPLE   I usually go for a walk at **four o'clock** in the afternoon. I return home at **a quarter to five.**

EXAMPLE   The first bell rang at **8:42** A.M., and the last one rang at **3:12** P.M.

RULE 8 Use numerals to write dates, house numbers, street numbers above ninety-nine, apartment and room numbers, telephone numbers, page numbers, amounts of money of more than two words, and percentages. Write out the word *percent.*

EXAMPLE On June **10, 1999,** I met Jan at **41** East **329th** Street in Apartment **3G.** Her telephone number is **555-2121.**

EXAMPLE Our class meets in Room **12; 55 percent** of the students are girls.

EXAMPLE I found **two dollars** between page **250** and page **251** in this book. The book's original price was **$12.95.**

PRACTICE Writing Numbers

Write each sentence. Use the correct form for each number. If the sentence is already correct, write correct.

1. I have added 43 new stamps to my collection.
2. From 1999 to 2000, corporate profits grew from one hundred twelve million dollars to one hundred sixty million dollars, an increase of forty-three percent.
3. It is exactly 399 miles from our door to Grandma's.
4. Bring $7 for the field trip by November second.
5. Send 10 pizzas to Apartment Four A, two thousand forty-six South Lincoln Avenue.
6. The fall sale will last from November eighteen to November 23 and will offer twenty-five % off all regular-priced merchandise.
7. Call one-eight hundred-Get-Thin to order our plan for just eighty-nine dollars and ninety-nine cents.
8. 34 students participated in the math contest; Robin won two 1st-place trophies and one 2nd-place ribbon.
9. By half past 10, all thirty-four thousand one hundred twenty-seven fans had filed out of the stadium.
10. Can you account for your whereabouts on July 9 between 7:15 and 10:15 P.M.?

Rewrite the following passage, correcting errors in spelling, capitalization, grammar, and usage. Add any missing punctuation. Write legibly to be sure one letter is not mistaken for another. There are ten mistakes.

Carl Sandburg

[1]Carl Sandburg might be called the peoples poet. [2]He was born on January 6 1878 in Galesburg, Illinois. [3]He left school after eighth grade and worked at many jobs delivering milk, harvesting ice, laying bricks, threshing wheat. [4]For a time, he was even a hobo his travels made him aware of the poor.

[5]After serving as a soldier Sandburg went to college. [6]Sandburg worked as a journalist, and he remained concerned about working people. [7]His well received book Chicago Poems with the poem Chicago, which described the city as the "City of the Big Shoulders," was published in 1916. [8]It made Sandburg famous however, a biography of Lincoln gave him financial success. [9]He won two Pulitzer Prizes one for his poetry and one for a biography entitled *Abraham Lincoln: The War Years.*

Write each sentence. Add commas, semicolons, colons, and end punctuation where needed.

1. Yippee Did you see the prizes Mom won at the school raffle

2. This new bike looks sleek fast and sturdy enough to ride off-road

3. Until we get home from the fair we will have to wait to try it out

4. "I loved riding the Ferris wheel" said Marianne "and the carousel too."

5. "Well I disagree" said Dan. "The roller coaster gives you a better ride goes faster and packs more thrills."

6. Frank Gruber Ph.D. is a safety expert with the university moreover he has studied the safety of carnival rides

7. "Wasn't the first state fair in our state held on September 21 1895?" Della asked.

8. I was asked to judge the following competitions quilting pie baking and jam making

9. "Mr. Jordahl which exhibit hall has the livestock?" asked Matt who was showing his prize rooster.

10. In fact it's exhibit hall 4. I'm pleased by how many entries we have how enthusiastic the owners are and how excited the crowd is.

11. The sheep and goats are located right by the front door cows and chickens are close to the rear

12. That Rhode Island red comes from Pekin Illinois which is the hometown of the late Senator Dirksen.

13. Chewing lazily on its cud one sleek cow seemed to enjoy being washed by its owner.

14. By the end of the day our family had enjoyed the rides the agriculture exhibits and the truck pull and we had avoided the side shows and political booths

15. The day after the fair grounds were empty and the carnival workers a colorful bunch of characters had disappeared

---

POSTTEST **Quotation Marks, Italics, and Apostrophes**

Write each sentence. Add quotation marks, underlining (for italics), apostrophes, and other punctuation marks where they're needed. If the sentence is already correct, write correct.

16. Many exotic species said Mr. Hanna have become endangered for a number of reasons

17. You know that the population has grown he said.

18. What happens to wildlife habitats he asked.

19. Did you say They are destroyed

20. The elephant has seen its habitat almost disappear.

21. Its also true that rangers cant prevent determined poachers from killing endangered animals

22. Biologists studies tell us that many wild populations are dwindling under these pressures he added.

23. Weve got to do something exclaimed Barbara.

24. Ill send my essay Is It Too Late for the Leopard? to the Chicago Tribune or to National Geographic.

25. Protecting animals rights should be everyones concern, or else our childrens world will be dreary.

POSTTEST **Hyphens, Dashes, Parentheses, and Numbers**

Write each sentence. Add hyphens, dashes, and parentheses where they're needed. Use the correct form for each number.

26. A prairie dog population of 25,000 lived on two thirds of the ranch land and crippled one tenth of the herd.

27. There were over 300 applicants for 5 full time positions at the factory on 1516 South Locust Street.

28. 3 members of the team made the all American team because of their success this season.

29. Havar's father in law, who is 52, entered Room 107 of the immigration service on October 12, 2001, to apply for U.S. citizenship.

30. Can you calculate 25% of 155 and 7 % of 95?

31. Your tryout is scheduled for one fifteen P.M.; it could actually be anytime between one and two o'clock.

32. The article about six ways to win friends began on page 41 and continued on page ninety-four.

33. The dunk tank it was hilarious to watch earned one hundred seventy five dollars for charity.

34. That five gallon gas tank has at least two gallons (8 quarts) of gas in it.

35. In 1790 the U.S. population was nearly 4,000,000.

Sentence Combining

• • • • • • • • • • • • • • •

PRETEST **Compound Elements**

Combine the sentences in each numbered item by using a coordinating conjunction. Add commas where they're needed. (Hint: Combine the elements listed in brackets at the end of each pair of sentences.)

1. a. Tasha watched the homecoming parade.
   b. Rob watched the homecoming parade. [subjects]
2. a. H. G. Wells wrote *The Time Machine*.
   b. He also wrote *The War of the Worlds*. [direct objects]
3. a. Aleda went to the mall with Jasmine.
   b. Aleda went to the mall with Kayte. [objects of prepositions.]
4. a. Luis put away the dishes.
   b. Luis cleaned the counters. [predicates]
5. a. Phil offered the ducks some bread.
   b. Phil offered the geese some bread. [indirect objects]
6. a. The week had come to an end.
   b. Everyone awaited the weekend fun. [sentences]

7. a. Kevin thought about going to the pool.

  b. He couldn't find his swim suit. [sentences]

8. a. Danielle plays the oboe.

  b. Her sister Amie plays the saxophone. [sentences]

9. a. Geri had planned to ask Ryan to the spring dance.

  b. She felt too shy. [sentences]

10. a. You could use this time to do extra-credit work.

  b. You could do your other homework. [sentences]

PRETEST **Prepositional Phrases and Appositive Phrases**

Combine the sentences in each numbered item by adding the new information in the second sentence to the first sentence in the form of a prepositional phrase or an appositive phrase.

11. a. I wore the stage makeup.

  b. It was on my face and neck.

12. a. Joe Montana played for the Forty-Niners.

  b. He was an enormously talented quarterback.

13. a. Harry Houdini was a legendary magician.

  b. He was renowned for his underwater escapes.

14. a. I am learning to play a piano piece.

  b. It is by Frederic Chopin.

15. a. The Hancock Building draws many Chicago sightseers.

  b. It is a skyscraper with an observatory at the top.

16. a. The student council is planning a bake sale.

  b. It will be held at the bank.

17. a. The mayor presented the key to the city to Mr. Choteau.

  b. Mr. Choteau is mayor of our sister city in France.

18. a. My brother cleaned up the mess.

  b. He did it for me.

19. a. I counted fifteen people on roller blades.

b. I counted them on our walk.

20. a. Anne Boleyn was queen of England for only a thousand days.

b. She was the second wife of Henry VIII and the mother of Queen Elizabeth I.

PRETEST Adjective and Adverb Clauses

Combine the sentences in items 21–25 by changing the new information in the second sentence to an adjective clause and adding it to the first sentence. Begin your clause with the word in brackets. Add commas if they're needed.

Combine the sentences in items 26–30 by changing the information in one sentence to an adverb clause and adding it to the other sentence. Begin your clause with the word in brackets. Add a comma if it's needed.

21. a. Our next speaker needs no introduction.

b. You all know him and love him. [whom]

22. a. John Keats died at twenty-five of tuberculosis.

b. He was one of the greatest British poets. [who]

23. a. Grape juice is a refreshing drink.

b. It is rich in antioxidants and vitamins. [which]

24. a. The shirt was not expensive.

b. I like it best. [that]

25. a. Pablo Neruda won the Nobel Prize for Literature.

b. His poetry moves me tremendously. [whose]

26. a. Arturo attended night classes in English. [After]

b. He felt more comfortable talking to others at work.

27. a. I feed the cats and dog.

b. I make breakfast for my family. [before]

28. a. You are at the dentist's office. [While]

b. I will run my errands.

29. a. I'm going to raise your allowance.
   b. You can pay for your own clothes. [so that]

30. a. You've never been in trouble before. [Because]
   b. I'll give you the benefit of the doubt.

14.1 COMPOUND SENTENCES

When you have written a few simple sentences that are closely related in meaning, try combining them to form compound sentences. A compound sentence often states your meaning more clearly than a group of simple sentences. By using some compound sentences, you can also vary the length of your sentences.

EXAMPLE   **a.** Sam had three sisters.

b. Matt had only one. **[but]**

Sam had three sisters, **but** Matt had only one.

In this example, simple sentence *a* is joined to simple sentence *b* with the coordinating conjunction *but*. Note that a comma is used before the conjunction.

A **compound sentence** is made up of two or more simple sentences. You can combine two or more simple sentences in a compound sentence by using the conjunction *and, but,* or *or.*

PRACTICE **Combining Simple Sentences**

Combine the sentences in each numbered item by using a comma and a coordinating conjunction. For the first three items, use the coordinating conjunction shown in brackets at the end of the first sentence.

1. a. Peter may take algebra this year. [or]
   b. He may wait until next year.

2. a. Candice is an excellent golfer. [and]
   b. She expects to receive an athletic scholarship.

3. a. Mrs. O'Fallon had been an only child. [but]
   b. She loved big families and had six children herself.
4. a. Grandpa washes the windows outside.
   b. Grandma washes them from inside the house.
5. a. Jon pretended to be angry.
   b. A slight smile gave him away.
6. a. We enjoyed a beautiful sunset on the deck.
   b. Then we went inside for a gourmet dinner.
7. a. For the raffle prize, we might give a gold watch.
   b. We might offer a ruby ring with diamonds.
8. a. Imelda demonstrated the way to make flautas.
   b. Natalie explained what ingredients were used.
9. a. Mr. West advised us to avoid the corner of Main and Appleton.
   b. He drove that way himself.
10. a. I could use my birthday money to buy CDs.
    b. I could add it to my summer camp fund.

14.2 COMPOUND ELEMENTS

Sometimes several sentences share information—for example, the same subject or verb. By combining such sentences and using compound elements, you can avoid repeating words. Sentences with compound elements also add variety to your writing.

EXAMPLE **a.** Helen wore a purple dress. **[and]**

b. She **carried a red handbag.**

Helen wore a purple dress **and carried a red handbag.**

Sentences *a* and *b* share information about Helen. The combined version takes the new information from sentence *b*, *carried a red handbag*, and joins it to sentence *a*, using the coordinating conjunction *and*.

You can avoid repeating information by using **compound elements.** Join compound elements with the conjunctions *and, but,* or *or.*

Combine the sentences in each numbered item by using a coordinating conjunction to form a compound element. Add the new information from the second sentence to the first sentence. For the first three items, the new information is in italics, and the conjunction you should use is shown in brackets at the end of the first sentence.

1. a. I gave old T-shirts to the Salvation Army store. [and]
   b. I also gave *outgrown jeans* to the Salvation Army store.
2. a. Mr. Huerta sells life insurance. [but]
   b. He does *not* sell *homeowner's insurance.*
3. a. Tabetha has the ability to become a doctor. [or]
   b. She could become *a systems analyst.*
4. a. A scientist relies on keen observations.
   b. He or she also relies on exact measurements.
5. a. For the reception, we might hire a band to play.
   b. We could ask Tony to act as DJ.
6. a. Mrs. Takemoto served us sushi.
   b. She did not serve tea.
7. a. The breeze off the lake was refreshing.
   b. It was cool.
8. a. You can have french fries as a side order.
   b. You can have cole slaw as a side order.
9. a. Ashley served as an usher at the play.
   b. Dana also served as an usher at the play.
10. a. We charged our gasoline purchases.
   b. We also charged our hotel room.

14.3 PREPOSITIONAL PHRASES

Prepositional phrases are useful in sentence combining. Like adjectives and adverbs, they present more information about nouns and verbs. Because prepositional phrases show relationships, they can often express complicated ideas effectively.

EXAMPLE **a.** The family took a trip.

b. It was a **hot summer day. [on]**

c. They went **to the beach.**

On a hot summer day, the family took a trip **to the beach.**

The new information in sentence *b* is added to sentence *a* as a prepositional phrase, and the new information in sentence *c* is moved to sentence *a*. In the new sentence, the prepositional phrase *On a hot summer day* modifies the verb, *took*. The phrase *to the beach* modifies the noun *trip*. Notice that a prepositional phrase that modifies a noun follows the noun it modifies. Prepositional phrases that modify verbs can occupy different positions in a sentence. (For a list of common prepositions, see page 174.)

A **prepositional phrase** is a group of words that begins with a preposition and ends with a noun or a pronoun. Prepositional phrases most often modify nouns and verbs.

| **PRACTICE** | **Combining Sentences with Prepositional Phrases** |

Combine the sentences in each numbered item by adding the prepositional phrase from the second sentence to the first sentence. For the first three items, the prepositional phrase in the second sentence is shown in italics. In the last item, you will need to combine three sentences.

1. a. The sign for our turnoff was hidden.
   b. The sign was *behind branches.*
2. a. The ducklings followed their mother.
   b. They went *across the highway.*
3. a. A puma watched alertly.
   b. It watched *from a cliff.*
4. a. Mrs. Ross vacations every year.
   b. She vacations with her best friend.

5. a. The next play will begin its run on November 3.

b. The play is at the Paladium.

6. a. Let's move the picnic table.

b. Let's move it into the shade.

7. a. The two-year-old was hiding his broccoli.

b. He was hiding it under his plate.

8. a. Her flight is coming from Roanoke, Virginia.

b. It is coming to Kansas City, Missouri.

9. a. I have several moving boxes.

b. They are for you.

10. a. The sauce will be done.

b. It is for the spaghetti.

c. It'll be done in another four minutes.

14.4 APPOSITIVES

You can use appositives to combine sentences in a compact and informative way. Appositives and appositive phrases identify or rename nouns.

EXAMPLE **a.** Maya Lin designed the Vietnam Veterans Memorial.

b. She was **an architecture student.**

Maya Lin, **an architecture student,** designed the Vietnam Veterans Memorial.

The appositive phrase *an architecture student* identifies the noun *Maya Lin.* Note that the appositive phrase is set off with commas because it gives nonessential information about Maya Lin. If an appositive or an appositive phrase gives information that is essential for identifying a noun, it's not set off with commas. (For more information about appositives, see pages 89–90.)

An **appositive** is a noun placed next to another noun to identify it or give additional information about it. An **appositive phrase** includes an appositive and other words that modify it.

Combine the sentences in each numbered item by changing the new information in the second sentence to an appositive or an appositive phrase and adding it to the first sentence. For the first three items, the appositive or appositive phrase in the second sentence is shown in italics. Add commas where they're needed.

1. a. Gwendolyn Brooks won a Pulitzer Prize for *Annie Allen.*
   b. She was *poet laureate of Illinois.*
2. a. The *Daily Chronicle* is hiring reporters.
   b. It is *our local newspaper.*
3. a. Dr. Hobbes has decided to retire.
   b. He is *our family physician.*
4. a. Robert Frost wrote "The Death of the Hired Man."
   b. He was one of the twentieth century's greatest poets.
5. a. Phyllis is moving to her own apartment.
   b. She is the Scott's youngest child.
6. a. Jezebel seems to understand what I say to her.
   b. She is my pet parakeet.
7. a. The Griffins' new house is in the country.
   b. It is a Tudor-style house.
8. a. He hopes to find work in Puerto Vallarta.
   b. It is a beautiful resort town in Mexico.
9. a. Mount McKinley rises 20,320 feet into the air.
   b. It is the highest mountain in North America.
10. a. Our hockey team is ranked third in the state.
   b. Our team is the Bruins.

14.5 ADJECTIVE AND ADVERB CLAUSES

When two sentences share information, one of the sentences can often be made into an adjective clause modifying a word in the other sentence.

a. Carla and Darla entered the dance contest.

b. Carla and Darla **are identical twins. [, who . . . ,]**

Carla and Darla**, who are identical twins,** entered the dance contest.

The new information (in blue type) in sentence *b* becomes an adjective clause modifying *Carla and Darla*. *Who* now connects the clauses. Notice the commas in the new sentence. Adjective clauses that add nonessential information are set off with commas. Those that add essential information are not. (For more information about adjective clauses, see page 195.)

An **adjective clause** is a subordinate clause that modifies a noun or a pronoun in the main clause. A relative pronoun, such as *who, whom, whose, which,* or *that* is used to tie the adjective clause to the main clause. The words *where* and *when* can also be used as connectors.

You can also use adverb clauses to combine sentences. Adverb clauses are especially effective in showing relationships between actions. For example, an adverb clause can show when one action takes place in relation to another.

EXAMPLE **a.** Lee read a great deal as a boy.

b. He was recovering from an accident. **[while]**

Lee read a great deal as a boy **while he was recovering from an accident.**

In the new sentence, the adverb clause *while he was recovering from an accident* modifies the verb *read*. The adverb clause tells when Lee read a great deal. Note that the subordinating conjunction *while* makes the relationship between the two actions clear. An adverb clause may occupy different positions within a sentence. If it begins the sentence, it's followed by a comma. (For more information about adverb clauses, see pages 198–199.)

An **adverb clause** is a subordinate clause that often modifies the verb in the main clause. Adverb clauses are introduced by subordinating conjunctions, such as *after, although, as, because, before, if, since, unless, until, when, whenever, where, wherever,* and *while.*

PRACTICE **Combining Sentences with Adjective and Adverb Clauses**

Combine the sentences in items 1–5 by changing the new information in the second sentence to an adjective clause and adding it to the first sentence. For items 1–3, the new information in the second sentence is shown in italics. Begin your clause with the word in brackets. Add commas if they're needed.

Combine the sentences in items 6–10 by changing the information in one sentence to an adverb clause and adding it to the other sentence. Begin your clause with the word in brackets. Add a comma if it's needed.

1. a. Martin would only eat a certain kind of bread.
  b. The bread *came from San Francisco.* [that]
2. a. The Lakota followed the herds.
  b. They *depended on buffalo for food.* [who]
3. a. Flora was named after her grandmother.
  b. The *name means "flower."* [whose]
4. a. The brother and sister earn twenty dollars a week.
  b. They mow our yard. [who]
5. a. The golfer was Tiger Woods.
  b. We wanted him to win. [whom]
6. a. I bring out the bridle. [Whenever]
  b. The pony runs away.
7. a. Everyone waited restlessly.
  b. The band appeared on stage. [until]
8. a. He had played before crowds many times. [Because]
  b. The young violinist was not nervous.

9. a. Everyone in the boat remains calm. [As long as]

   b. We will ride out the storm safely.

10. a. Our basement invariably gets wet.

   b. We have a heavy rain. [after]

PRACTICE Proofreading

Rewrite the following passage, combining sentences that are closely related in meaning.

Pearl S. Buck

Pearl S. Buck was born in West Virginia. The year was 1892. Until 1934, she lived most of her life in China. Her parents were missionaries there.

Buck spent her childhood in Chinkiang. It is on the Yangtse River. She attended college in Virginia. She returned to China after graduation. She did missionary work. She also took care of her home and children. What is more, she taught English literature in Chinese universities.

In the 1920s, Buck began to write. She had a gift for conveying the life of ordinary Chinese peasants vividly. She conveyed it compassionately too. In 1931 she published *The Good Earth*. It is an epic story of peasant life in China. She won a Pulitzer Prize in 1932 for this novel. It has been translated into thirty languages. It is considered her finest work. Buck wrote over seventy books in all. In 1938 she became the first woman to win a Nobel Prize in Literature.

Combine the sentences in each numbered item by using a coordinating conjunction. Add commas where they're needed. (Hint: Combine the elements listed in brackets at the end of each pair of sentences.)

1. a. Rosario is giving his report today.
   b. Rosie is giving her report today. [subjects]
2. a. Mr. Heredia rides his motorcycle on weekends.
   b. Mr. Heridia rides his jet ski on weekends. [direct objects]
3. a. Tom Hanks has proven his talent as an actor.
   b. He has also proven his talent as a director. [objects of preposition]
4. a. Anne-Marie plays soccer.
   b. Anne-Marie runs on the track team. [predicates]
5. a. Helen made Mia a puppet.
   b. Helen made Noah a puppet. [indirect objects]
6. a. Mom loves to wear perfume.
   b. Dad is allergic to most fragrances. [sentences]
7. a. Jeannine does the catering for large parties.
   b. Bob provides the entertainment. [sentences]
8. a. Courtney may go for a swim in the lake.
   b. She might just lie on the beach. [sentences]
9. a. The library will extend the lending period to three weeks.
   b. The fine for overdue books will double. [sentences]
10. a. H. H. Munro preferred to be anonymous as an author.
    b. He took the pen name Saki. [sentences]

Combine the sentences in each numbered item by adding the new information in the second sentence to the first sentence in the form of a prepositional phrase or an appositive phrase.

11. a. Joy, Jacob, and Natasha carried the supplies.
    b. They carried them into camp.
12. a. Jesse Stuart wrote *The Thread That Runs So True.*
    b. It is a book about his teaching days in Kentucky.
13. a. Norm poured birdseed.
    b. He poured it into the bird feeder.
14. a. Evelyn drank the lemonade.
    b. She drank it with great enjoyment.
15. a. The Washington Monument towers over the landscape.
    b. It is a white marble obelisk over 555 feet tall.
16. a. This episode explores black holes.
    b. It is an episode of the science program *Nova.*
17. a. The class was held in the apartment's recreation lounge.
    b. The lounge was a large room with tables, chairs, and game tables.
18. a. Delores Huerta is a hero to her people.
    b. She is a tireless activist for the rights of migrant workers.
19. a. Joanie dangled her blistered feet.
    b. She dangled them in the cool river water.
20. a. At Rosita's Restaurant, I order guacamole.
    b. Guacamole is a dip made with avocados.

GRAMMAR/USAGE/MECHANICS

Combine the sentences in items 21–25 by changing the new information in the second sentence to an adjective clause and adding it to the first sentence. Begin your clause with the word in brackets. Add commas if they're needed.

Combine the sentences in items 26–30 by changing the information in one sentence to an adverb clause and adding it to the other sentence. Begin your clause with the word in brackets. Add a comma if it's needed.

21. a. A person is not kind or likable.
    b. The person is mean to animals. [who]

22. a. My phone is a digital cordless machine.
    b. I purchased it at the electronics store last week. [which]

23. a. Someday there will be an electric car.
    b. It will travel just as fast as a gas-powered car. [that]

24. a. The librarian told us to be quiet.
    b. Her face had grown stern. [whose]

25. a. The chief of police will be retiring this year.
    b. Everyone agrees he has done a fine job. [who]

26. a. The parents are both long-haired cats. [Although]
    b. Their kitten has short hair.

27. a. We finally arrived at the concert.
    b. The band was playing its finale. [as]

28. a. I use ammonia-based cleaners. [Whenever]
    b. I break out in a rash.

29. a. No one is to leave the mansion.
    b. We check everyone's alibi. [until]

30. a. Felicia took a child-care class.
    b. She wanted to be a better baby-sitter. [because]

Chapter 15

Spelling and Vocabulary

● ● ● ● ● ● ● ● ● ● ● ● ● ● ●

15.1 SPELLING RULES

English spelling often seems to make no sense. Usually there are historical reasons for the spellings we use today, but you don't need to study the history of the English language to spell correctly. The rules in this section work most of the time, but there are exceptions to every rule. When you're not sure how to spell a word, the best thing to do is check a dictionary.

Spelling *ie* and *ei*

An easy way to learn when to use *ie* and when to use *ei* is to memorize a simple rhyming rule. Then learn the common exceptions to the rule.

Frank and Ernest

RULE	EXAMPLES
WRITE *I* BEFORE *E*	achieve, believe, brief, chief, die, field, friend, grief, lie, niece, piece, pier, quiet, retrieve, tie, yield
EXCEPT AFTER *C*	ceiling, conceit, conceive, deceit, deceive, receipt, receive
OR WHEN SOUNDED LIKE *A,* AS IN *NEIGHBOR* AND *WEIGH.*	eight, eighty, freight, neigh, reign, sleigh, veil, vein, weigh, weight

Some exceptions: caffeine, either, foreign, forfeit, height, heir, leisure, neither, protein, seize, species, their, weird; words ending in *cient (ancient)* and *cience (conscience)*; plurals of nouns ending in *cy (democracies)*; the third-person singular form of verbs ending in *cy (fancies)*; words in which *i* and *e* follow *c* but represent separate sounds *(science, society)*

Words Ending in *cede, ceed,* and *sede*

The only English word ending in *sede* is *supersede.* Three words end in *ceed: proceed, exceed,* and *succeed.* You can remember these three words by thinking of the following sentence.

EXAMPLE   If you **proceed** to **exceed** the speed limit, you will **succeed** in getting a ticket.

All other words ending with the "seed" sound are spelled with *cede: precede, recede, secede.*

Adding Prefixes

Adding prefixes is easy. Keep the spelling of the root word and add the prefix. If the last letter of the prefix is the same as the first letter of the word, keep both letters.

un- + happy = unhappy	co- + operate = cooperate
dis- + appear = disappear	il- + legal = illegal
re- + enlist = reenlist	un- + natural = unnatural
mis- + spell = misspell	im- + migrate = immigrate

Adding Suffixes

When you add a suffix beginning with a vowel, double the final consonant if the word ends in a **single consonant following a single vowel** *and*

- the word has one syllable

mud + -y = muddy	sad + -er = sadder
put + -ing = putting	stop + -ed = stopped

- the word is stressed on the last syllable and the stress remains on the same syllable after the suffix is added

occur + -ence = occurrence	repel + -ent = repellent
regret + -able = regrettable	commit + -ed = committed
begin + -ing = beginning	refer + -al = referral

Don't double the final letter if the word ends in *s, w, x,* or *y: buses, rowing, waxy, employer.*

Don't double the final consonant before the suffix *-ist* if the word has more than one syllable: *druggist* but *violinist, guitarist.*

Adding suffixes to words that end in *y* can cause spelling problems. Study these rules and note the exceptions.

When a word ends in a **vowel and y,** keep the *y.*

play + -s = plays	joy + -ous = joyous
obey + -ed = obeyed	annoy + -ance = annoyance
buy + -ing = buying	enjoy + -ment = enjoyment
employ + -er = employer	enjoy + -able = enjoyable
joy + -ful = joyful	boy + -ish = boyish
joy + -less = joyless	coy + -ly = coyly

SOME EXCEPTIONS: gay + -ly = gaily, day + -ly = daily, pay + -d = paid, lay + -d = laid, say + -d = said

When a word ends in a **consonant and y,** change the *y* to *i* before any suffix that doesn't begin with *i.* Keep the *y* before suffixes that begin with *i.*

carry + -es = carries	deny + -al = denial
dry + -ed = dried	rely + -able = reliable
easy + -er = easier	mercy + -less = merciless
merry + -ly = merrily	likely + -hood = likelihood
happy + -ness = happiness	accompany + -ment =
beauty + -ful = beautiful	accompaniment
fury + -ous = furious	carry + -ing = carrying
defy + -ant = defiant	baby + -ish = babyish
vary + -ation = variation	lobby + -ist = lobbyist

SOME EXCEPTIONS: shy + -ly = shyly, dry + -ly = dryly, shy + -ness = shyness, dry + -ness = dryness, biology + -ist = biologist, economy + -ist = economist, baby + -hood = babyhood

Usually a **final silent e** is dropped before a suffix, but sometimes it's kept. The following chart shows the basic rules for adding suffixes to words that end in silent *e.*

ADDING SUFFIXES TO WORDS THAT END IN SILENT *E*

RULE	EXAMPLES
Drop the *e* before suffixes that begin with a vowel.	care + -ed = cared dine + -ing = dining move + -er = mover type + -ist = typist blue + -ish = bluish arrive + -al = arrival desire + -able = desirable accuse + -ation = accusation noise + -y = noisy
Some exceptions	mile + -age = mileage dye + -ing = dyeing
Drop the *e* and change *i* to *y* before the suffix *-ing* if the word ends in *ie.*	die + -ing = dying lie + -ing = lying tie + -ing = tying
Keep the *e* before suffixes that begin with *a* and *o* if the word ends in *ce* or *ge.*	dance + -able = danceable change + -able = changeable courage + -ous = courageous
Keep the *e* before suffixes that begin with a vowel if the word ends in *ee* or *oe.*	see + -ing = seeing agree + -able = agreeable canoe + -ing = canoeing hoe + -ing = hoeing
Some exceptions	free + -er = freer free + -est = freest
Keep the *e* before suffixes that begin with a consonant.	grace + -ful = graceful state + -hood = statehood like + -ness = likeness encourage + -ment = encouragement care + -less = careless sincere + -ly = sincerely

RULE	EXAMPLES
Some exceptions	awe + -ful = awful judge + -ment = judgment argue + -ment = argument true + -ly = truly due + -ly = duly whole + -ly = wholly
Drop *le* before the suffix *-ly* when the word ends with a consonant and *le.*	possible + -ly = possibly sniffle + -ly = sniffly sparkle + -ly = sparkly gentle + -ly = gently

When a word ends in *ll,* drop one *l* when you add the suffix *-ly.*

dull + -ly = dully   full + -ly = fully

chill + -ly = chilly   hill + -ly = hilly

Compound Words

Keep the original spelling of both parts of a compound word.

Remember that some compounds are one word, some are two words, and some are hyphenated. Check a dictionary when in doubt.

foot + lights = footlights   fish + hook = fishhook

busy + body = busybody   with + hold = withhold

book + case = bookcase   book + keeper = bookkeeper

light + house = lighthouse   heart + throb = heartthrob

Spelling Plurals

A singular noun names one person, place, thing, or idea. A plural noun names more than one. To form the plural of most nouns, you simply add *-s.* The following chart shows other basic rules.

GENERAL RULES FOR FORMING PLURALS

NOUNS ENDING IN	TO FORM PLURAL	EXAMPLES
ch, s, sh, x, z	Add *-es.*	lunch → lunches bus → buses dish → dishes box → boxes buzz → buzzes
a vowel and *y*	Add *-s.*	boy → boys turkey → turkeys
a consonant and *y*	Change *y* to *i* and add *-es.*	baby → babies penny → pennies
a vowel and *o*	Add *-s.*	radio → radios rodeo → rodeos
a consonant and *o*	Usually add *-es.*	potato → potatoes tomato → tomatoes hero → heroes echo → echoes
	Sometimes add *-s.*	zero → zeros photo → photos piano → pianos
f or *fe*	Usually change *f* to *v* and add *-s* or *-es.*	wife → wives knife → knives life → lives leaf → leaves half → halves shelf → shelves wolf → wolves thief → thieves
	Sometimes add *-s.*	roof → roofs chief → chiefs cliff → cliffs giraffe → giraffes

GRAMMAR/USAGE/MECHANICS

The plurals of **proper names** are formed by adding *-es* to names that end in *ch, s, sh, x,* or *z.*

EXAMPLE   The **Woodriches** live on Elm Street.

EXAMPLE   There are two **Jonases** in our class.

EXAMPLE   Have you met your new neighbors, the **Gomezes**?

Just add *-s* to form the plural of all other proper names, including those that end in *y.*

EXAMPLE   The **Kennedys** are a famous American family.

EXAMPLE   I know three **Marys.**

EXAMPLE   The last two **Januarys** have been especially cold.

To form the plural of a **compound noun written as one word,** follow the general rules for plurals. To form the plural of **hyphenated compound nouns** or **compound nouns of more than one word,** usually make the most important word plural.

EXAMPLE   A dozen **mailboxes** stood in a row at the entrance to the housing development.

EXAMPLE   The two women's **fathers-in-law** have never met.

EXAMPLE   The three **post offices** are made of brick.

Some nouns have **irregular plural forms** that don't follow any rules.

man → men

woman → women

child → children

foot → feet

tooth → teeth

mouse → mice

goose → geese

ox → oxen

Some nouns have the same singular and plural forms. Most of these are the names of animals, and some of the plural forms may be spelled in more than one way.

deer → deer

sheep → sheep

head (cattle) → head

Sioux → Sioux

series → series

species → species

fish → fish *or* fishes

antelope → antelope *or* antelopes

buffalo → buffalo *or* buffaloes *or* buffalos

PRACTICE Spelling Rules

Find the misspelled word in each group and write it correctly.

1. sleigh, niether, quiet
2. shutting, slammed, fited
3. radioes, folios, pillows
4. seed, excede, intercede
5. fancyful, sleepiness, wearying
6. Clintons, Bushs, Mondays
7. posing, likelihood, glanceing
8. hometown, lifeboat, hommaker
9. teeth, mice, gese
10. inattentive, misspoken, restablish

15.2 IMPROVING YOUR SPELLING

You can improve your spelling by improving your study method. You can also improve your spelling by thoroughly learning certain common but frequently misspelled words.

"Do me a favor, chief. Next time you carve
something in stone have it spell checked first."

HOW TO STUDY A WORD

By following a few simple steps, you can learn to spell
new words. Pay attention to unfamiliar or hard-to-spell
words in your reading. As you write, note words that you
have trouble spelling. Then use the steps below to learn to
spell those difficult words.

1. Say It
Look at the word and
say it aloud. Say it again,
pronouncing each syllable
clearly.

2. See It
Close your eyes. Picture
the word in your mind.
Visualize the word letter
by letter.

3. Write It
Look at the word again
and write it two or three
times. Then write the
word without looking at
the printed spelling.

4. Check It
Check your spelling.
Did you spell the word
correctly? If not, repeat
each step until you can
spell the word easily.

Get into the habit of using a dictionary to find the correct spelling of a word. How do you find a word if you can't spell it? Write down letters and letter combinations that could stand for the sound you hear at the beginning of the word. Try these possible spellings as you look for the word in a dictionary.

SPELLING PROBLEM WORDS

The following words are often misspelled. Look for your problem words in the list. What words would you add to the list?

Often Misspelled Words

absence	cemetery	February
accidentally	changeable	foreign
accommodate	choir	forty
achievement	college	fulfill
adviser	colonel	funeral
alcohol	commercial	genius
all right	convenient	government
analyze	courageous	grammar
answer	curiosity	guarantee
athlete	definite	height
attendant	descend	humorous
ballet	develop	hygiene
beautiful	discipline	imaginary
beginning	disease	immediate
believe	dissatisfied	incidentally
beneficial	eligible	incredibly
blaze	embarrass	jewelry
business	envelope	judgment
cafeteria	environment	laboratory
canceled	essential	leisure
canoe	familiar	library

license	parallel	sense
maintenance	permanent	separate
medicine	physical	similar
mischievous	physician	sincerely
misspell	picnic	souvenir
modern	pneumonia	succeed
molasses	privilege	technology
muscle	probably	theory
necessary	pronunciation	tomorrow
neighborhood	receipt	traffic
niece	receive	truly
ninety	recognize	unanimous
noticeable	recommend	usually
nuisance	restaurant	vacuum
occasion	rhythm	variety
original	ridiculous	various
pageant	schedule	Wednesday

PRACTICE **Spelling Problem Words**

Find each misspelled word and write it correctly.

1. You must reconize the importance of car maintnence.
2. Dancers must have a good sence of rithum.
3. He has an appointment for a phisical exam tommorow.
4. If pronounciation is poor, you may mispell words.
5. Even with the advantages of modern medecine, pnumonia is a serious illness.
6. Are you familliar with the esential rules of grammar?
7. It will not be conveeient to accomodate more people.
8. We accidentaly overturned our canew in the rapids.
9. The game won't be canseled on a beutiful day like this.
10. That ninty-day garantee is worthless.

15.3 USING CONTEXT CLUES

The surest way to learn the meaning of a new word is to use a dictionary. However, you won't always have a dictionary handy. You can often figure out the meaning of an unfamiliar word by looking for clues in the words and sentences around it. These surrounding words and sentences are called the context.

USING SPECIFIC CONTEXT CLUES

Writers often give clues to the meaning of unfamiliar words. Sometimes they even tell you exactly what a word means. The following chart shows five types of specific context clues. It also gives examples of words that help you identify the type of context clue.

INTERPRETING CLUE WORDS IN CONTEXT

TYPE OF CONTEXT CLUE	CLUE WORDS	EXAMPLES
Definition The meaning of the unfamiliar word is given in the sentence.	in other words or that is which is which means	Jamake *inscribed* his name; **that is,** he wrote his name on the card. Jaleesa put the wet clay pot in the *kiln,* **or** oven, to harden.
Example The meaning of the unfamiliar word is explained through familiar examples.	for example for instance including like such as	Some people are afraid of *arachnids,* **such as** spiders and ticks. The new program has been *beneficial* for the school; **for example,** test scores are up, and absences are down.

chart continued on next page

Chapter 15 Spelling and Vocabulary **311**

TYPE OF CONTEXT CLUE	CLUE WORDS	EXAMPLES
Comparison The unfamiliar word is compared to a familiar word or phrase.	also identical like likewise resembling same similarly too	Maria thought the dress was *gaudy*. Lisa, **too,** thought it was flashy. A *rampant* growth of weeds and vines surrounded the old house. The barn was **likewise** covered with uncontrolled and wild growth.
Contrast The unfamiliar word is contrasted to a familiar word or phrase.	but however on the contrary on the other hand unlike	Robins are *migratory* birds, **unlike** sparrows, which live in the same region all year round. Martin didn't *bungle* the arrangements for the party; **on the contrary,** he handled everything smoothly and efficiently.
Cause and effect The unfamiliar word is explained as part of a cause-and-effect relationship.	as a result because consequently therefore thus	**Because** this rubber raft is so *buoyant,* it will float easily. Kevin is very *credulous;* **consequently,** he'll believe almost anything.

USING GENERAL CONTEXT

Sometimes there are no special clue words to help you understand an unfamiliar word. However, you can still use the general context. That is, you can use the details in the words or sentences around the unfamiliar word. Read the following sentences:

Joel was chosen student **liaison** to the faculty. Everyone hoped his appointment would improve communication between the students and the teachers.

GRAMMAR/USAGE/MECHANICS

The first sentence tells you that Joel is serving as a kind of connection between the students and the faculty. The word *communication* helps you figure out that being a liaison means acting as a line of communication between two groups.

Frank and Ernest

© 1994 Thaves/Reprinted with permission.
Newspaper dist. by NEA, Inc.

PRACTICE Using Context Clues

Use context clues to figure out the meaning of the italicized word. Write the meaning. Then write definition, example, comparison, contrast, cause and effect, *or* general *to tell what type of context clue you used to define the word.*

1. The pirate's treasure was thought to be *irrecoverable,* but through technology, it was brought to the surface.
2. Early people discovered that meat left untreated would *putrefy;* thus, they learned to preserve it in salt.
3. On payday, Frank likes to *splurge.* His friend Bill also likes to go out and spend his money freely.
4. My great-grandmother was a keen *suffragist;* that is, she worked for women's right to vote.
5. The *depletion* of resources is cause for concern. For example, petroleum reserves are running low.
6. The theater critic loved to *hobnob* with celebrities, chatting and partying with them whenever she could.

7. Some monkeys have *prehensile* tails. Most animals, however, cannot grasp objects with their tails.

8. We finally found the antique iron in the attic after we had *foraged* for it for an hour.

9. These instructions are truly *nebulous;* in other words, they are simply too vague to make any sense.

10. Miriam *gloated* when she got an A on the test; Hassim, likewise, told everyone about how well he had done.

15.4 ROOTS, PREFIXES, AND SUFFIXES

You can often figure out the meaning of an unfamiliar word by dividing it into parts. The main part of the word is called the root, and it carries the word's basic meaning. A root is often a word by itself. For example, *read* is a word. When a prefix or a suffix is added to it, *read* becomes a root, as in *unreadable.*

Prefixes and suffixes can be added to a root to change its meaning. A prefix is added to the beginning of a root. A suffix is added to the end of a root. A word can have both a prefix and a suffix: *un + read + able = unreadable.*

ROOTS

The root of a word carries the main meaning. Some roots, like *read,* can stand alone. Other roots may have parts added to make a complete word. For example, the root *port* ("carry") by itself is a place to which ships carry goods. Combined with a prefix, it can become *report, deport,* or *transport.* Add a suffix and you can get *reporter, deportment,* or *transportation.*

Learning the meanings of common roots can help you figure out the meanings of many unfamiliar words. The following chart shows some common roots.

ROOTS	WORDS	MEANINGS
bio means "life"	biography	a written story of a person's life
	biosphere	the part of the atmosphere where living things exist
dec or *deca* means "ten"	decade	ten years
	decathlon	an athletic contest consisting of ten events
dent means "tooth"	dentist	a doctor who treats the teeth
	trident	a spear with three prongs, or teeth
dict means "to say"	dictionary	a book of words
	dictator	one who rules absolutely
	predict	to say before (something happens)
duc or *duct* means "to lead"	conductor	one who leads or directs
	produce	to bring into existence
flect or *flex* means "to bend"	flexible	able to bend
	reflect	to bend back (light)
graph means "to write" or "writing"	autograph	one's own signature
	biography	a written story of a person's life
lect means "speech"	lecture	a speech
	dialect	the speech of a certain region
miss or *mit* means "to send"	omit	to fail to send or include
	missile	something sent through the air or by mail
phon means "sound" or "voice"	phonograph	an instrument for playing sounds
	telephone	a device for transmitting voices over a distance
port means "to carry"	transport	to carry across a distance
	porter	one who carries baggage

GRAMMAR/USAGE/MECHANICS

Chapter 15 Spelling and Vocabulary **315**

ROOTS	WORDS	MEANINGS
script means "writing"	prescription	a written order for medicine
	postscript	a message added at the end of a letter
spec or *spect* means "to look" or "to watch"	spectator	one who watches
	inspect	to look closely
	prospect	to look for (mineral deposits)
tele means "distant"	telephone	a device for transmitting voices over a distance
	television	a device for transmitting pictures over a distance
tri means "three"	triathlon	an athletic contest consisting of three events
	tricycle	a three-wheeled vehicle
vid or *vis* means "to see"	vision	the ability to see
	videotape	a recording of visual images
voc or *vok* means "to call"	vocation	an inclination, or call, to a certain pursuit
	revoke	to recall or take back

PREFIXES

The following chart shows some prefixes and their meanings. Notice that some prefixes, such as *dis-*, *in-*, *non-*, and *un-*, have the same or nearly the same meaning. A single prefix may have more than one meaning. The prefix *in-*, for example, can mean "into," as in *inject*, as well as "not," as in *indirect*. The prefix *re-* can mean "again" or "back."

Note that *il-*, *im-*, *in-*, and *ir-* are variations of the same prefix. *Il-* is used before roots that begin with *l (illegal)*; *im-* is used before roots that begin with *m (immature)*; and *ir-* is used before roots that begin with *r (irregular)*. *In-* is used before all other letters.

PREFIXES

CATEGORIES	PREFIXES	WORDS	MEANINGS
Prefixes that reverse meanings	*de-* means "remove from" or "reduce"	defrost devalue	to remove frost to reduce the value of
	dis- means "not" or "do the opposite of"	disagreeable disappear	not agreeable to do the opposite of appear
	in-, il-, im-, and *ir-* mean "not"	incomplete illegal immature irregular	not complete not legal not mature not regular
	mis- means "bad," "badly," "wrong," or "wrongly"	misfortune misbehave misdeed misjudge	bad fortune to behave badly a wrong deed to judge wrongly
	non- means "not" or "without"	nonathletic nonfat	not athletic without fat
	un- means "not" or "do the opposite of"	unhappy untie	not happy to do the opposite of tie
Prefixes that show relationship	*co-* means "with," "together," or "partner"	coworker coexist coauthor	one who works with another to exist together an author who writes as a partner with another
	inter- means "between"	interscholastic	between schools
	post- means "after"	postseason	after the regular season
	pre- means "before"	preseason	before the regular season

CATEGORIES	PREFIXES	WORDS	MEANINGS
	re- means "back" or "again"	repay recheck	to pay back to check again
	sub- means "under" or "below"	submarine substandard	under the sea below standard
	super- means "more than"	superabundant	more than abundant
	trans- means "across"	transport	to carry across a distance
Prefixes that show judgment	*anti-* means "against"	antiwar	against war
	pro- means "in favor of"	progovernment	in favor of the government
Prefixes that show number	*bi-* means "two"	bicycle	a two-wheeled vehicle
	semi- means "half" or "partly"	semicircle semisweet	half a circle partly sweet
	uni- means "one"	unicycle	a one-wheeled vehicle

SUFFIXES

A suffix added to a word can change the word's part of speech as well as its meaning. For example, adding the suffix *-er* to *read* (a verb) makes *reader* (a noun). Adding *-less* to *faith* (a noun) makes *faithless* (an adjective).

The following chart shows some common suffixes and their meanings. Notice that some suffixes, such as *-er, -or,* and *-ist,* have the same or nearly the same meaning. A single suffix may have more than one meaning. The suffix *-er,* for example, can also mean "more," as in *bigger.*

CATEGORIES	SUFFIXES	WORDS	MEANINGS
Suffixes that mean "one who" or "that which"	-ee, -eer	employee	one who is employed
		charioteer	one who drives a chariot
	-er, -or	worker	one who works
		sailor	one who sails
	-ian	physician	one who practices medicine (once called physic)
		musician	one who plays or studies music
	-ist	pianist	one who plays the piano
		chemist	one who works in chemistry
Suffixes that mean "full of" or "having"	-ful	joyful	full of joy
		suspenseful	full of suspense
		beautiful	having beauty
	-ous	furious	full of fury
		famous	having fame
		courageous	having courage
Suffixes that show a state, a condition, or a quality	-hood	falsehood	quality of being false
	-ness	happiness	state of being happy
	-ship	friendship	condition of being friends
Suffixes that show an action or process or its result	-ance, -ence	performance	action of performing
		conference	process of conferring
	-ation, -ion	flirtation	action of flirting
		invention	result of inventing
	-ment	argument	result of arguing
		arrangement	result of arranging
		enjoyment	process of enjoying

GRAMMAR/USAGE/MECHANICS

CATEGORIES	SUFFIXES	WORDS	MEANINGS
Suffixes that mean "relating to," "characterized by," or "like"	*-al*	musical	relating to music
		comical	relating to comedy
	-ish	childish	like a child
		foolish	like a fool
	-y	witty	characterized by wit
		hairy	characterized by hair
Other common suffixes	*-able* and *-ible* mean "capable of," "fit for," or "likely to"	breakable	capable of being broken
		collectible	fit for collecting
		agreeable	likely to agree
	-ize means "to cause to be" or "to become"	visualize	to cause to be made visual
		familiarize	to become familiar
	-less means "without"	hopeless	without hope
		careless	done without care
	-ly means "in a (certain) manner"	easily	in an easy manner
		sadly	in a sad manner

Notice that sometimes the spelling of a word changes when a suffix is added. For example, when *-ous* is added to *fury*, the *y* in *fury* changes to *i*. See pages 301–304 to learn more about spelling words with suffixes.

More than one suffix can be added to a single word. The following examples show how suffixes can change a single root word.

peace **[noun]**

peace + ful = peaceful **[adjective]**

peace + ful + ly = peacefully **[adverb]**

peace + ful + ness = peacefulness **[noun]**

Divide the following words. Write their parts in three columns headed prefix, root, *and* suffix. *In a fourth column, write another word that has the same prefix or the same suffix or both. Then write a definition for each word.*

1. reducible
2. nonresistance
3. invocation
4. antiterrorist
5. interviewer
6. semiconsciousness
7. untimely
8. professional
9. mistakable
10. desalinize

DILBERT reprinted by permission of United
Feature Syndicate, Inc.

Part Three

● ● ● ● ● ● ● ● ● ● ● ● ● ● ● ●

Composition

The Writing Process

• • • • • • • • • • • • • • •

Writing is a process done in different stages. These stages are listed below.

- prewriting
- drafting
- revising and editing
- proofreading
- publishing and presenting

These stages may be repeated several times during the Writing Process, and they need not necessarily follow one another in order. You can go back and forth between steps as often as you wish. You can repeat whichever steps you need to repeat until you get the result you want. The diagram on the next page shows you how the Writing Process works for most people.

THE WRITING PROCESS

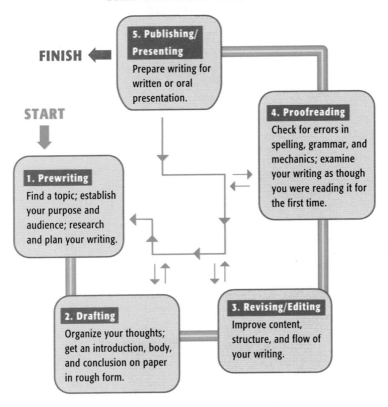

START

FINISH

5. Publishing/ Presenting
Prepare writing for written or oral presentation.

1. Prewriting
Find a topic; establish your purpose and audience; research and plan your writing.

4. Proofreading
Check for errors in spelling, grammar, and mechanics; examine your writing as though you were reading it for the first time.

2. Drafting
Organize your thoughts; get an introduction, body, and conclusion on paper in rough form.

3. Revising/Editing
Improve content, structure, and flow of your writing.

STAGE 1: PREWRITING

During Prewriting, you decide what you want to write about by exploring ideas, feelings, and memories. Prewriting is the stage in which you not only decide what your topic is, but

- you refine, focus, and explore your topic
- you gather information about your topic
- you make notes about what you want to say about it
- you think about your audience and your purpose

Your audience is whoever will read your work. Your purpose is what you hope to accomplish through your writing.

After you've decided on a topic and explored it, making notes about what you will include, you will need to arrange

COMPOSITION

and organize your ideas. This is also done during the Pre-writing stage, before you actually draft your paper.

There are many techniques you can use to generate ideas and define and explore your topic.

Calvin and Hobbes
by Bill Watterson

CHOOSING AND EXPLORING YOUR TOPIC

Keeping a Journal

Many writing ideas come to us as we go about our daily lives. A journal, or log, can help you record your thoughts from day to day. You can then refer to this record when you're searching for a writing topic. Every day you can write in your journal your experiences, observations, thoughts, feelings, and opinions. Keep newspaper and magazine clippings, photos, songs, poems, and anything else that catches your interest. They might later suggest questions that lead to writing topics. Try to add to your journal every day. Use your imagination. Be inventive and don't worry about grammar, spelling, or punctuation. This is your own personal record. It's for your benefit only, and no one else will read it.

Freewriting

Freewriting means just what it says: writing freely without worrying about grammar, punctuation, spelling, logic, or anything. You just write what comes to your mind. Choose a topic and a time limit and then just start writing ideas as they come to you. If you run out of ideas, repeat the same word over and over until a new idea occurs to you. When the time is up, review what you've written. The ideas that most interest you are likely to be the ones that will be most worth writing about. You can use your journal as a place for freewriting, or you can just take a piece of paper and start the process. The important thing is to allow your mind to follow its own path as you explore a topic. You'll be surprised where it might lead you.

1. Let your thoughts flow; write ideas, memories, anything that comes to mind.
2. Don't edit or judge your thoughts; just write them down. You can evaluate them later. In fact, evaluating your ideas at this point would probably dry up the flow. Accepting any idea that comes is the way to encourage more ideas.
3. Don't worry about spelling, punctuation, grammar, or even sense; just keep writing.
4. If you get stuck, just keep writing the same word, phrase, or sentence over and over until another idea occurs to you.

Brainstorming

Brainstorming is another technique you can use to generate ideas. It's often effective to do your brainstorming with other people because one idea can spark other ideas. Start with a key word or idea. Then list other ideas as they occur to you. Don't worry about the order. Just let your ideas flow freely from one to the next.

1. Choose someone to list ideas as they are called out. Use a chalk-board or a large pad of paper on an easel so that everyone can see the list.
2. Start with a topic or a question.
3. Encourage everyone to join in freely.
4. Accept all ideas; don't evaluate them now.
5. Follow each idea as far as it goes.

Clustering

Write your topic in the middle of a piece of paper. As you think about the topic, briefly write down everything that comes to mind. Each time you write something, draw a circle around it and draw lines to connect those circles to the main idea in the center. Continue to think about the secondary ideas and add offshoots to them. Draw circles around those related ideas and connect them to the secondary ideas. (See the model on the facing page.)

Clustering TIP

1. Start with a key word or phrase circled in the center of your paper.
2. Brainstorm to discover related ideas; circle each one and connect it to the central idea.
3. Branch out with new ideas that add details to existing ideas. Use as many circles as you need.
4. Review your chart, looking for ideas that interest you.

COMPOSITION

Clustering

Collecting Information

Whether you're deciding on your topic or exploring a topic you've already chosen, you need to get information about it. You can begin the process of collecting information with one or more of the following activities: asking questions, doing library research, observing, and interviewing. You may find that you'll want to use all four of these methods to gather information.

Asking Questions To discover the facts you need, begin by writing a list of questions about your topic. Different questions serve different purposes, and knowing what kind of question to ask can be as important as knowing how to ask it clearly. The chart on the following page will help you categorize your list of questions.

PERSONAL QUESTIONS	ask about your responses to a topic. They help you explore your experiences and tastes.
CREATIVE QUESTIONS	ask you to compare your subject to something else or to imagine observing your subject as someone else might. Such questions can expand your perspective on a subject.
ANALYTICAL QUESTIONS	ask about structure and function: How is this topic constructed? What is its purpose? Analytical questions help you evaluate and draw conclusions.
INFORMATIONAL QUESTIONS	ask for facts, statistics, or details.

Library Research If your topic requires information you don't already have, your school or public library is the best place to find what you need. The following tips can aid you in your search.

Library TIP

1. Search for books by title, author, and subject, using either the card catalog or the online computer system.
2. Use the subject headings for each listing as cross-references to related material.
3. Browse among other books in the section in which you locate a useful book.
4. Jot down the author, title, and call number of each book you think you will use.
5. Record the titles of books that don't provide help (so you won't search for them again).
6. Examine each book's bibliography for related titles.
7. Try to be an independent researcher but ask a librarian for help if you can't locate much information on your topic.

If you do your research on the Internet, evaluate your sources carefully and always find at least one more source to verify each point. The reliability of Internet information varies a great deal. It's a good idea to use print sources to verify information you find on the Internet, if possible.

Observing One good starting point for exploring a topic is simply to observe closely and list the details you see. After you've listed the details, arrange them in categories. The categories you choose depend on the details you observe and your writing goal. For example, you might want to organize your details by space order, by time order, or by order of importance.

Interviewing Get your information directly from the source: Interview someone. By asking questions, you can get the specific information you need or want. Follow these steps:

BEFORE THE INTERVIEW	Make the appointment.
	Investigate your topic and learn about your source.
	Prepare four or five basic questions.
DURING THE INTERVIEW	Ask informational questions (who, what, where, when, why, and how).
	Listen carefully.
	Ask follow-up questions.
	Take accurate notes (or tape-record with permission).
AFTER THE INTERVIEW	Write a more detailed account of the interview.
	Contact your source to clarify points or to double-check facts.

IDENTIFYING PURPOSE AND AUDIENCE

Purpose

Before you start to write, you must determine the primary purpose for your writing: to inform or explain, to persuade, to amuse or entertain, to narrate, or to describe. Sometimes you might want to accomplish more than one purpose, so you will have a primary purpose and a secondary purpose. To determine the primary purpose, answer these questions:

1. Do I want to tell a story?
2. Do I want to describe someone or something?
3. Do I want to inform my readers about the topic or to explain something about it?
4. Do I want to persuade my readers to change their minds about something or take some action?
5. Do I want to amuse or entertain?

Audience

Your audience is anyone who will be reading your writing. Sometimes you write just for yourself. Most often, however, you write to share information with others. Your audience might include a few friends or family members, your classmates, the population at large, or just your teacher. As you write, consider these questions:

1. Who will my audience be? What do I want to say to them?
2. What do my readers already know about my topic?
3. What types of information will interest my audience?

ARRANGING AND ORGANIZING IDEAS

Once you've gathered your information and ideas, you can choose from many kinds of details—examples, facts, statistics, reasons, and concrete and sensory details—to support your main idea. As a writer, you need to organize these details and put them in order. Your purpose and main idea will determine which kinds of supporting details you include as well as the order in which you arrange them. Some possible patterns of organization are

- chronological order (by time)
- spatial order (relationships based on space, place, or setting)
- order of importance
- cause and effect (events described as reason and result, motive and reaction, stimulus and response)
- comparison and contrast (measuring items against one another to show similarities and differences)

The technique you choose to organize details might be as simple as making a list or an outline that shows how the details will be grouped under larger subtopics or headings. You can also organize details visually by making a chart. You might better be able to see a plan for organizing your paper when you see the relationships among the parts of your topic.

STAGE 2: DRAFTING

When you write your draft, your goal is to organize the facts and details you have accumulated into unified paragraphs. Make sure each paragraph has a main idea and does not bring in unrelated information. The main idea should be stated in a topic sentence, and it must be supported by details that explain and clarify it. Details can be facts and statistics, examples or incidents, or sensory details.

Writing a draft, or turning your ideas into paragraphs, is a stage in the Writing Process and a tool in itself. During Prewriting, you started to organize your details. You will continue to do this as you write your draft because you might find links between ideas that give new meanings to your words and phrases. Continue to organize your details using one of the methods discussed in Prewriting.

To make your sentences interesting, vary their length. Don't use too many short sentences. Doing so will make your writing sound choppy. Use some short sentences and some long ones, but don't connect all your ideas with the word *and*.

You can use the ideas on sentence combining in Chapter 14 to combine and vary your sentences. You can use prepositional phrases, appositive phrases, and adjective and adverb clauses to make your sentences more interesting.

Your writing will also be easier for your audience to understand if you follow the Writing Tip below.

Writing Tip

Your composition should consist of three parts: the introduction, the body, and the conclusion (see the outline on page 370). Begin your paper with an **introduction** that grabs the reader's interest and sets the tone. The introduction usually gives the reader a brief explanation of what your paper is about and often includes the **thesis.** The thesis states your paper's main idea. The main idea is what you're trying to prove or what you're supporting.

Each paragraph in the **body,** or main part, of your paper should have a topic sentence that states what the paragraph is about. The rest of the paragraph should include details that support the topic sentence. Similarly, each topic sentence should support the thesis, or main idea of the paper.

End your paper with a good **conclusion** that gives a feeling of completeness. You might conclude your paper in any of the following ways:

- Summarize what you've said in the body of your paper.
- Restate the main idea (using different words).
- Give a final example or fact.
- Make a comment on the topic or give a personal reaction to it.
- End with a quotation that sums up the topic or comments on it.
- Call for some action (especially in persuasive papers).

STAGE 3: REVISING/EDITING

The purposes of Revising are to make sure that your writing is clear and well organized, that it accomplishes your goals, and that it reaches your audience. The word *revision* means "seeing again." You need to look at your writing again, seeing it as another person might. To accomplish this, you might just read your paper very carefully, or you might tape-record yourself reading your paper aloud and then listen to the tape to evaluate what you've written. The revision phase, however, often includes other people. You might share your writing with another student, a small group of students, or your teacher, who can suggest improvements. The ideas and opinions of others will tell you whether you're achieving your goals. After you evaluate your work, you might want to move some sentences around or change them completely. You might want to add or cut information. Mark these changes right on your draft and then include them in your final copy.

The revision stage is the point at which you can

- improve paragraphs
- use self-evaluation and peer evaluation
- check content and structure
- make sure the language is specific and descriptive
- check unity and coherence
- check style and tone

For Better or For Worse®   **by Lynn Johnston**

© Lynn Johnston Productions, Inc./Distributed
by United Feature Syndicate, Inc.

The phrases and clauses of a sentence must be parallel. This means that elements that have the same function in a sentence must be written in the same form.

The bears like napping under a tree and to splash in the lake. In this sentence, *napping under a tree and to splash in the lake* is a compound direct object. It tells what bears like. However, the first element, *napping under a tree,* is a gerund phrase. The second, *to splash in the lake,* is an infinitive phrase. To make the elements parallel, make both gerund phrases or infinitive phrases.

The bears like napping under a tree and splashing in the lake.

The bears like to nap under a tree and to splash in the lake.

Identify the elements that should be parallel in each sentence below. Then revise the faulty parallelism in each sentence.

1. Going to college and to get a teaching job are my goals.

2. The team's assets are a great offense and having a positive attitude.

3. The new magazine published articles to educate young voters about the issues and getting them familiar with the candidates.

4. To direct traffic and investigating accidents were the police officer's duties.

5. Beautiful beaches and having good weather draw visitors to Hawaii.

Writing Tip

It was once acceptable to use the masculine pronouns *he, him,* and *his* to refer to nouns that might be either male or female. This practice is now considered unfair and outdated. Instead of writing *A reporter must check his facts,* you can write *Reporters must check their facts* or *Reporters must check the facts* or *A reporter must check his or her facts.* Of course, if you're writing about a specific person, you should use a suitable pronoun: *This reporter loves her work.*

STAGE 4: PROOFREADING

The purposes of Proofreading are to make sure that you've spelled all words correctly and that your sentences are grammatically correct. Proofread your writing and correct mistakes in capitalization, punctuation, and spelling. Refer to the following chart for Proofreading symbols to help you during this stage of the Writing Process.

Proofreading Marks		
Marks	**Meaning**	**Example**
∧	Insert	My gra$\overset{d}{\wedge}$nmother is eighty-six years old.
℘	Delete	She grew up on a dair$\overset{\text{/}}{r}$y farm.
# ∧	Insert space	She milked$\overset{\text{\#}}{\wedge}$cows every morning.
⌒	Close up space	She fed the chickens in the bar$\overset{\frown}{n}$yard.
=	Capitalize	$\underset{=}{\text{times}}$ have changed.
/	Make lowercase	Machines now do the /Milking.
⟳ sp	Check spelling	Chickens are fed ⟨automatically.⟩ $\overset{sp}{\wedge}$
⁀	Switch order	Modern farms are⟨like⟩more factories.
¶	New paragraph	¶Last year I returned to the farm.

STAGE 5: PUBLISHING/PRESENTING

This is the stage at which you share your work with others. You might read your work aloud in class, submit it to the school newspaper, or give it to a friend to read. There are many avenues for Presenting your work.

Chapter 17

Modes of Writing

●●●●●●●●●●●●●●●●

17.1 DESCRIPTIVE WRITING

An effective written description is one that presents a clear picture to the reader. You can use descriptive writing to help your reader see what you see, hear what you hear, and feel what you feel. Good descriptive writing involves these skills:

- using your senses to observe
- selecting precise details
- organizing your ideas

OBSERVING AND TAKING NOTES

Writing a good description begins with careful observation. You use your sight, touch, smell, hearing, and taste to experience the world. These sensory details can add richness to your descriptions of people, places, things, and experiences. Before you take notes, close your eyes and picture what you want to describe. Then list words and phrases that tell how it looks, feels, smells, sounds, or tastes.

If you can't find just the right word, turn to a **thesaurus.** A thesaurus is a reference book that groups together words with similar meanings.

Using Your Experience and Imagination

You are able to describe people, places, things, and situations because you first perceive the details through your senses. You see that your friend has curly red hair. You smell the hot, buttered popcorn at the movies. You can take those details from your own experience and use them in descriptive writing.

Focusing on the Details

Descriptive writing often starts with a memory or an observation—something that catches your attention. The details that make someone or something stay in your mind become the raw material for composing a description.

Start with your first impressions—the things you first notice about a person, a place, a thing, or an experience. Then start gathering details. One way is to identify the small things that help produce each impression.

Asking yourself questions can also help you choose details. For example, you might ask how something appears at different times of the day, what senses you use to observe it, or to what you might compare it.

WRITING THE DESCRIPTION

Using Specific Words

A good description includes specific nouns, vivid verbs, and exact adjectives.

- A specific noun, *beagle* or *Rover,* is more informative than the general noun *dog.*
- A vivid verb such as *stroll, amble, saunter, march, tramp,* or *hike* tells the reader more than a pale verb like *walk.*

- Exact adjectives—*seventy-six* rather than *many; lanky, gaunt, bony,* or *gangly* instead of *thin*—give a clearer picture than vague, indefinite ones.

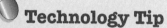

Technology Tip

Your word-processing program may have a built-in thesaurus to help you find the precise word you need.

Ordering Descriptive Details

When details are presented in a sensible order, readers get a picture in their minds. To order your own descriptive details, you might think of your eye as a camera lens. First, choose a starting point. Then decide on the best way to move your eye's camera across your subject. One way is to start at the front and move toward the back. Another way is to start at one side and move toward the other side. Still another way is to start from a far point and move to a near one. The order you use should be one that will make sense to your readers. When you're writing a description, make a sketch of the scene. The sketch can help you decide how to order your details.

A painter arranges details so the viewer sees an ordered picture. A writer describes details so the reader imagines a scene clearly. Writers, like painters, arrange the details of a scene in a certain order and for a particular reason. How you order your details depends on your purpose. Describing a skyscraper from bottom to top emphasizes the building's height. A description of the Grand Canyon might show details in the order a descending hiker sees them. Writers can order details in several ways, depending on the point in space that seems a logical starting place. Details can be ordered from top to bottom, from near to far, or from left to right. Ordering your details according to their place in the picture is called **spatial order**.

Using Transitions

When you use spatial order, you must give your audience a way to picture the scene as you move from one detail to the next. Transition words, such as *under, to the right,* and *behind,* help link details so readers can follow the path you've made.

Transition words show how the details in a description are related, and they make the description easier to follow. Transitions are powerful tools. Without them, you just have a list of details—not a description. Transition words and phrases can turn the details into vivid images. The chart on the next page shows some additional transition words and phrases you can use.

COMPOSITION

TRANSITION WORDS AND PHRASES

above	between	nearby
among	beyond	over
around	in back of	overhead
before	in front of	past
behind	in the distance	to the left of
below	inside	to the right of
beside	near	under

SUMMARY

As you write your description, use sensory details to bring your subject to life. Remember these tips:

- Use precise language.
- Follow spatial order.
- Include transitions.

17.2 NARRATIVE WRITING

A narrative is a story or an account of an event. There are historical narratives, fictional narratives, and real-life narratives. When you write a story, or narrative, you answer the question *What happened?* Your story will need a beginning, a middle, and an end. It will also need a setting, a conflict and solution, characters, and, perhaps, dialogue.

Plot Suppose you've seen a movie, and a friend asks you what the movie was about. You would probably tell what happened through a series of events. What happens in a narrative is called the **plot.**

Characters As you talk about the events of the plot, you will find yourself talking about the **characters.** Characters are the people or animals that take part in the events.

Setting A story also has a **setting.** The setting puts the characters in a certain place at a certain time. Stories can be set in the present, the past, or the future. What happens in the story and how characters look and act often depend on the time when the events take place.

EXPLORING NARRATIVE IDEAS

The plot of most good stories centers on a problem faced by a character. Focusing on a problem that needs solving is one good way to come up with story ideas.

Once you have an idea you like, you can start developing it into a full-length story. Asking yourself questions like those listed in the chart below will help you plan a series of events. Some events will help solve the problem in your story. Others may make the solution more difficult.

QUESTIONS ABOUT STORY IDEAS
1. What is the problem?
2. What characters are involved?
3. What happened before?
4. What will happen next?
5. What is the solution to the problem?

Planning Your Story

Plan some elements of your story before you begin writing. Think about the characters and events and how the setting affects them. Writing down some details about the important story elements—plot, characters, and setting—can ease you into writing.

COMPOSITION

Establishing Your Point of View

In narrative writing, the point of view is important. Some stories are told by a main character in the first person—using *I* or *we.* First-person narratives tell only what the narrator witnesses and thinks. The reader sees all the events through the narrator's eyes and views them as the narrator views them. Other stories are told by an observer in the third person—using *he, she,* or *they.* The narrator of a third-person story may describe events from a single character's view, or the narrator may reveal the thoughts and feelings of all the characters.

WRITING YOUR STORY

Your narrative will eventually bring together plot, setting, and characters. As you write, focus on one of these three elements. Choose the element that seems most striking. Then start writing about this element and notice how the other elements find their way into the story.

Writing Tip

1. Start writing and keep writing.
2. Let your story tell itself.
3. Try to see and hear your story as you write. Think of your story as a movie unfolding before your eyes.
4. Take a break if you get stuck.

Beginning Your Story

A good story begins by grabbing the reader's attention. Think about what makes you keep reading a story. Is it an exciting plot? Intriguing characters? An unusual writing style? Some writers work and rework the beginning of a story until they get it just the way they want it. Other writers draft the entire story first. Then they look for the catchiest line or the first dramatic moment and move that to the beginning.

Sometimes revising a story opening means looking at the rest of what you've written to find the best place to start. You might look for the most engaging sentences and start your story at that point.

Other times you may keep the beginning you have but make a few changes. Cutting unimportant words or adding descriptive details can give more impact to your story beginning. Remember that a good story beginning is what gets your readers interested and keeps them reading.

Keeping a Story on Track

When you begin to write your narrative, you may find that you have too many details to tell. Choose only the details that are essential to your story. If you do this, your readers won't get confused by ideas that don't really matter. Sometimes you may have to cut out some details in order to keep the most important details clear. You may be able to use the details you cut out at another time in another story.

Putting Events in Order

To tell a story that is clear, the events and details must be arranged in a logical order. After you've chosen the important events for your narrative, you need to place them in some particular order. **Chronological order** is an effective way to organize your story. A story is in chronological order when the events are presented in the time order in which they occurred. When you use time order, you tell what happened first, second, and so on. You may use words like *then, next,* and *later* or phrases like *in the meantime, early in the morning,* and *about nine o'clock that night.* These words will help your readers follow your story.

MUTTS

BY PATRICK M^CDONNELL

Using Transitions

Certain words and phrases, called **transitions,** can help readers keep track of the order of events in your writing. Some examples of transitions are *before, after, until then, next, first, later, afterward,* and *finally.*

Writing Tip

In writing a narrative, vary your transitions. If you always use *first, next,* and *finally,* your writing may sound dull.

Writing Dialogue

Dialogue is the words spoken by the characters in a narrative. Well-written dialogue can help bring characters and events to life. What characters say, and how they say it, will often reveal what they're like. Dialogue can help show the moods, interests, and personalities of different characters.

Your dialogue will sound natural if your characters talk the way real people talk. You can use slang, sentence fragments, contractions, and descriptions of facial expressions and body language.

When you write dialogue, you need to help your readers keep track of who is speaking.

- Enclose the exact words of a speaker in quotation marks.
- Use phrases such as *Molly said* or *Jake replied.*
- Begin a new paragraph for each speaker.

Finishing the Job

Every well-written narrative has a conclusion. One type of conclusion sums up the story and reflects on what happened. The conclusion should give your audience the feeling that the story is complete.

SUMMARY

A narrative has plot, characters, and setting. These three elements contribute to a conflict and a solution. In writing a narrative, remember these tips:

- Establish a point of view.
- Reveal your characters' personalities through appropriate dialogue.
- Make the order of the events clear with transitions.

17.3 EXPOSITORY WRITING

The goal of expository writing is to explain or inform. The following chart shows four approaches to expository writing.

These approaches can be used alone, or they can be combined in any expository piece of writing.

APPROACHES TO EXPOSITORY WRITING	
APPROACH	**Example**
DEFINITION	*Sivuquad,* a name for St. Lawrence Island, means "squeezed dry." The islanders believed that a giant had made the island from dried mud.
COMPARE-CONTRAST	Coastal fishing fleets often stay at sea for days or weeks. Long-range fishing vessels may remain at sea for months.
PROCESS	To breathe, a whale surfaces in a forward rolling motion. For two seconds, it blows out and breathes in as much as twenty-one hundred quarts of air.
CAUSE-EFFECT	The discovery of oil and gas in Alaska in 1968 led to widespread development in that region of the world.

DEFINING

Defining a term or an idea is one approach to expository writing. You can give a formal definition or a personal definition. In a formal definition, you should provide specific qualities of the term you're explaining to help your audience understand it. For a personal definition, you might use real-life examples and vivid details. These examples and details will express your personal feelings about the idea or term.

Organize Your Definition Begin your research with a dictionary or other reliable source. After you've written the basic definition or idea, you can add details. When you write your draft, try different orders of organization. You might want to start with the basic definition and move to a broader sense of the term, or you could begin with details and examples and conclude with the basic definition.

COMPARING AND CONTRASTING

Comparison-contrast is another kind of expository writing. When you compare two things, you explain how they're similar. When you contrast two things, you explain how they're different. Comparing and contrasting two items can be a useful way of explaining them.

Examine Your Subjects A good way to begin your comparison-contrast piece is with a careful examination. First, think about one subject and list descriptive details that go with that subject. Then make a list of the same kinds of details for your other subject. For example, if you were going to compare Superman and Batman, you might note that Batman travels by car and wears a mask and a cape. Then you would make a list of the same kinds of details for Superman.

Sort What You See Once you've listed some details, you can sort them for comparison and contrast. At this point, some writers use a Venn diagram like the one below. A Venn diagram is made of two ovals or circles. Each circle contains the details of one of the subjects. Details that the two subjects have in common go where the circles overlap.

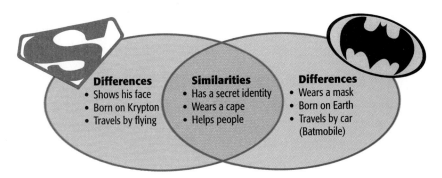

Differences
- Shows his face
- Born on Krypton
- Travels by flying

Similarities
- Has a secret identity
- Wears a cape
- Helps people

Differences
- Wears a mask
- Born on Earth
- Travels by car (Batmobile)

After you've made a Venn diagram, you're ready to write. Details you pull from the middle of the Venn diagram are similarities. Details pulled from the outsides are differences.

Organize the Details There are two ways to organize a comparison-contrast piece.

- One way is by subject. In this method, you discuss all the details about one subject first and then all the details about the other subject.
- The second way to organize your details is by feature. In this method, you choose one feature and discuss the similarities and differences for both subjects. Then you do the same thing for another feature and so on until you've covered all the features.

EXPLAINING A PROCESS

To explain a process, choose a topic you know well. Then identify your audience and what they may already know. Locate terms they'll understand and those you'll have to explain. Be clear about your purpose.

Make the Order Clear Before you write about a process, gather information through research, observation, or interviews. List the steps of the process in chronological order. Then write. Use transition words to help make the order of the steps clear for the reader. *First, then, after, next, later, while,* and *finally* are some useful transition words in explaining a process.

USING CAUSE-AND-EFFECT RELATIONSHIPS

Sometimes events are connected in a cause-and-effect relationship. A cause is an identifiable condition or event. An effect is something that happens as a direct result of that condition or event.

A cause-and-effect explanation may show one cause and one effect. It may explain a series of effects resulting from a single cause. It can also present multiple causes and multiple effects.

Sometimes a cause and its effect form part of a chain of events. One cause may lead to an effect, and that effect may in turn change circumstances and lead to another effect. The example below shows how this cause-and-effect chain works.

Below-freezing weather occurs. ➡ Frost damages the orange crop. ➡ Fewer oranges are available than in other years, but demand doesn't fall. ➡ Oranges and orange juice become more expensive.

Organize Your Explanation You can organize your cause-and-effect explanation in one of two ways. One method involves identifying a cause and then explaining its effects. The other method involves stating an effect and then discussing its cause or causes. After you've completed your draft, review it to be sure the cause-and-effect relationships are clear. Use transition words such as *so, if, then, since, because, therefore,* and *as a result* to clarify the relationships.

Using Details Supporting details are the heart of expository writing. The details you select will depend on the approach you've chosen. The chart below shows different kinds of details that might be included in a report about the planet Mercury.

KINDS OF DETAILS	
FACTS	Mercury is nearer the sun than any other planet in our solar system.
STATISTICS	Mercury rotates once in about fifty-nine Earth days. Its orbit around the sun takes about eighty-eight Earth days.
EXAMPLES/ INCIDENTS	The temperature on Mercury could melt lead.
REASONS	Because Mercury is so close to the sun, the daylight side of the planet is extremely hot.

Arranging Details Once you've selected supporting details for your explanation, you're ready to organize them. Ask yourself what you're trying to do in your essay. For example, are you going to show the cause and effect of tornadoes? Are you going to use a comparison-contrast essay to point out the similarities and differences between two planets? Questions such as these can help you organize your ideas—the supporting details—logically.

You might choose a number of ways to arrange information and supporting details. If you're defining something, you might arrange features from most to least significant. If you're writing about a process, then **chronological order,** or time order, might be more logical.

SUMMARY

Expository writing explains and informs. You can include one or more of these elements:

- definitions
- step-by-step processes
- comparison and contrast
- cause-and-effect relationships

You can support your explanation with facts, statistics, examples, incidents, and reasons. Use appropriate transition words and phrases to make relationships clear.

17.4 PERSUASIVE WRITING

Look around you. Magazines, newspapers, books, posters, letters, radio and television programs—almost anything you read, see, or hear can include persuasion. One purpose of persuasive writing is to make readers, listeners, or viewers think or feel a certain way about an idea or a product. Another purpose is to make people take action. Sometimes it does both. When you write to persuade, you try to convince your audience to think or act in a particular way. In order to persuade, you must catch and hold the attention of your audience.

Often persuasive writing begins by stating the writer's goal. Then evidence—information to support that goal—follows. Some supporting statements will make you think ("The rain forest is disappearing at the rate of. . . ."). Some supporting statements will make you feel a certain way ("You won't fit in unless you wear. . . ."). Finally, there is usually a reminder of what the writer wants you to do or think.

FORMING AN OPINION

In most persuasive writing, the writer states an opinion or urges an action and then offers reasons to convince readers to accept the opinion or support the action. Reasons are often supported by facts, statistics, and examples.

Once you take a stand on an issue, you must provide support for it. At the same time, you should also consider arguments your opponents might make against your position.

When you're searching for a topic, explore experiences from your daily life that inspire strong opinions. Make a list. Write names of people, places, or things and jot down your thoughts about each. Freewrite for about ten minutes to see where your writing leads you. Journal entries can also help you find a topic. Sometimes just reading your entries will remind you of something you feel strongly about.

When you have a topic or a goal you really care about, the challenge is to win over your audience. As you choose a goal for your persuasive piece, answer the questions in the chart below. If you can answer yes to each question, you've found a good topic.

FINDING A PERSUASIVE WRITING TOPIC
1. Do I feel strongly about this topic?
2. Do people disagree about this topic?
3. Do I have enough to say about this topic to persuade others to accept my position?

Once you have a topic, think about your position on it. Sometimes when you learn more about a topic, your position changes. Other times you may discover that your opinion is the same as everyone else's. Exploring a topic helps you discover whether it's a suitable one for a writing project.

In persuasive writing, a key ingredient is the statement of what you want your audience to do or think. You can express that in a topic sentence, which may appear either at the beginning or at the end of your opening paragraph.

One way to explore a topic is to list the reasons people might agree or disagree with you. You can put these reasons in a chart headed "Pro" and "Con." A pro-and-con chart can help you organize your thoughts, make your opinion clearer, and help you determine why or how others might argue against your opinion.

CONSIDERING YOUR AUDIENCE

Why should people adopt your ideas? You need to provide convincing reasons. Whenever you try to convince someone of something, you need to keep your audience in mind. Consider the following questions.

THINKING ABOUT YOUR AUDIENCE
1. Who is my audience?
2. How much does my audience know about my topic?
3. Does my audience care about this topic?
4. What evidence will be most interesting to my readers?
5. What evidence will be most convincing to my readers?

Different people have different interests and different levels of knowledge. Choose reasons that will appeal to your audience. When your goal is to influence opinions, you need to know who your readers are and how they think.

SUPPORTING YOUR OPINION

Research is an important step in persuasive writing. Your opinions will carry weight only if you can back them up. To gather support, investigate your topic by reading, observing, and discussing, and sometimes by interviewing experts— people with special knowledge about the issue.

One way to build an argument is to list reasons that support your opinion. Your list of pros and cons is a good source of reasons. The next step is to gather evidence to support your reasons. What kinds of evidence will you use to support your position and your reasons? Persuading people to change their attitudes or to take action requires evidence. Evidence comes in two forms: facts and opinions.

Facts Facts are statements that can be proved. For example, the statement "Snakes are not slimy" is a fact. You could prove it by touching a snake or by reading about snakes. Statistics, or facts expressed in numbers, are one form of factual support. Examples are another.

Opinions An opinion is a personal belief or feeling. It can't be proved. The opinions of experts, however, can be powerful evidence. Personal experience can also be good evidence.

Test your argument to discover possible arguments against it. Use your list of pros and cons to discover any weak links or places where your evidence is unconvincing. Decide how to strengthen any weaknesses you discover.

Calvin and Hobbes

by Bill Watterson

Chapter 17 Modes of Writing **355**

EVIDENCE IN PERSUASIVE WRITING		
KINDS	**Examples**	
FACT	Americans spent 33 billion dollars on the diet industry in 1990.	
STATISTIC	In 1990, 34 percent of men and 38 percent of women spent 33 billion dollars on diets.	
EXAMPLE	A preteen boy guzzles protein drinks, hoping to increase his size and strength.	
OPINION	Well-known diet specialist Dr. Luz Waite recommends regular exercise along with any weight-loss plan.	

Not all pieces of evidence are equally strong. Some "facts" are really opinions in disguise. When you write persuasively, check your facts to make sure they back up your point.

ORGANIZING YOUR ARGUMENT

After you gather your evidence, review it piece by piece. Which evidence is the strongest or most convincing? Sometimes you might want to put the strongest piece of evidence first in your paper. Other times you might want to save it until the end. Decide which order of evidence best supports your goal.

Make a list of your evidence in the order that seems most persuasive. Use this list to draft your persuasive argument. Of course, you may change the order of the evidence during revision.

The structure of a persuasive piece can resemble the three-part structure of a report. The introduction states the topic and your opinion on it. The body provides evidence to support your opinion. The conclusion summarizes your argument and suggests action.

Tips for Structuring a Persuasive Piece

1. Decide how to arrange your evidence.
2. Write a strong opening that states your position clearly.
3. Present suitable supporting evidence in the best order.
4. Anticipate and answer opposing arguments.
5. Begin or end with your strongest point.
6. Sum up your argument and give your conclusions.

SUMMARY

The goal of persuasive writing is to make people think or act in a certain way. Remember these tips:

- State your position clearly and forcefully.
- Consider your audience.
- Include suitable supporting details in the form of facts and opinions.
- Arrange your evidence in the most effective way.

Research Report Writing

• • • • • • • • • • • • • • •

When you write a research report, you investigate a topic and present information about the topic to your readers. You've probably seen such reports in newspapers and magazines. Journalists write these reports to investigate such topics as politics, environmental issues, and business concerns. They use a variety of sources to find information, and then they present this information to their readers.

To write a report, you should

- choose a topic that interests you
- decide on a purpose for your report
- gather information from sources
- take notes, organize your notes, and write an outline
- write about your purpose and main idea in a thesis statement
- present the information about your topic to your readers in your own words
- prepare a list of your sources

18.1 PREWRITING

CHOOSE A GOOD TOPIC

Keep two important things in mind when you're planning a research report.

1. Select a topic that interests you. Ask yourself, What are my favorite subjects? What would I like to know more about?

2. Narrow the topic so that you can cover it thoroughly.

When you prepare to write a research report, write down a list of things that interest you. You may find it helpful to freewrite in your journal to see where your thoughts lead you.

Calvin and **Hobbes**   by **Bill Watterson**

Narrow Your Topic

Every subject contains both broad general topics and narrower topics. Before you can begin writing your research report, you need to choose an appropriate topic.

COMPOSITION

- If you choose a topic that is **too broad**—such as sports—you won't be able to cover the topic thoroughly.
- If you choose a topic that is **too narrow**—such as a particular type of mountain bike—you may not find enough facts and statistics for your report.

Are you writing a two-page report or a five-page report? Use a chart like the one that follows to narrow your topic so that you can present it to your readers' satisfaction.

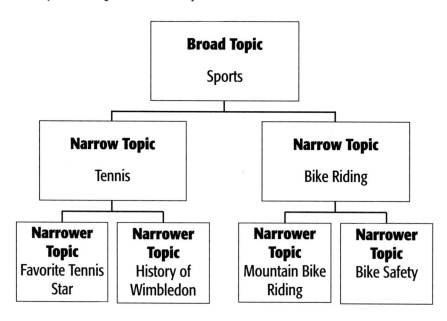

Answer the following questions to make sure you have chosen the right topic.

1. How long is your report supposed to be?
2. How much information about your topic can you find?
3. What element of the general subject interests you most?

FIND THE INFORMATION

Now it's time to gather the information you'll need to begin drafting your report. Reports are built on facts, statistics, examples, and expert opinions, so you'll need to do some research.

Encyclopedias and other reference books are a good place to begin looking. The information in these books can help you pinpoint your search. They can also help you to ask questions about your topic and lead you to other resources. Here is a list of the sources you can use to investigate your topic.

- reference books, such as encyclopedias, almanacs, atlases, and dictionaries
- books
- magazines
- newspapers
- pamphlets
- nonprint resources, such as videotapes and audiotapes
- Internet sources
- computer software programs
- experts—anyone who has valuable information about the topic you're investigating

Evaluate the Information

As you look for information from these sources, you must decide how reliable the information is. One way to do this is by identifying facts and opinions.

Facts Facts can be proved. Statistics and other information that can be proved true are facts.

Opinions Opinions cannot be proved; they are what people think about facts. You should include only the opinions of experts in your report. The opinions of experts are more reliable than the opinions of nonexperts.

Another way to decide if a source is reliable is to consider bias. Authors who are biased support a particular point of view. They'll probably include only information that supports their point of view. Because of this, you may not get a complete picture from a biased source.

Technology Tip

Evaluate Internet Sources Not all Internet sites contain accurate information. To make sure the information from a site is accurate, find another source with the same information.

Use Primary and Secondary Sources

Primary Sources Primary sources give you information that has not been gathered and shaped in a certain way by someone else. Examples of primary sources include these:

- A person close to the event or topic you're investigating. For example, someone who lives on a farm would be a primary source for a report on farm life.
- A real journal, a letter, or a document from the period you're investigating

Research TIP

A teacher may be a valuable primary source for you. For a report about tennis, for example, you might interview a school tennis coach.

Secondary Sources Books and magazines are generally considered secondary sources, which means that another writer has gathered the information and shaped it in a certain way. For example, a newspaper article about life on a farm would be a secondary source.

Conduct an Interview

When possible, your research should include primary sources. Interviews with people who know about your topic can give you firsthand information you probably couldn't find anywhere else.

Once you've identified an expert on your subject, contact him or her to see if and when an interview is possible. Prepare interview questions ahead of time. The most effective interview questions are open-ended; that is, they ask for more than a yes or no answer.

QUESTIONS THAT INVITE A YES OR NO ANSWER	OPEN-ENDED QUESTIONS
1. Is it dangerous to ride a bike without a helmet?	1. Why is it dangerous to ride a bike without a helmet?
2. Do young cyclists wear bike helmets?	2. What might happen to young cyclists who don't wear helmets?

INTERVIEW TIP

When you conduct an interview, use a notebook, a tape recorder, or both to help you remember important points.

Form a Purpose

You should have a purpose, or reason, for writing your research report. After surveying your topic, choose a purpose by

- writing down three questions you hope to answer in your report
- considering which question will guide your research

An example of a question that might guide your research is, What can cyclists do to make bike riding safer? The purpose of your report will be to show your readers how to ride a bike safely.

> ## Research TIP
>
> As you learn more about your topic, you may discover an element that looks more interesting than the one you originally chose. It's not too late to change direction.

Make Note Cards

After you've found some sources, you can start to gather information. As you read, think about what is important and worth remembering. Take notes on three-by-five index cards, being sure to jot down the title and the author of each source.

- Take notes as you read—not later!
- At the top of each note card, write the subject of the note. Later this heading will help you organize your note cards and find the information you need.
- At the bottom of each note card, write the author's name, the title of your source, and the page number where you found the information.
- Don't copy information word for word. This is called plagiarism. Instead, think about what you're reading, and then write your notes in your own words.
- If you do copy some words from a source, use quotation marks on your note card (and later in your report) to show that you're using someone else's words and ideas.
- Begin a new card each time you start a new topic or go to a new source.

Look at the following source, which was taken from a book on cycling.

Helmets come in more styles, shapes, and prices than most shops can handle. As I write this, there are at least a hundred models on the market competing for your attention. Average weight is about 9 ounces though some are as light as 6 or 7 ounces.

James C. McCullagh. <u>Cycling for Health, Fitness, and Well-being</u>, 182–183. New York: Dell Publishing, 1995.

Now look at the handwritten notes that one student made after reading the selection. Notice the differences.

Helmets
• different styles (This might encourage young people to wear them.)
• many weigh less than ten ounces

James C. McCullagh. <u>Cycling for Health, Fitness, and Well-being</u>, 182–183.

COMPOSITION

Editing TIP

Don't throw away your notes before your report is finished. If you need to check a fact as you edit your report, you can look back at your notes.

Writing Tip

When you're planning your report, remember that visual aids, such as photos, maps, and charts, can help your readers understand your points.

Make Source Cards

Keep a record of your sources (the books, magazines, encyclopedias, Internet sites, and people you interview) by using source cards. (A source card is simply a three-by-five index card.) On these source cards, you will list the information about the source. You should make a source card for each of your sources. Be sure to copy this information exactly. You will use it later to prepare a list of your sources. The information included on the example source cards that follow is recommended by the Modern Language Association.

Source Cards for Books List the author, the title of the book, the city where the book was published, the publisher, and the date of publication.

> McCullagh, James C. <u>Cycling for Health, Fitness, and Well-being</u>.
> New York: Dell Publishing, 1995.

Source Cards for Magazines Magazines can be useful for gathering up-to-date information. On your source card, list the author of the article, the title of the article, the title of the magazine, the date of the issue, and the first and last page numbers of the article. (If there's a break between the first and last pages, list only the first page number and a plus sign.)

> Rathbun, Mickey. "Play It Safe! What Is the Best Armor Against Kids' Sports Injuries? An Informed Parent." <u>Sports Illustrated for Kids</u> May 1, 1998: 10+.

Source Cards for Encyclopedias List the author (if he or she is named), the title of the article, the name of the encyclopedia, and the year of publication followed by the abbreviation *ed.,* which stands for *edition.* If the encyclopedia articles are arranged in alphabetical order, you don't need to write the volume and page numbers.

> Shepherd, Ron. "Cycling." <u>Encyclopedia of World Sport: From Ancient Times to the Present</u>. 1996 ed.

Source Cards for Online Sources Electronic resources are cited much as print resources are, but additional information is needed. You must indicate whether your source is online, CD-ROM, diskette, magnetic tape, or DVD.

Cite the information in the order that it is given in the following list. You might not be able to find everything in the list. If you can't find all the information listed here, provide as much information as you can find.

1. Author, editor, or compiler of the source
2. Title of an article, poem, or short work (in quotation marks) or title of a book (underlined); or title of a posting to a discussion line or forum followed by the phrase *Online posting*
3. Title of the scholarly project, database, or professional or personal site (underlined). If the professional or personal site has no title, use a description such as *Home page.*
4. Editor or director of the scholarly project or database

5. Date of electronic publication, of the last update, or of the posting
6. Name of the institution or organization sponsoring the Internet site or associated with it
7. Date you used the source
8. Electronic address of the source (in angle brackets)

"A Consumer's Guide to Bicycle Helmets." Bicycle Helmet Safety Institute. Mar. 8, 1998. Bicycle Helmet Safety Institute. July 15, 1998 <http://www.bhsi.org/webdocs/guide.htm>.

Interviews List the name of the person you interviewed, the type of interview (personal, telephone, or e-mail), and the date of the interview.

Smith, John. Personal Interview. July 17, 1998.

CHOOSE AN APPROACH

When you prepare your research report, decide what approach you want to take toward your topic. Here are some common approaches. You may want to look at the chart on page 348 for more information about these approaches.

- Explain how something works, using a step-by-step process.
- Compare and contrast.
- Define something.
- Point out a cause-and-effect relationship.

Different approaches work with different topics. For example, if you want to tell your readers how to use the Internet, you may find that a step-by-step approach works best.

Write a Thesis Statement

As you were doing your research, you chose a purpose for your report. Now you should write about your purpose in the form of a thesis statement. A thesis statement is a sentence that tells briefly and clearly the main idea you want your readers to understand. It tells what you want to show, prove, or explain, and it gives your report a focus.

Answer the following questions to help you compose a thesis statement for your research report:

- What is your report's purpose or main idea?
- What are some of the most important ideas you learned in your research?
- What exactly do you want your readers to know?

After you've written a thesis statement that explains exactly what you want your readers to know, you're ready to write an outline.

Write an Outline

Make a list of ideas that support your thesis statement; then organize the ideas to form an outline.

1. Review your note cards and sort them into groups with similar headings.
2. Ask yourself, What main idea does each group represent?
3. Think of the most logical way to arrange your main ideas.
4. Read every note card in each group. Which ideas support other ideas? Identify the **main headings,** or main ideas, and then identify the **subheadings,** or supporting details.
5. When you write your outline, use roman numerals to indicate main headings and capital letters to indicate subheadings.

Bicycle Safety

I. Introduction
Thesis statement: Bike safety
includes careful riding,
common sense, regular
maintenance, and proper
equipment.

These are the main headings, or main ideas.

II. Traffic Rules
  A. Hand signals
  B. Right-hand side
III. Common Sense
  A. Earphones
  B. Other passengers
  C. Night riding
IV. Maintenance

These are subheadings, or supporting details.

  A. Inspection
  B. Repairs
V. Helmets
  A. Reasons people don't wear
     them
  B. Statistics
  C. Reasons to wear one
VI. Conclusion

Study Your Draft Outline Ask yourself the following questions as you study your draft outline:

1. Is every subheading, or supporting detail, under the correct main heading, or main idea?
2. Does every main heading have at least two subheadings? If not, either do more research or delete the main heading.
3. Is your outline as complete as it can be? You should be able to write your report directly from your outline by adding details about your main headings and your subheadings.

18.2 DRAFTING

KNOW YOUR AUDIENCE

Who will read your report? You should have a certain audience in mind as you write your report. Consider this audience's interests as well as their knowledge of the subject. Remember that your readers don't have the benefit of all the background research you've done. Be sure to explain any term or process your audience might not know.

ORGANIZE YOUR REPORT

A report has three parts: an introduction, a body, and a conclusion.

1. In the **introduction,** you will catch your readers' interest and show your position on your topic. You can begin your report in several ways.
   - with a question
   - with a surprising fact or statistic
   - with a fascinating story related to the topic
   - with a striking quotation
2. In the **body** of the report, you will develop your topic. As you write the body, answer the question, What did I discover? You should include at least one paragraph for each main heading in your outline.

3. In the **conclusion,** you will summarize your topic or state your final thoughts about it.

WRITE YOUR DRAFT

Use your outline and your note cards to write a draft of your research report. To begin, arrange your note cards in the same order as the ideas in your outline. Read each roman numeral heading on your outline and skim your notes for information about that heading. As you write, you may find that you need to put your information in a different order. Your outline is only a guide. You can always change it as you write.

Don't worry about details of punctuation, spelling, or grammar as you write your draft. You can fix those later. The important thing is to express your ideas in a clear, organized way.

LIST YOUR SOURCES

When you were doing research for your report, you made source cards. These cards contain the sources of your information. Now it's time to make a list of these sources. This list will appear on a separate page at the end of your report. First, arrange the entries in alphabetical order according to the author's last name (or the work's title if there is no author indicated). Then copy the information for each source in the order in which it appears on your source card. Include the page numbers for magazine and newspaper articles. You may want to look at the sample source cards on pages 366–368 and the model list of sources on pages 378 and 379 for help.

18.3 REVISING/EDITING

EVALUATE YOUR DRAFT

When your draft is finished, set it aside for a while before you read it again. When you return to your draft, evaluate it to decide what you need to improve. Answer the questions on the following checklist to decide how to revise your draft to make it clearer and more accurate.

- Do I grab my readers' attention in the introduction?
- Do I stick to my topic?
- Do I accomplish my purpose?
- Do I keep my audience in mind?
- Does my main idea come across clearly?
- Does the information in the body fit the main idea of each paragraph?
- Have I followed my outline? Is there a paragraph in my report for each main heading in my outline?
- Do I give enough details? Too many?
- Are all dates, names, and numbers correct?
- Are all quotations accurate?
- Have I written a good conclusion that summarizes or restates my main idea?

GET A SECOND OPINION

One of the best ways to evaluate a draft is to have a class-mate examine it. Share your draft with a partner and ask him or her the following questions.

- Is anything unclear?
- Where could I add more information?
- What do you find most interesting about my topic?
- What would you like to know more about?

You may want to ask your partner to write down his or her responses to these questions. Then you can refer to these responses as you revise.

18.4 PROOFREADING

After revising your draft, type or print a new copy of it with your corrections included. Then proofread your report one final time. You should check for one type of error at a time. For example, the first time you proofread, check for spelling errors. The second time you proofread, check for punctuation.

Proofreading Checklist

1. Have I explained or defined any words that may be unfamiliar to the reader?
2. Have I corrected all grammar errors?
3. Have I corrected all spelling errors?
4. Have I used correct punctuation?
5. Have I capitalized everything correctly?
6. Have I documented my sources properly?
7. Is my final copy neat and easy to read?
8. Have I indented each paragraph?
9. Have I left a one-inch margin on all four sides of each page?
10. Have I numbered the pages and included my name on each one?

18.5 PUBLISHING/PRESENTING

After completing your report, you're ready to share what you've learned. You can share your work in a variety of ways.

- Bind your report in book form.
- Present it on a computer disk.
- Put it into a notebook binder.
- Post it on a bulletin board.
- Print it as part of a class newsletter or magazine.

Think of things to include—covers, drawings, diagrams, clippings, or photographs—that will make your report attractive. Then share it with others!

SAMPLE RESEARCH REPORT

Clark Kent

Ms. Lane

Period 3

March 15, 2000

Bicycle Safety

Every year, millions of Americans take to the streets to ride their bikes. They ride them to and from work or school or on the weekend as a hobby. Although bike riding can be an enjoyable way to exercise, it's important to remember that bike riding can also be dangerous. More than a million Americans injure themselves seriously each year while riding a bicycle. The good news is that many bicycle injuries can be avoided through bike safety. Bike safety includes careful riding, common sense, regular maintenance, and proper equipment.

> The thesis statement expresses the main idea of the report.

One of the most important ways that cyclists can avoid accidents is by knowing and obeying all traffic rules. Not knowing

COMPOSITION

these rules can be dangerous. Cyclists are at fault in nearly 90 percent of all biking accidents. When turning a corner, cyclists should use hand signals to let others know which way they are going. If there is no bicycle lane, cyclists should ride on the far right-hand side of the road.

Cyclists should also use common sense when riding. They should never wear earphones when they ride because earphones may prevent them from hearing warning signals from other traffic. They should never allow others to ride on the handlebars. A passenger can block the cyclist's vision and distract the cyclist. When riding at night, cyclists should have lights and special reflectors on their bikes so that drivers can see them.

One safeguard that people often ignore is proper bike maintenance. Cyclists should inspect their bikes regularly to make sure the tires, brakes, handlebars, seats, and spokes are in good condition. Some repairs

can be done easily by the cyclist, but regular
inspections at a bike shop are also
recommended.

    The most important part of bicycle
safety is wearing a helmet. Many young
people don't wear helmets because they
believe helmets are unattractive and not
"cool." Statistics indicate that up to 85 percent of all bicycle injuries could be prevented if people would simply wear helmets.
Many manufacturers produce helmets in
attractive designs and styles, and helmets
are now much lighter than they used to be.
The Bicycle Helmet Safety Institute recom-
mends that parents buy "snazzy" helmets to
encourage their children to wear them. There
is no longer any excuse for people not to
wear helmets.

    Bike riding can be fun, but it also
carries important responsibilities. By following the proper precautions and making safety a habit, cyclists can be sure
that biking remains fun for everyone.

> The topic sentence of each paragraph supports the thesis statement. The rest of the paragraph supports the topic sentence.

> The conclusion summarizes or restates the thesis statement.

COMPOSITION

SOURCES

"A Consumer's Guide to Bicycle Helmets."
Bicycle Helmet Safety Institute. Mar. 8,
1998. Bicycle Helmet Safety Institute.
July 15, 1998 <http://www.bhsi.org/
webdocs/guide.htm>.

Fine, Kenneth C. "Bicycle Safety." The
Columbia University College of Physi-
cians and Surgeons Complete Home
Medical Guide. New York: Crown
Publishers, 1995.

McCullagh, James C. Cycling for Health,
Fitness, and Well-being. New York: Dell
Publishing, 1995.

Pessah, Jon. "Bicycle Helmets Are As
Important As Seat Belts in Preventing
Injuries. But How Do You Convince Your
Kids to Wear Them?" Newsday Nov. 20,
1993: 21.

Rathbun, Mickey. "Play It Safe! What Is the
Best Armor Against Kids' Sports
Injuries? An Informed Parent." Sports
Illustrated for Kids May 1, 1998: 10+.

COMPOSITION

Shepherd, Ron. "Cycling." <u>Encyclopedia of</u>
<u>World Sport: From Ancient Times to the</u>
<u>Present</u>. 1996 ed.

COMPOSITION

Chapter 19

Business Writing

• • • • • • • • • • • • • •

19.1 WRITING A REQUEST LETTER

Have you ever written to someone you didn't know to ask for something? Maybe you wrote to an author to ask why she wrote a book you liked. Perhaps you wrote to the staff of a summer camp for information about a special program that interested you. Maybe you need information for a school report. You might decide to write a request letter to get the facts you need.

TIPS FOR WRITING A REQUEST LETTER

Here are some tips that will help Susan—and you—write a request letter that will get the results you want:

Be Brief Don't wander off the subject or include details that the reader doesn't need (or want) to know. Remember that business people are busy. They expect you to explain the reason for your letter in the first sentence or two. If you don't, they might not continue reading, or they might misunderstand why you're writing.

Explain Your Request Clearly Provide all the necessary information. If you have several questions or are asking for several things, number them. That way, the reader will be more likely to answer all your questions and not overlook one.

Respect the Reader's Time and Effort You shouldn't ask someone to provide basic information you could easily find in an encyclopedia or a library reference book. You shouldn't ask your favorite author, who lives several states away, to visit your school to talk to your class—for free. Be reasonable in your requests and make it easy for the reader to respond.

Ask Politely Request, don't demand. Show that you appreciate anything the reader can do to meet your request or answer your questions.

Use Business Style Include all the parts of a business letter: the heading, inside address, salutation, body, closing, and signature. Using the correct form will make a good impression on your reader. If you take your letter seriously, the reader is more likely to take it seriously too.

Proofread You should read your letter several times before you mail it. If you don't take the time to find and correct any errors in your letter, why should the reader take the time to answer it?

Include a heading: your own address and the date.

16A Portage Road
Portland, Maine 34567
May 10, 2002

Education Department
Columbus Zoo

Address the letter to a specific person or department, if possible.

9990 Riverside Drive
Columbus, Ohio 44344

Include an inside address: the reader's name and address.

Explain your request clearly in the first sentence or two.

Dear Education Department Staff:

    Please send me information about your breeding program for gorillas. I'm writing a science report about how zoos are helping to preserve endangered species, and I understand that your zoo has been very successful with gorillas.

Give the reason for your request.

    I have learned quite a bit about gorillas in my research, but I would like to know more about your program. Could you please answer the questions below?

Show that you've made an effort to learn about the topic.

Write your questions in a list if there are several.

1. What species of gorillas are in your program?

2. Where do you get the gorillas for your program?

3. How many babies have been born and in what years?

4. Do you keep all the babies that are born at your zoo?

    I'd also be interested in any other information that you have available about the gorillas and your program. I know you are very busy, but I'd appreciate getting the information as soon as possible. I've enclosed a large stamped, self-addressed envelope.

Make it easy for the reader to fulfill your request.

Thank you very much for your time and the information.

Show your appreciation.

Sincerely,

Susan Workman

Write your signature above your typed name.

Susan Workman

COMPOSITION

USING THE CORRECT FORM

Business letters, including request letters, can be written in two forms: block or modified block. Susan used the modified block form. Notice how she placed her heading, closing, and signature toward the right side of the page. She also indented each paragraph.

In the block form, all the parts of a letter begin at the left margin. Nothing is indented. Both the modified block and block form should be single-spaced and should include a blank line between the paragraphs (not shown in Susan's letter).

BEING BUSINESSLIKE

To write a business letter, you don't have to use long sentences. You also don't have to use old-fashioned words, such as *herein* and *the undersigned,* meaning "the writer." Business writing is supposed to communicate, to share information. Simple language does that best. A business letter should sound more like a conversation than a textbook.

Your business letters, including your request letters, will be much better if you make these kinds of substitutions:

INSTEAD OF THIS	WRITE THIS
this letter is written for the purpose of requesting	please send me
enclosed please find	I am enclosing
at this point in time	now/today
in the near future	soon
if you are in a position to	if you can
will you be kind enough	please
I would like to express my appreciation	thank you
thanking you in advance for your help	thank you

At the same time, a business letter should not sound exactly like a conversation. "Thanks a lot!" is fine for e-mail or letters to friends, but it's a little too informal for a business letter. A simple "Thank you" is more appropriate. In other words, your language should be polite but not stiff, friendly but not overly casual. You should write as you would to an adult whom you respect.

Everyone needs information and help from time to time. Now you know how to write a letter that will explain what you need, show that you respect the reader, and get you what you want!

19.2 WRITING DIRECTIONS FOR A PROCESS

Do you always read the instructions before you use a new compact-disc player or a headset or new computer software? No? You're not alone. Many people avoid reading instructions. They expect the instructions to be too confusing or too long, or maybe the instructions will be too short, leaving out important steps. Many people don't expect instructions to be helpful, so they don't bother to read them. Of course, this can lead to mistakes, wasted time, frustration, and even damaged equipment. Still, trying to figure out poorly written instructions can have the same result.

If you learn to write clear instructions, you'll gain a valuable skill. The ability to write clear instructions will help you in school and at work for the rest of your life. This section will help you develop that skill.

Frank and Ernest

© 1996 Thaves / Reprinted with permission.
Newspaper dist. by NEA, Inc.

GETTING STARTED

Before you write anything, including instructions, the first step is always the same: Think about your readers. Ask yourself these questions:

- Who is my audience?
- What does my audience know about the topic?
- What terms will they understand? What terms will I need to explain?

If you assume that your audience understands certain things, you may fail to explain them in your instructions. If you don't explain these things, some of your readers might get stuck at a certain step and not know how to continue. On the other hand, if you explain too much, experienced readers may get impatient. "Why should I read more of this?" they may ask themselves. "I already know how to do these steps!" However, if they stop reading at Step 3, they might do Step 4 incorrectly.

How do you avoid explaining too little or too much? Find out what most of your intended readers already know about the topic. Let's say you're explaining how to get from one place to another. First, you need to find out how well your readers know your town or city. Maybe you're lending your cousin your compact-disc player, and she has asked you to write down instructions for using it. Before you start writing, ask your cousin if she has ever used a compact-disc player. Then you will know what to put in your instructions and what to leave out.

Find out what terms your readers know and use. If you're explaining how to program a videocassette recorder, will they understand such terms as *INPUT/SELECT, SP, EP, timer set mode,* and *program memory?* If you're writing the steps for adding a phone number to a speed-dial program, which of these terms are your readers likely to understand: *type, input, program?* If you're not sure whether your readers will be familiar with a certain term, it's probably best to explain it.

CHOOSING A TITLE

Start your instructions with a clear title that specifically describes what the reader will learn.

INSTEAD OF THIS	WRITE THIS
How to Use Your Videocassette Recorder	How to Set Your Videocassette Recorder to Record Automatically

WRITING AN INTRODUCTION

An introduction tells the purpose of the instructions. It explains who should follow them and perhaps when and why. For example, suppose a set of instructions in a business office tells how to reorder parts. The introduction should explain who is responsible for reordering the parts and when they should be reordered. Otherwise, everyone in the office might assume that someone else is responsible for following the steps.

In your introduction, list any needed materials or equipment so that readers can gather what they need before they begin the steps. Include any general warnings or cautions, such as "Unplug the videocassette recorder before changing the connections." Then repeat the warnings at the appropriate steps in the instructions. This is also a good time to explain any terms that may be new to readers, such as *initialize* or *airway*.

ORGANIZING THE STEPS

Now it's time to ask yourself these questions:

- What steps should readers complete?
- What other information does my audience need?

List all the steps in the process. Leave out obvious ones, such as "Locate your videocassette recorder." Then put the steps in chronological order—that is, in the order readers should complete them—and number them.

INSTEAD OF THIS	WRITE THIS
1. Insert the disk in the slot after turning on the computer.	1. Turn on the computer. 2. Insert the disk in the slot.

List each step separately. If you try to combine two or more instructions in a single step, your readers may become confused.

INSTEAD OF THIS	WRITE THIS
1. Turn on the computer before inserting the disk in the slot.	1. Turn on the computer. 2. Insert the disk in the slot.

Start each step with a verb. A verb will tell your readers what to do.

INSTEAD OF THIS	WRITE THIS
1. The CONTROL key and the F1 key are pressed at the same time.	1. Press the CONTROL key and the F1 key at the same time.

Number only the steps that readers should complete. Below each step, add any other information they might need. For example, you may want to explain what should happen at that point in the process, or you might want to stress why that step is important. If you want to include this kind of information, indent these explanations under the steps or underline them or put them in italics or parentheses. Make it easy for readers to find and follow each step without getting confused by explanations. Below is an example of how to include an explanation.

INSTEAD OF THIS	WRITE THIS
1. After you press 3, the screen will show a menu.	1. Press 3. (The screen will show a menu.)

Sometimes a step should be carried out only under certain conditions. In that case, describe the conditions first. Otherwise, readers might carry out a step before they realize they should do it only at certain times. (This time, you will not start a step with a verb.)

INSTEAD OF THIS	WRITE THIS
1. Press ENTER if the light is flashing.	1. If the light is flashing, press ENTER.

If a diagram will help explain what to do, include it. For example, you might want to draw a diagram of the control panel of the videocassette recorder. Then you could label each knob and button.

CONSIDERING A CONCLUSION

If you wish, end your instructions with a brief conclusion. You might write one of the following:

- Tell what readers should have accomplished by following the instructions.
- Name some sources of help if readers have problems following the instructions.

Compare the following sets of instructions. It's difficult to find the steps in the first set. Notice how much easier it is to follow the numbered steps in the second set.

EXAMPLES

Confusing

Taking a Test

Be sure to take along a pencil to mark the answer form. Fill in the whole circle and stay within the lines, or the computer might make a mistake in scoring your test. Read all the answers before making your choice. One choice may seem correct, but another one may be more correct. You also need to learn all you can about the test. For example, is it going to be timed? Are you expected to complete the test? Should you guess if you're not sure, or do incorrect answers count against you? The directions should always be read before you begin each section of the test. Directions may change from section to section. Skip a space on the answer form if you skip a question. The best approach is usually to answer all the questions you're sure of first. If there's time, go back and answer the rest.

Clear

How to Take a Standardized Test

Begin with a clear, descriptive title.

The tips below will help middle school students improve their scores on standardized tests, such as state achievement tests.

Explain the purpose of the instructions and who should follow them.

1. First, find the answers to these questions:

   Put the steps in chronological (time) order and number them.

   - Is the test going to be timed? Are you expected to complete the whole test?
   - Should you guess if you're not sure, or do incorrect answers count against you?

2. Take along a pencil to mark the answer form. Start all steps with a verb.

3. Read the directions before you begin each section of the test. (Directions may change from section to section.)

   Use parentheses (or underlining, italics, or indention) for explanations.

4. Read all the possible answers before choosing one. (One may seem correct at first, but another answer may be more accurate.)

5. Fill in the whole circle for the answer you choose and stay inside the lines. (Computers have trouble scoring messy answer forms.)

6. Answer all the questions you're sure of first. (If there's time, go back and answer the rest.)

7. If you skip a question, skip that space on the answer form.

   Describe any special conditions before explaining a step.

COMPOSITION

19.3 MAKING A PRESENTATION

Making an oral presentation can be a rewarding experience, but it can also make your stomach flutter. You're up there all alone, and everyone's looking at you. You're sure you're going to embarrass yourself somehow. Probably you'll forget what you were going to say. Maybe you'll remember, but everyone will get bored and start yawning. What if your hands shake and people notice?

But what if you walk to the front of the room, full of confidence, and give a presentation that really fascinates your audience? It could happen! This section will help it happen to you. You'll learn how to prepare for an oral presentation so that you can do it well and feel comfortable. You'll even look forward to it!

You've given oral presentations before, of course. You probably started with book reports in elementary school. In middle school, you might be asked to give oral reports in language arts or science class. You'll also have to give them in high school and in college or other training programs after high school. When you begin working, sooner or later you'll probably have to give more oral presentations. Now is the time to develop the skills and the confidence to give these presentations. You'll use these skills for many years to come and in many different settings.

Here are the steps you will learn in this section:

1. Think About Your Topic and Your Purpose
2. Analyze Your Audience
3. Decide What to Say
4. Organize Your Presentation
5. Add Visuals
6. Practice
7. Present Yourself Well

THINK ABOUT YOUR TOPIC AND YOUR PURPOSE

You might be assigned a topic, or you may get to choose your own. First, make sure you know what is expected from your presentation. Are you simply supposed to inform the audience about a topic, or are you expected to persuade the audience to do something?

Suppose your purpose is to inform. If you chose your own topic, make sure it's not too broad for a short presentation. You might want to present just one or two aspects of it. For example, if your topic is television, you might decide to talk about how commercials influence our buying decisions, or you might explain why and how the networks are trying to reduce the amount of violence on television.

Think of an approach that will interest your audience. If your topic was assigned, find out what the assigner (probably your teacher) wants the audience (probably your class) to learn about the topic.

Maybe your purpose is to persuade the audience to do something. Perhaps you're supposed to convince them to volunteer for a community clean-up campaign or enter a short-story contest. In either case, you will need to think of ways to persuade your audience. How would they benefit from helping in the campaign or participating in the contest?

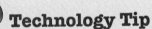

Technology Tip

If you don't know your topic well, your next step will be to learn more about it. Besides the library, a good source for current information is the Internet. Before using information from the Internet, however, be sure your source is accurate. Sites sponsored by well-known organizations, such as news networks, are your best bet. Avoid home pages posted on the Internet by individuals.

ANALYZE YOUR AUDIENCE

To analyze your audience, answer these questions:

- How will your listeners respond to this topic? Will they be eager to learn about it? Will they be bored unless you can think of a new approach?

- What does this audience already know about the topic? Have they studied it in school? What terms will they understand? Which ones will you have to explain? If your topic is television commercials, for example, which ones will be familiar to your audience? If you will be talking about television violence, which shows does your audience watch that tend to contain violence?
- How can you show your audience that the topic is important in their lives? For example, have students in your school bought products advertised by commercials and been disappointed? Has something happened in your community that might have been inspired by violence on television?

Analyzing your audience will help you decide what your presentation should include. You can first gain your audience's interest and then inform or persuade them, depending on your purpose in speaking.

DECIDE WHAT TO SAY

Knowing a great deal about your topic and your audience will help you decide what to include in your presentation. The amount of time you have to speak will also help you decide how much information you can include.

Instead of saying a little about many elements of your topic, choose two or three main points that will be meaningful to your audience. They will not remember a large number of details. However, they are likely to remember two or three points if you offer interesting examples.

While you're planning what to say, ask yourself one or both of these questions:

- What do I want the audience to learn?
- What do I want the audience to do after my presentation?

ORGANIZE YOUR PRESENTATION

A presentation has a beginning, a middle, and an end. An effective presentation begins with a strong opening to interest the audience in the topic. Then the speaker tells the audience the points he or she will cover so that they know what to expect. Next, the speaker presents those points in an organized way. The speaker ends with a strong closing to remind the audience of what they've learned or to motivate them to act.

The Beginning

Plan an opening that will grab your audience's attention. It should also introduce your topic. Here are some ways to do this:

Tell a Story It can be a true story about yourself or others, but make sure it won't embarrass anyone else. (You can embarrass yourself if you want to!) For example, you might mention a recent news story that relates to your topic, or you could tell about a time when you believed a commercial's claims and spent your whole allowance on a useless product.

Ask a Question Questions can get the audience thinking about the topic. For example, you might ask, "When was the last time you bought a product because it was advertised on television?" or "Did you watch television last night? How many times did you see a character hit, punch, shove, kick, shoot, or stab someone?"

Offer a Surprising Fact Get the audience's attention with a fact that startles them. For example: "By the time you are legally old enough to drink alcoholic beverages, you will have seen more than 100,000 beer commercials on television."

Tell a Joke Do this only if you're good at it. Choose your joke carefully. Select one that relates to your topic, and *make sure it doesn't insult any person or group of people.* Most libraries have books of jokes written especially for speakers to use. After you choose a joke, try it out on friends to see if they think it's funny, doesn't insult anyone, and isn't too silly. Telling a joke can relax both the audience and you, but be careful. You may embarrass yourself if the joke flops.

The Middle

After you've decided how to begin your presentation, organize your main points into a logical order. Writing them in an outline helps. Then you will locate examples, quotations, or statistics to back up each point and add them to your outline. Here are some ways to organize your points:

Chronological Explain a series of events in the order they occurred or give steps in the order they should be completed. For example, you might tell what was done over the past few years during the school clean-up campaign, or you could explain the steps in writing a short story.

Priority Arrange the reasons to do something from least to most important. For example, here are three reasons we should ignore television commercials:

Least important:	They waste our money on products that don't work as promised. ("Buy this face cream, and your pimples will disappear!")
Next important:	They encourage our fears. ("Use this mouthwash, or no one will want to be near you!")
Most important:	Some advertised products can harm our health. For example, drinking beer leads to thousands of automobile accidents.

Problem/Cause/Solution Describe a problem, explain why it is happening (or will happen), and offer a solution. For instance, you might point out specific areas at school where trash has accumulated, such as the outdoor areas near the cafeteria. Next, you will explain the cause of this problem: students dropping trash from their lunches. Then you will describe the solution: the clean-up campaign, more trash containers, signs to remind students not to litter.

Compare and Contrast Show how two events, people, or objects are similar and different. Using this approach, you might compare the amount of violence in two popular television shows. If one show can be popular without violence, is violence necessary in the other one?

Categories Divide your topic into categories and explain each one. You might use this approach to explain several of the persuasive techniques used in television commercials.

The Ending

The ending of your presentation is as important as the beginning. Here are two effective endings:

Summarize Restate your main points and then go back to your opening. Finish the story you started, repeat the question you asked, or show the audience how the fact or joke you shared relates to your main points.

Repeat Your Strongest Point Rephrase your strongest point and then ask the audience to do something specific. For example, you might urge them to sign up for the clean-up campaign or write a short story for the contest.

After organizing your opening, your main points, and your closing, write them on note cards. Put each main point on its own card and include any important details you want to mention, along with any quotations or statistics you have gathered.

Writing Tip

Write on your note cards in words and phrases, not sentences. You're not going to *read* these cards. The cards will just remind you of what you planned to say. Number the cards so you can keep them in order during your presentation.

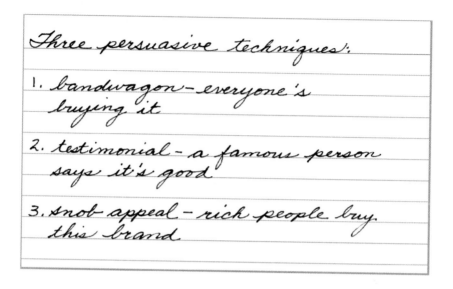

Three persuasive techniques:

1. bandwagon—everyone's buying it

2. testimonial—a famous person says it's good

3. snob appeal—rich people buy this brand

ADD VISUALS

Different people prefer to learn in different ways. Some people like to listen to someone tell them new information. Other people would rather see new information printed out, perhaps in a book or on a chart. Most people, especially the second group, will be more interested in your presentation—and understand it better—if you use some visuals.

A visual can be as simple as a list printed on poster board. It can be as complicated as animated computer graphics. Visuals can include charts, tables, graphs, maps, models, samples, videotapes, drawings, photographs, and diagrams. They can be presented on individual sheets of paper to be distributed to the audience, on poster board, or on slides. Visuals can be made by hand or by computer.

If your presentation is about television commercials, you might videotape two or three of them. Then you could show them to your audience and discuss the persuasive techniques used in each one, or you could make a line graph to show the decrease in television violence and display the graph using an overhead projector or an opaque projector.

Visuals should not only give the audience something to look at. They should also help explain your points. If you use a number of visuals, they can serve as an outline for your presentation. Then you can use the visuals as reminders of what you were going to say instead of looking at note cards. Using visuals makes you look well organized. Visuals also give you something to do with your hands!

Designing Visuals

- Explain only one point on each visual. Keep the visual simple so that your audience will immediately understand its point. Don't make your audience struggle to figure out what your visual means.
- Give every visual a title that helps explain it.
- Use big letters so your audience can read the words on your visual. But don't use all capital letters. WRITING THAT'S IN ALL CAPITAL LETTERS IS MUCH HARDER TO READ!

Writing Tip

Keep it simple!

- Use only one idea for each visual.
- Use no more than thirty-five words on one visual.
- Give each visual a title.

- Don't try to include every detail from your note cards on visuals. Focus on your main points.
- Don't make your visuals too cluttered. That is, don't use too many colors, sizes of letters, or pictures. Three colors are plenty, and two sizes of letters are enough. Choose pictures to help explain your points, not to decorate your visual.
- Don't forget to proofread. If you skip this step, an overhead might display a misspelled word in three-inch letters!

COMPOSITION

Using a Computer Presentation Program

If you have a computer and software available, they can help with your presentations. PowerPoint software, for example, can produce slides and send them directly from your computer to an overhead screen for your audience to see. PowerPoint allows you to make words, paragraphs, or pictures appear and disappear from the slide. You can also add sound effects. In addition, PowerPoint can make overhead transparencies and print handouts for the audience.

ARE YOUR VISUALS

- easy to understand?
- interesting?
- related to your topic?
- neat?

Using Visuals

Visuals can add a great deal to your presentation. However, they do require some planning so that your presentation will flow smoothly. Follow these tips:

- Check any equipment you plan to use. Just before the presentation, check it one more time to make sure it still works. A computer program that worked at home may not work in another setting. The bulb on the overhead projector may have burned out. Be ready with another way to share the information in case of problems.
- Don't show a visual until you're ready to talk about it. Then leave it displayed until you're ready for the next one. Turning equipment on and off can annoy an audience. Empty white screens can also be distracting.

- Face your audience and stand to one side of your visual so that everyone can see it. *Do* explain your visuals, but *don't* read them to the audience.

PRACTICE

Rehearse your speech two or three times. Use your visuals so you can figure out when to show each one to the audience. After the opening of your speech, tell the audience the points you will cover so they know what to expect. Then practice moving smoothly from one point to the next. Finally, close with the strong ending you have planned.

Ask a few friends or family members to listen to you and give you their opinions. Ask them to pay attention to the way you organized your presentation and the way you gave it. You might videotape yourself and watch the tape. Listen for times when you were difficult to understand or you didn't clearly explain what you meant. Were any of your points a little boring? If so, find more interesting examples to liven them up.

Check your timing to make sure your presentation is not too long or too short. Remember that you might speak more quickly in front of a larger audience. Don't practice so many times that you memorize your presentation. You want it to be fresh and interesting for you and for the audience.

Calvin and Hobbes   by Bill Watterson

Calvin & Hobbes © 1989, 1993 & 1994 Watterson. Reprinted with permission of Universal Press Syndicate. All rights reserved.

COMPOSITION

PRESENT YOURSELF WELL

If you feel nervous before speaking to a group, congratulations! You're just like most speakers! You can still make an excellent presentation. Just admit to yourself that you're feeling a little nervous. Then use that energy to do your best. Many professional athletes also feel nervous just before a competition begins. They welcome their nervousness because it gives them extra energy.

Getting Ready

Get a good night's sleep. To prevent burps, avoid drinking any kind of carbonated beverage for several hours before your presentation.

Just before you speak, help yourself relax by taking several deep breaths. Next, tighten and relax your muscles, one set at a time. Start at your toes and work to the top of your head. Then take a few more deep breaths for good measure. Finally, gather your note cards and your visuals and take your place in front of the group. Pause and smile at the audience. DON'T apologize for being nervous—and begin.

Looking Good

- Stand up straight, but don't be stiff.
- Look at the audience. Pick out one person and pretend you are talking just to him or her. Then pretend you are talking to a different person. Keep changing so you look at people in every part of the audience. Audiences like speakers who look at them. They believe that speakers who look at them are better informed, more experienced, friendlier, and more sincere than speakers who do not make eye contact.
- Use gestures, just as you would during a conversation. They help show your enthusiasm for your topic.
- Move around. Unless you're standing on a stage or must stay close to a microphone, try walking among the audience members. It will help make you and them feel more relaxed.

Sounding Good

- Speak clearly and slowly. Let your voice rise and fall naturally, as if you were having a conversation. Try not to rush.
- Speak loudly enough to reach people in the back of the room. If you're using a microphone, let it do the work. Don't shout.
- Get excited about your topic! Your audience will catch your excitement. Enthusiasm is contagious.

PUTTING IT ALL TOGETHER

Now you know how to do well on your next presentation. If you still feel nervous about it, imagine the worst thing that could happen. Here are some disasters that might come to your mind:

- You'll forget what you were going to say, or you'll lose your place. (No, you won't. Your note cards and your visuals will keep you on track.)
- Your presentation will be boring. (Not after all the planning you've done! You know your audience and your topic well. You've thought of an interesting opening, and you've found good examples to support your main points. You have also designed excellent visuals.)

So when *is* your next presentation? Think about how you can use the steps in this section to get ready for it. Then you will feel confident and comfortable as you make your presentation. You might even look forward to it!

Part Four

• • • • • • • • • • • • •

Resources

So much has already been written about everything that you can't find out anything about it.

—James Thurber

Chapter 20

The Library or Media Center

• • • • • • • • • • • • • • • •

Although you've probably been in a library, you might not realize all the resources the library has to offer or how to find them. This chapter will guide you through the library and help you understand how and where to find what you need.

CIRCULATION DESK

At the circulation desk, you'll find a library worker to answer your questions and check out your books.

CATALOG

A computer or card catalog will tell you what books are available in the library and where to find them. You'll learn more about using both kinds of catalogs in Chapter 21.

THE STACKS

The stacks are rows of bookshelves. They're called the "adult section" in some libraries, but you usually need not be an adult to use these books. In most libraries, the stacks are divided into these sections:
- fiction (novels and short stories)
- biography (books about the lives of real people)
- nonfiction (everything that is not included in fiction or biography)

YOUNG ADULT AND CHILDREN'S SECTION

The young adult and children's section includes picture books for very young readers, but you can also find excellent resources here for your school reports and for fun. Fiction, biographies, and nonfiction are usually grouped separately, as in the adult section. All these books are listed in the library's computer or card catalog.

REFERENCE AREA

The reference area might include encyclopedias, dictionaries, almanacs, and other reference materials. Books in the reference area can be used only in the library. The library doesn't allow anyone to check them out. Thus, these materials are always available when someone needs them.

NEWSPAPERS AND PERIODICALS

In the newspapers and periodicals section, you can read newspapers from your town or city, from other major cities, and perhaps from other countries. You can also look through periodicals, which include magazines and journals. You probably can't check out the most recent issues. However, you can usually check out older issues to read at home. You'll learn more about finding articles in newspapers and periodicals in Chapter 21.

AUDIO-VISUAL MATERIALS

From the audio-visual section of the library, you can borrow books on tape, videotapes, and audiocassettes and compact discs (CDs) of your favorite music.

COMPUTER AREA

Many libraries offer personal computers you can use for research. Some computers might also be available for writing reports and papers and for using the Internet.

STUDY AREAS

Your library might have quiet areas set aside for people who want to read or study.

SPECIAL COLLECTIONS

Some libraries set up special displays and change them every few weeks. A display might consist of rare books, student art, or a collection of antique dolls, carved figures, or items from another country.

Reprinted with special permission
of King Features Syndicate.

Using Print Resources

In the course of doing research for a report, you will no doubt look at books and periodicals. One reason that print resources, especially books, are tremendous sources of information is that they survive for years, enabling you to gain access to information from the past.

Periodicals, because they're printed more quickly and more often than books, are sources of current information and opinion. You can use periodicals to find varying viewpoints on the same subjects. In this chapter, you'll learn about some of the different kinds of print resources available to you.

21.1 UNDERSTANDING CATALOGING SYSTEMS

Maybe you're looking for information on a particular subject. Maybe you want to see books by a certain author, or you want to check out a specific book. The library's catalog will help you find what you're looking for. Most libraries now use computerized catalogs, but some still have card catalogs.

COMPUTER CATALOGS

Each computer catalog is different. Before you use one for the first time, read the instructions. They might be posted beside the computer or printed on the screen. If you need help, ask a librarian.

Most catalog programs begin by asking whether you want to search by author, title, or subject. If you want to search for an author's name, type the last name first, followed by a comma and the first name. Here is an example:

Thurber, James

If you want to search by title, start with the first important word in the title. Ignore *A, An,* and *The* at the beginning of a title. For the book *A Thurber Carnival,* you would type the following:

Thurber Carnival

When you're entering names and titles, be sure the words you enter are spelled correctly. A computer catalog can't recognize misspelled words. It will search for exactly what you type.

For a subject search, you will use a key word. A key word is a word that names or describes your topic. Whenever you search a computer database, such as a library catalog or the Internet, the key word you use will greatly affect the results you get. On the next two pages are several tips to help you get the best results from a subject search.

Search TIP

1. **Be specific.** A general key word, such as *experiments,* will get you many screens of sources, sometimes called matches or hits. Although these sources will relate in some way to your key word, few of them will be mainly about your topic. To save time, choose a key word that better names or describes your topic, such as *cloning.* You will get a much shorter list of hits, but more of them will be useful to you.

2. **Use Boolean search techniques.** Boolean search techniques can help you look for books in a computer catalog, find articles in magazine databases, or locate information on the Internet. (You'll learn to search magazine databases and the Internet later in this chapter.) Boolean techniques use the words *and, or, not,* and sometimes *near* or *adj (adjacent).*

    And: You can combine two key words with *and,* such as *cloning and animals.* Then the computer will list only sources that contain both words. This kind of search results in far fewer hits, but more of them will relate to your topic. (Some programs use + instead of *and,* as in *cloning + animals.*)

    Or: If you want information on two different topics, link them with *or,* as in *cloning or twins.* The word *or* tells the computer to conduct two searches at once.

    Not: To stop the computer from searching for information you don't want, use *not.* For example, if you wanted information about cloning but not about cloning sheep, you could enter *cloning not sheep.*

    Near or *adj:* Some computer programs allow you to use *near* or *adj (adjacent).* These words tell the computer to locate sources with two key words near each other. For example, you might use *cloning near dog.* (You could also enter

RESOURCES

cloning and dog. However, the computer might then list articles that contain the word *cloning* and the word *dog*— but nothing about cloning dogs.)

Not all computer programs recognize Boolean search instructions. For some programs, you must begin a Boolean search with *b/* (for Boolean search), as in *b/cloning near dog.*

3. **Use quotation marks.** Enclosing a phrase in quotation marks tells the computer to find every book or article with *exactly* those words. For instance, you might enter *"cloning dogs."*

4. **Try truncating.** You can truncate, or shorten, your key word by using an asterisk (*). Then the computer will search for all words that begin with the letters before the asterisk. For example, you might use *clon** as a key word. The computer will list books or articles containing the words *clone, clones, cloning,* and *cloned.* By truncating your key word, you make sure the computer doesn't overlook various forms of the word.

You can also use this technique when you aren't sure how to spell a word. For example, you could use *Doll** as a key word if you weren't sure whether the first cloned sheep was named *Dollie* or *Dolly.*

If you need help with the computer catalog of your library, you can always ask a librarian for help. Many libraries also offer classes on how to use the computer catalog.

Understanding Search Results

To use a library computer catalog, type in the author's name, the book title, or a key word for a subject search. The screen will list related sources that are available at that library. Let's say you start a subject search by typing in *cloning.* The screen shows you a list similar to the one on the next page.

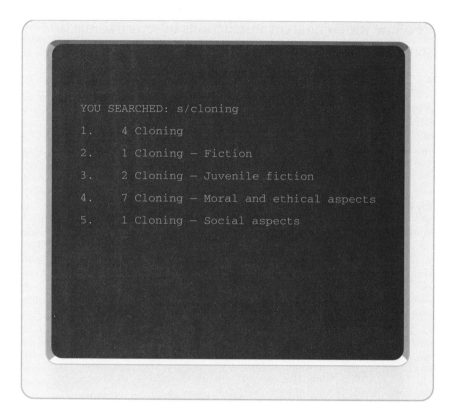

```
YOU SEARCHED: s/cloning
1.      4 Cloning
2.      1 Cloning — Fiction
3.      2 Cloning — Juvenile fiction
4.      7 Cloning — Moral and ethical aspects
5.      1 Cloning — Social aspects
```

The first listing (1) tells you the library has four books about cloning in general. Because they aren't marked "fiction," they're nonfiction. Because they aren't marked "juvenile," they're meant for adults. The second (2) and third (3) listings are fictional books, one for adults and two for young readers. The fourth (4) and fifth (5) listings are adult nonfiction books.

You don't know much about cloning yet, so you were hoping the library would have some books on this topic in the "juvenile nonfiction" category. Those books would give you the basic information you need. You don't want to read a fictional story about cloning, even one meant for young readers. You need facts for your report, not a story. You decide to try a different but closely related key word.

Follow the computer's instructions to return to the first page and type in your new key word: *genetics.*

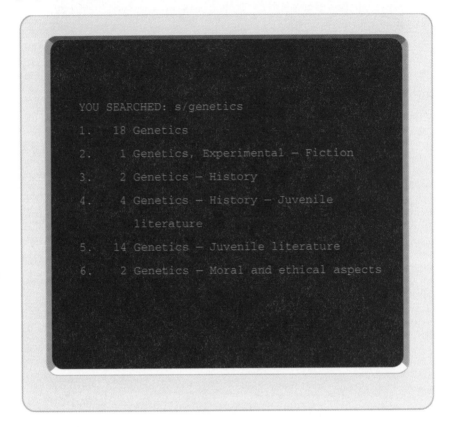

```
YOU SEARCHED: s/genetics
1.   18 Genetics
2.    1 Genetics, Experimental - Fiction
3.    2 Genetics - History
4.    4 Genetics - History - Juvenile
         literature
5.   14 Genetics - Juvenile literature
6.    2 Genetics - Moral and ethical aspects
```

You're glad to see listings 4 and 5; they offer a total of eighteen nonfiction books about genetics for young readers. You follow the directions on the screen to see what books are listed under 4 and 5. The computer instructions tell you how to move forward and backward through a library listing. For example, you might enter *ns* (next screen) or *f* (forward) to see the next page of a listing. To go backward, you might enter *ps* (previous screen) or *b* (backward). Each catalog program is different, so carefully read the onscreen instructions.

You decide to find out more about a book that was listed under 5. The screen on the next page offers this information about that book:

```
CALL NO: 576.5 BAE

AUTHOR: Baeuerle, Patrick Alexander

MAIN TITLE: Ingenious genes: learning about

the fantastic skills of genetic engineers

and watching them at work / by Patrick A.

Baeuerle.

PUBLISHER: New York: Barron's, c1997

LOCATION                      STATUS

1.    J NON-FICTION OVER      Available

2.    J NON-FICTION OVER      Available
```

This book may provide the basic information you need. The library has two copies. The status column on the screen indicates that no one has checked out either copy, so both should be in the library. If someone had checked one out, the status column would list the date it was due back at the library.

Some catalog entries also include the number of pages in the book. Some tell whether the book is illustrated or has a bibliography. Some state whether the work is a book or a videotape. Many entries list additional headings you could use as key words to find more information about the same topic.

Write down the call number shown at the top of the listing. (Call numbers are numbers and letters used to classify books. They're explained on pages 414–417.) Then go to the location listed: the oversized shelves in the young readers' nonfiction area. (The word *OVER* in the listing means "oversized.") Oversized books are located in their own section because they need taller shelves than most books.

Find the shelf in the oversized section with call numbers between 570 and 580. Then look along the rows for the book marked 576.5 BAE. The books are in numerical order, so it's easy to find the one you're looking for. As you glance through the table of contents, you're sure this book will help you learn more about cloning.

CARD CATALOGS

Card catalogs are stored in long, narrow drawers. The drawers hold two or more small cards for every book in the library. The cards are arranged alphabetically. Fiction books have two cards each. One lists the book by its author, and one lists the book by its title. Nonfiction books have at least three cards each. These cards list the book by its author, its title, and its subject or subjects.

The cards list the same information as the computer catalog. However, they don't tell you whether someone has checked out the book. A library may separate its card catalog into two categories: subject cards in one category and author and title cards in another.

21.2 LOCATING BOOKS: DEWEY DECIMAL SYSTEM OF CLASSIFICATION

The purpose of call numbers is to help you locate books. Most school and community libraries use call numbers based on the Dewey Decimal System of Classification. The Dewey Decimal System divides nonfiction books into ten categories.

DEWEY CATEGORIES

NUMBERS	CATEGORY	EXAMPLES OF SUBCATEGORIES
000–099	General Works	encyclopedias, bibliographies, periodicals, journalism
100–199	Philosophy	philosophy, psychology, personality
200–299	Religion	mythology, bibles
300–399	Social Sciences	sociology, education, government, law, economics, vocations, customs
400–499	Language	dictionaries, languages, grammar
500–599	Pure Sciences	chemistry, astronomy, biology, mathematics
600–699	Technology and Applied Sciences	medicine, engineering, agriculture, home economics, business, radio, television, aviation
700–799	Arts	architecture, painting, music, photography, recreation
800–899	Literature	poetry, plays, essays, criticism
900–999	Geography and History	geography, history, travel

Let's say you want to know more about James Thurber. You'd begin by entering his last name as a key word in a computer catalog or by looking under *T* in a card catalog.

The library might have many books by Thurber and about Thurber. One book might be *My Life and Hard Times,* a book by James Thurber. This book is placed in the 800 category, literature. Literature is broken into subcategories; for example, 810 is American literature, and 820 is English literature.

James Thurber was an American author, so *My Life and Hard Times* has a call number in the 810s: 817 THU. Some subcategories of the Dewey system contain hundreds of books. To make sure each book has its own call number, a decimal point and more numbers (and sometimes letters) are added to the number of the subcategory. For example, the book about genetics by Patrick Baeuerle has a call number of 576.5 BAE. Many libraries also add the first three letters of the author's last name to the call number, such as THU for Thurber or BAE for Baeuerle.

Library TIP

Two librarians may assign the same book to different Dewey categories. That's why books may have different call numbers in your library than those noted here.

Our imaginary library has another book, called *Remember Laughter: A Life of James Thurber,* by Neil A. Grauer. Its call number is *B Thurber James. B* stands for biography. Many libraries group their biographies together in a separate section of the library. Often there is one biography section in the adult stacks and another in the young adult and children's section. Biographies are shelved alphabetically according to the subject of the book. *Remember Laughter: A Life of James Thurber* is located in the *T* section of the biographies.

The library also has a book called *Thurber: A Biography,* by Burton Bernstein. It, too, has a call number of *B Thurber James.* Two biographies with the same call number but different authors are shelved alphabetically by the last name of the author. That puts Bernstein's book before Grauer's book in the *T* section of the biographies.

One book of short stories by James Thurber, *92 Stories,* is located in the fiction section. Most libraries using the Dewey system identify fiction with the call number *F, Fic,* or *Fiction.*

The call number also includes the first three letters of the author's last name or the author's entire last name. The call number of *92 Stories* is *Fic Thurber.*

Fiction is shelved alphabetically by the authors' last names. Books by the same author are shelved by the first important word in each title, ignoring *A, An,* and *The.* (The book *92 Stories* is shelved as if the number were spelled out: *Ninety-two.*)

Reference books, such as encyclopedias, have an *R* or *Ref* before their call numbers. This means you cannot check out these sources and must use them in the library.

21.3 LOCATING ARTICLES IN NEWSPAPERS AND OTHER PERIODICALS

You can find the latest information on a topic in newspapers, magazines, and journals. The two tools described below will make your search easier.

COMPUTER DATABASES

You may be able to use the library's computers to locate magazine and newspaper articles on your topic. These articles are organized and stored in a database. The library may store databases on CD-ROMs, or it may subscribe to an online service that provides databases. Some libraries do both. Most databases allow you to search by topic, by type of publication (magazine or newspaper), or by specific publication, such as the *New York Times.*

To search for information in a database, begin by entering a key word. The database will then list articles about that topic. The listing usually includes the title, the author, the publication, the date, and a sentence or two about the article. You can select any articles that seem useful. Then the database will allow you to read a brief summary or the whole article on the computer screen. For a small fee, you can print a copy of the article.

READERS' GUIDE TO PERIODICAL LITERATURE

Not every library can subscribe to computer databases. However, nearly every library has the print edition of the *Readers' Guide to Periodical Literature.* This guide includes titles of articles from about two hundred magazines and journals. Both subjects and authors are listed alphabetically and cross-referenced.

An update of the print edition of *Readers' Guide* is published every two weeks. Information about all the articles published that year is reprinted in a hardbound book at the end of the year. The guide is also available on a CD-ROM that you can search using a computer.

Libraries often keep issues for the current year in their newspapers and periodicals section. Issues from the previous one to five years may be stored in a different area. Older issues may be on **microfilm** (a roll or reel of film) or **microfiche** (a sheet of film). Both types of film must be inserted into special projectors that enlarge the pages so that you can read them easily. You can usually make copies of these articles to take home.

Not every book in the library or article in library databases offers current, reliable information. The tips below will help you avoid sources that have outdated information or biased opinions.
1. **Evaluate the author of each source of information.** Look for information about the author's background. Consider whether this person is an expert or just someone with many opinions.
2. **Make sure the information is directly related to your topic.** If you try to include facts that are slightly off your topic, your report will seem unorganized.

3. **Check the publication date.** You may use older sources for information that's not likely to change, such as facts about the battles of World War II. However, your sources must be as recent as possible for topics that are in today's headlines, such as cloning.
4. **Evaluate the author's thinking.** Are the "facts" in a source really facts, or are they just opinions? Can they be proved or disproved? Does the author offer evidence to support his or her ideas?
5. **Gather information on the same topic from several sources.** By doing this, you'll discover different opinions on the issue or topic, but the facts should remain the same.

21.4 USING OTHER REFERENCE SOURCES

General reference sources are easy to use and provide information on thousands of topics. Below are some excellent examples of these sources.

TYPE OF REFERENCE	EXAMPLES
General Encyclopedias General encyclopedias fill many volumes. Subjects are arranged alphabetically. An index at the end helps you find topics.	*World Book Encyclopedia* *Encyclopaedia Britannica* *Collier's Encyclopedia* *Grolier Encyclopedia* *Encarta Encyclopedia*
Specialized Encyclopedias Specialized encyclopedias focus on specific topics. You might be surprised at the number of specialized encyclopedias available.	*Encyclopedia of World Art* *Van Nostrand's Scientific Encyclopedia* *Encyclopedia of World Crime* *Encyclopedia of the Opera* *Encyclopedia of the Third Reich* *Encyclopedia of Vitamins, Minerals, and Supplements* *Encyclopedia of Western Movies* *Encyclopedia of the Geological Sciences*

TYPE OF REFERENCE	EXAMPLES
Almanacs and Yearbooks Almanacs and yearbooks are usually published annually. They provide current facts and statistics. Check the most recent issues for the latest information.	*Information Please Almanac* *World Almanac and Book of Facts* *Guinness Book of Records* *Statistical Abstract of the United States*
Atlases Atlases may contain current or historical information. They include maps and statistics about countries, climates, and other topics.	*Hammond World Atlas* *Cambridge Atlas of Astronomy* *Historical Atlas of the United States* *Goode's World Atlas* *National Geographic Atlas of the World* *Atlas of World Cultures*
Biographical References Biographical reference works include brief histories of notable people, living or dead.	*Contemporary Authors* *American Authors 1600–1900* *Cyclopedia of Literary Characters* *Webster's New Biographical Dictionary* *Biographical Dictionary of World War I* *Biographical Dictionary of World War II* *Biographical Dictionary of Scientists (by field)* *Biographical Dictionary of Artists*

Government Publications
Some large libraries have government publications on agriculture, population, economics, and other topics.
	*Monthly Catalog of United States
	  Government Publications*
	*United States Government Publications
	  Catalog*
	(Both are also available on CD-ROMs and as online publications.)

Books of Quotations In a book of quotations, you can find quotations by famous people or about certain subjects. The quotation from James Thurber at the beginning of Part Four can be found in *The International Thesaurus of Quotations*.	*Bartlett's Familiar Quotations* *The Harper Book of Quotations* *The Oxford Dictionary of Quotations* *The International Thesaurus of Quotations*

21.5 MAKING THE MOST OF WORD RESOURCES

A dictionary and a thesaurus can help you put more words on the tip of your tongue and at the tip of your pencil. Both references are essential tools for writers.

DICTIONARIES

A dictionary contains entries in alphabetical order. An entry is a single word or term along with its pronunciation, definition, and other information.

B.C.   by johnny hart

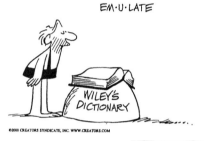

EM·U·LATE

©2000 CREATORS SYNDICATE, INC. WWW.CREATORS.COM

WHAT UNCLE HENRY SAID WHEN AUNTIE EM ARRIVED TOO LATE TO SAVE TOTO.

©2000 CREATORS SYNDICATE, INC.
WWW.CREATORS.COM
By permission of Johnny Hart
& Creators Syndicate, Inc.

Finding Words in a Dictionary

The guide words at the top of each dictionary page can help you find words quickly. Guide words are the first word and the last word on the page. If the word you're looking for falls between these words alphabetically, it will be on that page.

For example, let's say the guide words on a page are *lintel* and *lisp*. You'll find the words *lioness, lip-synch,* and *liquid* on this page. However, *linguistic* comes before *lintel,* so it will be on an earlier page. *Lithium* comes after *lisp,* so it will be on a later page.

If you're looking for a phrase beginning with *St.,* the abbreviation will be spelled out: *Saint.* Look for *Saint Bernard,* not *St. Bernard.*

Understanding Dictionary Entries

Let's analyze a dictionary entry to see what kinds of information it offers.

in•fer (in fur´) *v.* **in•ferred, in•fer•ring 1.** to conclude by reasoning from facts known or assumed: *I infer from your frown that you're angry.* **2.** to guess: *We inferred that the stranger was our new teacher.* —**in•fer•able** (in fur´ ə bəl) *adj.* —**in•fer•rer** (in fur´ər) *n.* [from Middle French *inferer,* from Latin *inferre,* literally, "to carry or bring into," from *in-* + *ferre* "to carry"]

Synonyms: *Infer, deduce,* and *conclude* all mean "to arrive at a conclusion." *Infer* implies arriving at a conclusion based on specific facts. *Deduce* includes the special meaning of drawing a conclusion from a general idea. *Conclude* suggests arriving at an inference based on a chain of reasoning.

1. *The Entry Word:* The entry word itself shows the correct spelling of the word. A raised dot or a blank space within the entry word shows where the word may be divided at the end of a line of writing. The entry word will also show you when a compound word should be written as one solid word (as in **landfill**), when it should be hyphenated (as in **land-poor**), and when it should be written as two words (as in **land mine**).

2. *The Respelling:* The respelling, or pronunciation, is shown immediately after the entry word. An accent mark follows the second syllable in *infer* to show that the second syllable should be stressed in pronouncing the word. So that you can check the pronunciation of the letters and symbols in the respelling, a pronunciation key is shown on every page or every other page in most dictionaries.

3. *Part of Speech Label:* An abbreviation in italic type gives the part of speech of the entry word. The abbreviation *v.* stands for *verb; adj.* stands for *adjective;* and *n.* stands for *noun.*

4. *Inflected Forms:* Inflected forms include plurals of nouns, principal parts of verbs (past, past participle, and present participle), and comparative and superlative forms of adjectives and adverbs. These forms are included in a dictionary entry only when they have irregular spellings. When the past and the past participle of a verb are the same, only one form is shown for both. The sample entry shows that *inferred* is the past form and the past participle of *infer,* and *inferring* is the present participle. These forms are considered irregular because the final consonant is doubled when the ending is added.

    This part of a dictionary entry can help you spell irregular plural forms, such as *quizzes* for *quiz* and *rodeos* for *rodeo.* This section will also show you when to double a final consonant *(stop, stopping; sad, sadder),* when to drop a final *e (dine, dining),* and when to change a final *y* to *i (easy, easiest)* before adding an ending.

5. *Definitions:* Definitions are the heart—and the longest part—of a dictionary entry. If an entry word has more than one meaning, each definition is numbered. Example sentences are often included to make meanings clearer.

6. *Run-on Entries:* Definitions in a dictionary entry may be followed by one or more run-on entries. A run-on entry is a form of the entry word to which a suffix has been added. In the sample dictionary entry, **in•fer•able** and **in•fer•er** are run-on entries. Each run-on entry is preceded by a dash and followed by its pronunciation and its part of speech. The meanings of these words can be inferred by combining the meaning of the entry word and the meaning of the suffix. (See the list of suffixes and their meanings on pages 319–320.)

7. *Etymology:* Many dictionary entries include an etymology, which gives the origin or history of the word. The entry for *infer* explains that this word is based on a Middle French word. The Middle French word was based on a Latin word with a literal meaning of "to carry or bring into." When you infer, you carry or bring your knowledge into a new situation. You use what you know to reach a conclusion. You can see that the Middle French and Latin versions of the word are both similar to the English spelling.

8. *Synonyms:* Some dictionary entries list synonyms, or words with the same or nearly the same meanings. Understanding small differences in meaning will help you use the right word in the right place. Some dictionaries also include antonyms, words with opposite meanings.

Some words have more than one meaning or word history; some may be used as more than one part of speech. In such cases, a dictionary may have multiple entries for a word. Let's look at three entries for the word *rest:*

¹**rest** (rest´) *n.* **1.** REPOSE, SLEEP **2.** freedom from activity or disturbance **3.** something that acts as a stand or a support **4.** a place for resting or lodging **5.** *Music.* a silence between musical notes **6.** a brief pause in reading [Middle English, from Old English; akin to Old High German *rasta* "rest"]

²**rest** *v.* **1.** to get rest by lying down or stopping activity **2.** to lie dead **3.** *Farming.* to remain idle or without a crop **4.** *Law.* to finish presenting evidence in a legal case: *The defense rests, Your Honor.*

³**rest** *n.* something that remains over; REMAINDER: *Jada ate the rest of the fruit salad.* [Middle English, from Middle French *reste,* from *rester* "to remain," from Latin *restare,* from *re-* + *stare* "to stand"]

Numbered Entries Notice the small raised numeral to the left of each entry word in the preceding dictionary sample. This number indicates there is more than one entry for the word. Some dictionaries show separate entries for each part of speech. Some show separate entries for each meaning that has a different word history, or etymology.

In the first and second entries, the meanings have to do with pausing, sleeping, or remaining idle, but the entry words are different parts of speech. The third entry word is the same part of speech as the first, but the word's meaning and its etymology are different.

Cross-References Synonyms within an entry are sometimes printed in small capital letters. In the entries for *rest,* the words *repose, sleep,* and *remainder* are synonyms for specific meanings of *rest.* You can learn more about these meanings of *rest* by looking up the words in small capital letters.

Subject Labels Some dictionary entries include subject labels. A subject label preceding a definition indicates that the definition applies to the subject named. In the sample entries for *rest,* there are three subject labels. In ¹*rest* definition 5 applies to music. In ²*rest* definition 3 applies to farming, and definition 4 applies to law.

The following chart gives examples of other kinds of information you may find in a dictionary entry.

TYPE OF INFORMATION	DESCRIPTION	EXAMPLE FROM AN ENTRY
Capitalization	Indicates that certain uses of a word should be capitalized	**earth** . . . *Often capitalized.* the planet that is third in order from the sun
Out-of-date label	Identifies meanings that are no longer used or used only in special contexts	**anon** . . . *Archaic.* at once; immediately
Style label	Indicates a meaning that is appropriate only in a very informal context	**cool** . . . *Slang.* very good; EXCELLENT
Regional label	Indicates a meaning used in a certain geographical area	**bon•net** . . . *British.* an automobile hood
Usage note	Offers guidelines for using—or not using—a word	**ain't** . . . Although inappropriate in formal speech or writing, *ain't* is sometimes used to attract attention or add humorous emphasis.

OTHER KINDS OF INFORMATION IN GENERAL DICTIONARIES

You can find other kinds of information in the back of some dictionaries. Here is a list of some of the kinds of information you may find in a dictionary.

Biographical Names

Do you remember James Thurber? Who was he? When was he born? When did he die? A section of biographical names gives the spelling and pronunciation of thousands of

people's names, from Berenice Abbott (an American photographer who lived from 1898 to 1991) to Stefan Zweig (an
Austrian writer who was born in 1881 and died in 1942).

Geographical Names

How do you pronounce *Kilimanjaro*? What is it, and
where is it? In a section of geographical names, you can find
the correct spelling, pronunciation, and location of countries, cities, mountains, lakes, rivers, and other geographical
features. Entries range from Lake Abitibi, in Ontario,
Canada, to Zimbabwe, a country in southern Africa.

Abbreviations, Signs, and Symbols

Is the postal abbreviation for Maine MA, MN, or ME? A
dictionary may include lists of abbreviations, signs, and
symbols. Check this section if you can't remember, for
example, what *NOAA* stands for (National Oceanic and
Atmospheric Administration) or what the symbol & means
(*and*).

Style Handbook

Some dictionaries include a style guide. This section may
include rules for spelling, punctuation, and capitalization. It
may also include other matters of writing style. Investigate
your dictionary to find out what it has to offer.

THESAURUSES

A thesaurus lists synonyms, words with the same or
nearly the same meaning. A thesaurus may be organized in
traditional style or in dictionary style.

Traditional Style

Let's say you've used the word *continue* several times in a
report, and you want to find a synonym. To use a traditional
thesaurus, begin by looking in the index. There you might
find these choices:

continue endure 110.6
  protract 110.9
  go on 143.3
  extend 201.9
  persevere 623.2

Let's say that *extend* seems like a good word to replace *continue* in your report. You could use *extend,* or you could look in the front of the book under 201.9 for more choices. Guide numbers at the top of each page help you find the number you want quickly. They're similar to a dictionary's guide words.

On the page with the guide numbers 201.3–203.7, you find paragraph 201.9, a group of synonyms for *extend.* The most commonly used words are printed in bold type.

> VERBS **9. lengthen, prolong,** prolongate, **elongate, extend,** produce [geom.], **protract,** continue, lengthen out, let out, **draw out,** drag out, string out [coll., U.S.], spin out; **stretch,** draw; tense, strain.

A page in the back of the thesaurus explains that *geom.* stands for *geometry* and *coll.* stands for *colloquial,* or *informal.*

Dictionary Style

A dictionary-style thesaurus is organized much like a dictionary. Using the guide words at the top of the page, locate the word *continue.* Checking the front of the book, you learn that an asterisk (*) indicates that a term is colloquial or slang.

CONTINUE

Verb. **1.** [To persist] persevere, carry forward, maintain, carry *or* roll *or* keep *or* go *or* run *or* live on, never stop, sustain, remain, press onward, make headway, move ahead, *leave no stone unturned; see also **ADVANCE.**

Antonyms: cease, end, give up

2. [To resume] begin again, renew, begin *or* carry over, return to, take up again, begin where one left off, be reinstated *or* restored; see also RESUME.

Antonyms: discontinue, halt, postpone

FoxTrot

by Bill Amend

Accessing Electronic Resources

• • • • • • • • • • • • • • •

When you're looking for up-to-date information, electronic resources can provide an excellent starting point. The Internet is an increasingly important source of information for people of all ages around the world. CD-ROMs and other electronic resources that are not connected to the Internet also offer vast amounts of information.

"Ray? It's Vern. The computers are down again."

22.1 USING THE INTERNET

The Internet is a computer-based, worldwide information network. The World Wide Web, or WWW, is software that determines what is displayed on the Internet. Working together, the Internet and the World Wide Web allow you to gather information without leaving your home, school, or library.

GAINING ACCESS

Computers in your library can probably link you to the Internet for free. If you're using a computer at home, you'll need a modem. A modem connects your computer to a telephone line. You must also subscribe to an Internet service, such as America Online or CompuServe. That service will connect you to the Internet for a monthly fee.

UNDERSTANDING ADDRESSES

The information on the Internet is organized by locations, or sites. Each site has its own address. An address is also called a Uniform Resource Locator, or URL.

ACCESSING WEB SITES

Let's say you're connected to the Internet, and you want to view the information at a certain site or address. You can enter the address on the computer screen and be connected to the site.

You can also access specific reference sources, such as the *New York Times* or *Encyclopaedia Britannica,* in this way. Some of these sources are free. For others you must subscribe and perhaps pay a fee. A screen will explain any extra charges that are required. Then you can choose whether to continue.

USING SEARCH ENGINES AND SUBJECT DIRECTORIES

If you don't have a specific address in mind, you can search by key word. A search engine or a subject directory can help.

Search Engines A search engine uses your key word to produce a list of related Web sites. Each Internet service provider uses a certain search engine, but you can switch to a different one by entering its address.

A key word that is too general may generate hundreds of thousands of possible Web sites. It will take you a very long time to search through them to find a few helpful sources!

Subject Directories If you haven't selected a specific topic yet, start with a subject directory. It will begin by listing general topics, such as arts and humanities, science, education, entertainment, recreation and sports, health, and other general subjects. After you choose one, the directory will offer a list of possible subtopics from which to choose. The directory then offers several more lists of subtopics for you to consider. In this way, you can narrow your topic. Finally, the directory will show a page of Web sites that are related to the specific topic you have chosen.

MOVING AROUND WEB SITES

Often words or phrases at one Web site provide links to related Web sites. These special words or phrases are called hyperlinks. They may be underlined or printed in a different color to make them easy to spot. When you click on a hyperlink, you will be transferred to another Web site. To get back, you can click on the back arrow at the top of the computer screen.

"It's a brand new theme park where all the rides are based on your favorite web sites!"

No one oversees Web sites to make sure they offer accurate information. You must evaluate each site yourself. First, review the "Evaluating Tip" on pages 418–419. The tips listed there also apply to Internet sources. The following tips will also help you evaluate Internet sources.

1. Determine whether a Web site actually relates to your topic. A search engine will use every possible meaning of your key word to produce its list of sites.

2. Check the source of the information at a Web site. (You may have to press the "move back" key several times to identify a source.) Many Web sites are personal pages. Just because you find information on the Web doesn't mean it's true or accurate.

22.2 USING CD-ROMS AND DVDS

CD-ROMs (Compact Disc Read-Only Memory) and DVDs (Digital Video Discs) can be used with a personal computer at home, at school, or at a library. They don't require a connection to the Internet.

CD-ROM databases store both sights and sounds. Some CD-ROMS offer short versions of historical events. Some have moving pictures that show, for example, how bees "dance" to communicate with one another.

One CD-ROM can store the same amount of information as seven hundred computer diskettes. Many dictionaries, encyclopedias, and other reference sources are now available as CD-ROMs. A DVD can store even more information, as much as a full-length movie.

Library computer catalogs are another example of electronic resources that are not part of the Internet. Some of the databases available at a library are also on CD-ROMs. Other databases on library computers are part of the Internet.

James Thurber died in 1961, long before the Internet existed and long before there was as much information available as there is today. He would be amazed to discover how much has been "written about everything" at this point, and more is being written every minute!

Now you know how to find the information you need. Use your new skills to gather information for school reports and to find out more about this challenging and exciting world!

INDEX

Entries with bold page numbers represent terms and definitions in the Glossary of Terms, pages 4–28.

M

Magazines
  capitalizing titles of, 254
  italics for titles of, 272
  locating articles in,
    417–418
  source cards for, 366–367
Mail, male, 43
Main, mane, 43–44
Main clauses, **17,** 192, 193
Main verbs, **18,** 104–105
Male, mail, 43
Mane, main, 43–44
Many, much, 44
May, can, 34
Measurements, abbreviations
  for, 57–59, 277
Meat, meet, 44
Microfiche, 418
Microfilm, 418
Might of, 37
Minute, 44
Misreading, comma to prevent,
  267
Modified block form for let-
  ters, 382–383
Months
  abbreviations of, 56
  capitalizing names of,
    253
Monuments, capitalizing
  names of, 252
Most, almost, 30, 165
Movies, italics for titles of,
  272
Much, many, 44

Music albums, italics for titles
  of, 272
Musical compositions, italics
  for titles of, 272
Must of, 37

N

Names, capitalizing, 250–254
Narrative writing, 342–347
  characters in, 343
  chronological order in, 345
  dialogue in, 347
  drafting in, 344–347
  plot in, 342
  prewriting in, 343–344
  setting in, 343
  transitions in, 346
Nationalities, capitalizing
  names of, 254
Need, knead, 41
Negative, double, **12**
Negative words, **18,** 166–167
New, knew, 41
Newspapers, 405
  capitalizing titles of, 254
  italics for titles of, 272
  locating articles in, 417
Night, knight, 41
Nonessential clauses, **18,** 197,
  293
Nonessential phrases, **18,** 207,
  291
Nonrestrictive clauses. *See*
  Nonessential clauses

in directions for process,
386–388
order of importance, 333
in persuasive writing,
356–357
for presentations, 392–395
priority, 394
in research report writing,
371–372
spatial order, 333, 340
summarizing, 395
Organizations, capitalizing
names of, 253
Ought to of, 45
Outline for research report,
369–371

Pair, pare, pear, 45
Parallelism, **336**
Parentheses, **19,** 276
Participial phrases, **20,**
206–207
definition, **20,** 207
diagraming, 242
essential, 207
nonessential, 207
punctuating, 263
Participles, **20,** 206–207, 242
definition, **20,** 206
diagraming, 242
past, **20,** 113–116, 206
present, **23,** 206
punctuating, 263
Passed, past, 45
Passive voice, **20,** 111–112

Past, passed, 45
Past participles, **20,** 206
as adjectives, 145
of irregular verbs, 113–116
Past perfect tense, **20–21,** 109
Past progressive form of verb,
21, 107
Past tense, **21,** 103
of irregular verbs, 113–116
Pause, paws, 45
Peace, piece, 45
Pear, pair, pare, 45
Peer editing, 373
Perfect tenses, **21**
Periodicals, 405
locating articles in, 417–418
*Readers' Guide to Periodical
Literature,* 418
Periods, **21**
with abbreviations, 56,
277, 278
as end marks, 66, 261
with quotation marks, 271
Personal pronouns, **21,**
125–126
with unknown gender, 336
Persuasive writing, 352–357
audience in, 354
facts in, 355–356
opinions in, 355–356
prewriting in, 353–356
research for, 355–356
Phrases, **22**
adjective, **5,** 178
adverb, **6,** 178
appositive, **7,** 89–90
essential, **13,** 207